Country Boy, But No Country Lawyer

Lives of great men all remind us
We can make our lives sublime,
And, departing, leave behind us
Footprints on the sands of time.

— Henry Wadsworth Longfellow

To my beloved wife, Martha.

ISBN: 978-0-578-79097-8

Printed in the United States of America

AUTHOR'S NOTE

Sometimes a book just finds you.

Here I was, minding my own business as the program speaker to the West Amarillo Rotary Club in early 2019. Afterward, Robert Templeton asked if he could have a few minutes. In that few minutes, he presented a proposal for a book on the top lawsuits in his long legal career.

I didn't commit immediately because projects like these are laborious.

I did suggest that if this were to happen, it needed to be more. It needed to be about his life too, not just his time in the courtroom.

As I have told many when I spent a career at the late Amarillo Globe-News, everyone has a story – everyone. And chances are, it's much more compelling than most believe.

Our paths had never really crossed. I didn't know Robert Templeton, but certainly knew of him. In legal circles, he had name recognition. He was a player, and I don't mean his favorite card games of poker and gin, either.

His legal career in Amarillo has spanned more than 60 years. At age 88, he's still at it. Few have had longer legal careers in the city. The remarkable Tom Morris comes to mind as does federal judge Mary Lou Robinson, both of whom were friends and advisors.

Templeton spent the first 10 years of his life in Amarillo. He moved briefly to Salt Lake City and Bridgeport, Conn., before his family moved to his father's tiny hometown of Frost near Waco. That's where he went to high school. Templeton then graduated from Baylor and Baylor Law School and served in the Air Force. After that, he was back in Amarillo almost by accident to start his legal career as the third of three rungs on the ladder in the Potter County attorney's office.

From prosecuting drunk drivers in the 1950s, he would eventually try cases with millions of dollars at stake. To say Robert Templeton is beloved would not in any way be true. No lawyer worth his salt is. It's like being a football coach or newspaper columnist. The very nature of the job is going to upset people, and certainly that's the case in the rough and tumble world of the courtroom.

But Templeton is respected and he is good at what he does, often very good. An argument could be made that some may have done it better, but not longer, and some may have done it longer, but not better.

He has been at the forefront of some groundbreaking cases in Amarillo. There's a saying, of which no one quite knows the origin: "May you live in interesting times." Robert Templeton has certainly done that.

Oh, and I decided to write his book.

Jon Mark Beilue
July 2020

Jon Mark Beilue and Robert (Bob) Templeton

PROLOGUE

My first motive to write a book was the experience I had with the bankruptcy of the American Housing Foundation. It was such an injustice that I wanted to expose what happens far too often in bankruptcies.

In January 2019, I listened to Jon Mark Beilue give a speech at the West Amarillo Rotary Club. I knew I had found someone who could help me write a book. So we got started and we worked two days a week for 1 ½ hours on Wednesday and Friday for well more than a year. Gradually, this evolved into stories of lawsuits I tried over the years. Then I expanded this into somewhat of a biography. He said he needed to try to make me look human so that readers would identify with me and pull for me.

It hasn't been easy to pull out the details of lawsuits tried 40 years ago and I don't know that it's been fun. But it doesn't hurt to leave a few footprints in the sands of time as Longfellow said. Inside every good trial lawyer there's a book, but they never take the time – or seldom take the time – to write one.

What the reader will find is that I have not pulled any punches. Every story is factual and names have seldom been changed. There was only one instance where that happened, and it was noted a different name was used. There's no fiction to it. I called it like I saw it. Most of these lawsuits were tried in Amarillo or the Panhandle. Some were important and some were just good stories.

I wrote this as best I could in the way I tell stories. I tried to make them simple, understandable and interesting. In a lifetime of practicing law, I've had help from great friends, great teachers, many of whom were my opponents, and my wife Martha, my best friend and most honest critic.

In many ways I was self-taught, but that's not entirely true either. My great friend Bill Attebury believed in me. Judge Mary Lou Robinson tried her best to regulate me – what a woman and judge she was. Tom Morris was a friend and advisor from the start.

The list is too long to include everyone.

Tom Templeton, my dad, taught me so much. He never met a stranger. He made friends with everyone. He was the greatest salesman and best shot with a firearm I ever saw.

He literally made me go to law school, which was mostly boredom. Not until I was 40 years old did I realize he knew what he was doing.

Robert Templeton
Amarillo, Texas
July 2020

TABLE OF CONTENTS

CHAPTER

I

Saturdays And The First Class In Law

It would be over 10 years before Robert Templeton would enter his first class at Baylor Law School in 1949, but he unwittingly got his first lesson in being a trial lawyer when he was just a kid in the 1930s.

Being a trial lawyer takes an array of skills, not the least of which is being a salesman. There's a jury of 12 and the bottom line is they have to believe you. Whether it's by the weight of evidence or the power of persuasion or relating to the jury as the neighbor next door, a lawyer has some convincing to do.

"I've always tried to understand and appeal to Joe Six Pack and how he sees life," Templeton said. "It's that simple and that difficult. It's always there. Sometimes it screams at you.

"Find a lawyer that has intellect and natural salesmanship and they will be tough in court. I've seen lawyers I don't know how they lost a case they were so good."

The professor in Templeton's first unofficial class in law school was his father. The classroom was small towns across the Texas Panhandle. The course? Call it Getting People to Believe in You.

When Robert Templeton was all of 7 years old, he and the family bird dog, Rex, would climb into the car of Remington Arms' top salesman in the country, leave Amarillo and head east on the Mother Road of Route 66 for points east.

That Remington's top salesman was also his dad, Thomas Jefferson

Templeton, made that pretty easy. The three would leave Amarillo and make stops in various Texas Panhandle towns in Templeton's vast selling territory.

"I learned right then how you can communicate with another person," he said, "and watching how my dad talked with people, it came natural for me in talking to a jury."

He was known as Tommy or Tom Boy when he was young, and signed his name as T.J. His mind was as sharp as his eye. When his oldest son was a boy, the elder Templeton was a manufacturer's representative for Remington Arms in a huge chunk of West Texas.

In the late 1930s, the Templetons lived at 4232 W. 13th Street. Tommy was gone much of the time during the week servicing his territory. At home was wife, Mary. Robert was the oldest, Mary Tom was 21 months younger, and Jeff was the baby, seven years younger than Robert.

Tommy Templeton made about as good a living as a fellow could as this part of the country was digging itself out of the Dust Bowl and the Depression. He was making about $300 a month. The family wasn't lavished upon, but they didn't go without either. For Christmases, Tommy bought his oldest son an erector set, a Lionel train. On one occasion, Robert received a $50 Schwinn bicycle. Fifty dollars around 1940, that was a lot of money.

On Saturdays, Tommy was often in his car making rounds in Texas Panhandle towns, trips in which he could get to several towns in a day and then be back home in the late afternoon. Free from school at Margaret Wills Elementary on those days, Robert couldn't wait to jump into the car with his dad.

On this Saturday, the destination was Shamrock. He had his case full of samples and order forms. Rex, the wonder dog that Tommy had acquired from a peddler, jumped in the car. So did Robert. They headed the 90 miles first to the hardware store in Shamrock.

It was times like this that young Robert could see up close what it was like to work a crowd, and in later life, how to work a jury. A man had to find something in some way to connect to others.

At the Shamrock hardware store, Tommy was met by the store

Summer in the 1930's. Bob, Tom, Sister Mary Tom, and Rex the bird dog.

owner. They shook hands, but there would be no sales today.

"Tommy, I'm not buying anything today. I haven't sold what you sold me last time," the store owner said.

Tommy Templeton told the store owner he wasn't there to make any sales. He was just there to visit a little bit. In addition to his knack for sales, Templeton was also among the country's top competitive shooters. Skeet, targets, shotguns, rifles, pistols. It didn't really matter. If it had a trigger, Templeton was among the most accurate anyone had seen. It was a gift he was born with and honed it along the way. He would later win championships in both trap and skeet shooting.

It wasn't long before a group would inevitably join in on the conversation in the back of the hardware store. They knew of Tommy's skill with a gun. The stories would start. Soon, it was time for some action. They asked to see Tommy perform.

"OK, Rex, you and Bob go back and get my gun," he said.

The young Templeton and the bird dog would trudge back to the car and get his dad's .22 rifle. It would be in a case with a handle on it. Bob gave the case to Rex, and slobber and all, Rex would take the case back to the amused crowd.

"OK, Rex," Tommy said, putting his hand underneath the case. "Let me have it." And with that, Rex would drop the case into Tommy's hand.

The crowd followed Tommy into the alley. He'd tell Bob to get him a lead washer, a flat washer with a hole in it. Tommy pitched the washer up and took a shot at it. It fell to the ground.

They were sure he had missed it. One thing was for sure. The washer wasn't dented. So what was it? Tommy took some tape, put it over the hole in the washer, and shot it again. When the washer fell to the ground, the tape had a hole in it. And he did it again and again. Throw up the washer, fire a shot, check the washer for a hole in the tape. Case closed.

He'd then take a .22 hollow point, and throw up a potato he just happened to have with him. The potato would explode.

"Then he did something I never saw anyone try to do, and don't know if anyone else could do," Templeton said.

He took a .22 short bullet, and would pitch it high in the air. Tommy Templeton shot the lead out of the bullet.

"He didn't hit all of them, but he did most of them," his son said.

So what's the secret, Tommy? How did you do it, the crowd asked?

"No trick to it," he said. "When you pitch up something like this, when it's as high as it's going to go, for just that moment, it's motionless. That's when you shoot it."

He had the crowd eating out of his hand. He then motioned his young son and Rex to go back to the car and get his order book. Dutifully, they'd trudge back to the car like they had done earlier to get his gun case. They would return with Rex holding the order book.

"OK, Rex, let me have it," Tommy said, and Rex would drop the order book into his hand.

"Jack," he said to the hardware store owner, "I noticed you were a little low on 12-gauge shells. Do you want one gross or two?"

Jack, who was not going to buy anything on this day earlier, would take one gross.

"My dad didn't ask him if he wanted to buy, but which one do you want, one or two gross?" Bob said. "You see, Jack couldn't say no with everyone there and what he just did. He never walked out of a hardware store to my knowledge at any time I was with him without getting an order of some kind."

Class dismissed.

Tommy Templeton was all of 5-6 ½, but he was a giant of man to his son. Every father should in some way be a hero to his son. Those trips with his father at the end of the 1930s would serve Bob Templeton well the rest of his life. At the time, he just liked being with his dad, but later, he saw those times for the lessons it taught him.

"I realized later in life how much I learned about people and selling that I've used all my life," he said. "He had a wonderful memory. He would see a fella he hadn't seen in 10 years and remember his name, but also call his wife and kids by name.

"He had a genuine interest in people. I've never been that good, but I've always liked people and enjoyed the human race – the good, bad and indifferent. I learned watching him how you communicate with another person. And it's worked. It's just come natural for me to be able to talk directly to a jury. My dad was a smart man.

"He used to say to treat everybody as your equal because no matter who, he can always do something better than you can. He would have made a heckuva lawyer."

As it was, in an indirect way, he was a heckuva law professor.

CHAPTER

2

Frogs And Fights

John Monroe Jameson was one of those men who saw opportunity in the late 1800s in the wide-open land that was the Texas Panhandle. He was born in 1868 in Grayson County, 65 miles north of Dallas. In 1894, he married Martha Jean Roling. Soon after, in a spirt of adventure, the two left home for the sparsely populated Texas Panhandle.

Jameson became a school teacher. He would become the largest stockholder in White & Kirk department stores, but more than anything, he was a rancher and a water well driller. He bought a section of land east of what was becoming the town of Canyon, bought another section in Carson County, a ranch near what would be Fritch, and a ranch in New Mexico.

Jameson was one of the most active drillers in the Panhandle. Many of the early windmills in the area were by his design. An accident in 1914 occured when he fell off a windmill and broke both legs. He was never really the same. But before that, his work made living on the high plains possible, but it did more than furnish water to people and livestock. They became a symbol of security. They spoke of freshness, of a new and possible way of life. They gave rhythm to life in the Panhandle.

A new way of life for Jameson also included a large family for he and Martha Jean. They would have seven children over 17 years, six of them were girls. The fourth girl was Mary Lillian, born in 1908.

At age 19 in 1927, she worked as a secretary at a hardware store in Canyon, not far from the Jameson place east of town. One day in walked Thomas Jefferson Templeton, or Tommy or T.J. He was new to the Panhandle.

Templeton was from Frost, a small town 55 miles northeast of Waco. He was a salesman for Remington Arms, one of the very best the company had. He was so good, in fact, that Remington moved him to the vast area of the Panhandle and South Plains as a regional salesman where need was great and competition few.

He went into the Canyon hardware store with a sale or two in mind, and left with something else on his mind – Mary. She caught his eye, and he caught hers. He called upon the store in Canyon more and more until they became pretty steady.

They were married on May 17, 1929. They settled into a little duplex at 17th Avenue and Hayden Street in Amarillo. Nearly three years later, on March 17, 1932, to be exact, their first child, Robert Lincoln Templeton, was born. He was named after his grandfather. Mary Tom, a sister, was born 21 months later.

"She and I were very close," Templeton said. "Mary Tom thought I was it. I was the big brother. We never had a disagreement of any kind. We just had that kind of relationship."

As he got older, Robert felt like he was the head of the household with his dad gone much of the time working his large Remington sales territory. Think of one of the boys in Little Rascals during the 1930s and early 1940s and that would be Templeton.

The duplex had a window in back, perfect for opening and slipping out to play when homework or chores might have been the priority. About three houses away were Bill and Sam Attebury at 1710 Hayden. Bill was 3 years older, while Sam was 18 months. Despite age differences as kids, they became fast friends. It didn't hurt that the two dads – Tommy and Arnold Attebury – were good friends as well.

"My dad was so kind and good to those Attebury boys that they never forgot it the rest of their lives," Templeton said. "Bill was a lifelong friend, from the time we first met until he died (in 2010)."

Tommy Templeton and wife, Mary in front of their Amarillo home.

Robert age 3.

Mary, Mary Tom, and Robert.

When Robert was just 5 years old, the three boys were messing around a nearby pond. Templeton went under and thrashed about before Bill went into the chest-deep water to pull out his friend.

"He claimed later he saved my life," Templeton said. "I have vague memory of something, but Bill is probably telling the truth."

In the 1950s, after Bill returned from Korea and the Navy, he, Sam and their father Arnold established Attebury Elevators around the Panhandle. Later, that experience led Bill to help found A&S Steel Buildings, a major player in the emerging pre-engineered steel building industry. Later, he was heavily involved in the beef industry. Bill Attebury would become a client of Templeton's.

"He was setting up a corporation, and said that I want you to have a part of it," Templeton said. "He said, 'I want you to have 25 percent of it.' I had always been told not to have any business with your clients. I said, 'Bill, I'm not going to do that.' I would have been a very rich man had I been smart enough to take him up on that. That's the kind of fellow Bill Attebury was."

In 1939, when Robert was 7 years old, his dad moved the family to a new house that developer Horace Scott had built at 4232 W. 13th Avenue. That was about the time Jeff, the youngest child, was born. Moving there meant Robert and Mary Tom went to school at Margaret Wills Elementary.

In moving, Robert became friends with the Martin boys, Joe and Danny. Those blocks around 13th Avenue became home. Robert found a niche at Margaret Wills. He had friends and he had a Schwinn bicycle. In the summers, he would spend much of the time in Frost, his dad's hometown, with his grandparents on their farm.

But boys will be boys, and that meant there were the occasional scrapes. His dad bought him a punching bag that was on a moveable pole that he could practice on. It stayed on the front porch where Robert's skinny arms and small fists would wail on it to be ready should the occasion arise.

It arose.

He got into an after-school dustup that best Robert could recall was about a draw. But it was not to be the end. There was strength in numbers, the class bully figured. He coerced two other friends to join in a plan that had them chasing Robert when he went home for lunch as was his daily custom.

"They almost caught me," he said. "There was a ladder on a neighbor's house that went up to a garage. It was one of those pull-up deals. I was fast enough, probably because I was scared, to climb that ladder and then pull the thing up so they couldn't get up too. I stayed up on the roof the whole time until they had to go back to school. It finally died out and they left me alone."

But another pugilist surfaced, one two years older than Robert and Danny Martin. He'd pounded on them on more than one occasion.

"I went to my dad to talk to him because I didn't know what to do," Robert said. "The kid lived a little bit down the street from us."

Tommy Templeton threw out the idea that his son and Danny should jump him when he walked down an alley on his way home from school. Two against one, maybe they'd have a chance.

"We were dumb enough to do what he said," Robert said. "We jumped him and scared the hell out of him and he never bothered us again."

But don't believe that Robert was always the innocent victim. He liked to pull a trick as much as the next kid. And it didn't help that Mary Tom had a mischievous spirit about her.

There was a boy, Baxter DeGrassi, who lived just east of the Templetons. His dad was in the insurance business, and Robert and Mary Tom believed he was a little bit coddled. When it finally started raining in the late 1930s, there came these gully-washers. And with it in the Templeton neighborhood came these little frogs that seemed like a Biblical plague.

"They just came out of nowhere," Robert said.

Out of curiosity, Robert, his sister, and Danny took out one day after a big rain to see just how many of those little frogs they could gather. They had a galvanized tub and found frogs everywhere near Western Street and Plains Avenue. They filled the tub up with frogs. And like the dog who finally catches the car, what do you do now?

"Let's leave some with Baxter," Mary Tom said.

Robert and Danny didn't argue. They walked by the DeGrassi home. Nobody seemed there. They knocked. No answer. They turned the doorknob. The door opened. At that point, Mary Tom knew what to do. They dumped about half the tub of frogs into the DeGrassi home and high-tailed it out of there.

It was left to their imagination as to what might have happened. They didn't have to imagine too long. The next day, Mrs. DeGrassi walked over to the Templetons. Robert and Mary Tom saw her coming, and went into the house and their bedroom like a good boy and girl.

Mary Templeton was outside when Mrs. DeGrassi approached. Robert opened the window to eavesdrop on the conversation. It didn't help their case the tub was still in the yard and some frogs were jumping in and out.

"I remember it to this day," Robert said. "She said, 'Mrs. Templeton, when we were gone yesterday, somebody opened the door to our house and let loose all these frogs. They were on my mantle, my sofa. They were all over the house. Would your kids know something about this?'"

Mary Templeton's response? "Oh, no, Robert and Mary Tom would never do anything like that," she said.

Since that was about 75 years before home security cameras were in vogue, Mrs. DeGrassi could do nothing but walk away. Years later, Templeton was back in Amarillo at a party that Baxter DeGrassi was at. He figured the statute of limitations had expired.

"You remember those frogs in your house when we were kids?" Templeton said. "That was me."

DeGrassi remembered it well. The admission did not surprise him at all.

Those early years in Amarillo were about as innocent as the time could be for a country coming out of the depression and the Panhandle coming out of the Dust Bowl. The Templetons, thanks to Tom's Remington job, had enough money. Robert had a bicycle, friends, a homemaker of a mom who made their clothes, and a good school. On Saturdays, he would often get a dime from his dad to go to the Paramount theater on Polk Street to see a cowboy western or Flash Gordon.

A young fellow could get used to a life like this. Then came December 1941. The Japanese attacked Pearl Harbor on Sunday, Dec. 7, 1941. The next day, Robert was home sick with a cold.

"My dad had us an RCA radio and I remember it was on and listening to President Roosevelt talk about the day of infamy and declaring war on Japan," Templeton said.

For millions of Americans, their world was changing. And it changed for the Templetons. World War II saw them moving across the country. Because of the war, Remington suspended selling guns and ammunition to the public. That put Tommy Templeton out of his sales job.

Instead, he was transferred to Remington's small arms munitions plant, the Utah Ordnance Plant in Salt Lake City. In March 1942, Robert turned 10. By April, they had moved from Amarillo to Utah.

Salt Lake City was a nice town with good people, almost all of them Mormons. Robert finished up fourth grade there. If he thought 880 miles would change the aggressive attitudes of young boys, he thought wrong. On his first day of school, Robert thought he had a new friend as he walked toward his new home with him after school was let out. He stopped short of Templeton's house.

"What are you stopping here for?" Templeton asked. "He said, 'Well, I guess this place is as good as any to whip you.'"

They wrestled to the ground with Robert on the bottom. The kid let Robert get up. With that, Robert, a southpaw, threw a left as hard as he could that hit the kid in the ribs. He fell down moaning. He got back up and wrestled Templeton through two yards. It was then that Mary Templeton came out of the house to put a stop to the wrestling and punching.

"I didn't want to see him again, and the next day at school, he wasn't there. That was a relief," Templeton said. "A lady then came to see the teacher and asked her what she was going to do with the bully that broke her son's ribs."

As it turned out, nothing.

Over the winter of 1942, Tommy Templeton smuggled five 30-caliber shells out of the plant. He shaved the points and made them hollow points. He went with friends to the Wasatch Mountains. He stationed himself in an area where the mountains blended into a valley and deer came through. With those five 30-caliber shells, he killed five deer. A young buck hung in the bedroom of their house where the family ate deer meat that winter.

The family adjusted to life in Salt Lake City, but things changed quickly during the war. Tommy Templeton was informed that after 18 months in Salt Lake, he was being transferred to Remington's corporate headquarters in Bridgeport, Conn. That was also the site of Remington's major ammunition plant.

The Templetons rented a house just outside of Easton, Conn., about 10 miles from Bridgeport. It was a roomy house and they were surrounded by dairy farms and orchards. But Tommy didn't like the move. He didn't like the Northeast.

He began to drink hard liquor more and more to cope. Finally, in March 1944, Remington fired him.

What were they going to do now? Tommy had a wife and three children, ages 12 to 5. The best thing – the only thing – he knew to do was to head back to his hometown of Frost.

They got on a passenger train, and Robert had a 12-year-old's adventure of roaming up and down the train as it made its way from Bridgeport to Chicago, to St. Louis and then to Dallas. Tommy got on the train drunk in Bridgeport, but didn't have a drink on the train and quit cold turkey once he got back to Texas.

"Everything I did, I did to excess but I never did anything long enough to kill me," Tom Templeton said.

He quit cold turkey when the family returned to Texas. "How many men could do that?" Robert said.

The family transferred from one train in Dallas for a short 55-mile train trek to Corsicana where Robert's aunt – his dad's sister – met them at 4 a.m.

It was a short drive to Frost. It had been a place to go in the summers, but now, for 12-year-old Robert Templeton, this was home.

— Reflection —

"The first day I was in Frost," Templeton said, "Billy Bonnett took me to the Frost water tower. We began to climb it. Part way up, Billy backed out. I was too scared to stop. Fear can be a great motivator."

CHAPTER

3

Life In A Small Town

Robert Lincoln "R.L." Templeton was in his 20s and was restless. The town of Soddy-Daisy in southeastern Tennessee near the Alabama and Georgia border was home, but home wasn't doing him any favors. It was becoming increasingly tough to make a living there in the late 1890s.

He'd heard stories of rich black soil south of Dallas, Texas, and it was available at a fair price for a man willing to roll up his sleeves and farm it. It may have been a risk to uproot himself and go sight unseen 850 miles to a little town called Frost, but as songwriter Bob Dylan would write 70 years later, "When you ain't got nothin, you got nothin' to lose."

As it turned out, the gamble was worth it. R.L. Templeton was able to make a living by acquiring two farms and eventually running a hardware store in Frost. He met his future wife Dosha Stegall in Sherman, Texas, and they had four children, including two daughters, and all were named after presidents or famous Americans – Benjamin Franklin, the oldest, two daughters, William McKinley, called, believe it or not, "Chicken Bill," and Theodore Roosevelt, called "Ted."

The other son was Thomas Jefferson Templeton. Tommy was born in 1903, grew up in Frost, and now in 1944, he moved back. Ted had picked up Tom and his family in Corsicana, and drove them to Frost to begin a new life in an old familiar place.

Frost had recovered from a horrific tornado that devastated the town in 1930. On May 6 of that year, around 3 p.m., a tornado later estimated at an F4 on the Fujita Scale where a maximum is 5, roared through Frost. It virtually destroyed downtown businesses and tore apart homes in the town of 748.

The tornado was estimated to be 500 yards wide with winds as high as 260 mph. The storm killed 41, including 27 in Frost, from a 9-month-old infant to an 82-year-old woman. Tragic as it was, it was fortunate more weren't killed. The Frost school, 90 years ago, had no safety shelter. Teachers took about 75 elementary school children out of the school, which was destroyed, and had them on their stomachs in the rows of a nearby cotton field. Miraculously, none were hurt.

Some took shelter in the Citizens State Bank vault. Everything around the bank, including the building, was destroyed. Others found refuge in the county jail. With any large tornado, there were peculiarities that showed the power and whims of the powerful force. A horse was found impaled by a 2-by-4 board. A Model T was blown 400 yards away, upright and unscratched. A house was destroyed, but a piano remained not only untouched, but the sheet music still on the piano.

But 14 years later, the scars from that storm were mainly a haunting memory each spring for those who survived. The main outward difference was it seemed every home had a storm cellar. For the Templetons, the town of Frost was a new beginning.

Tommy Templeton returned to Frost without a job, and jobs were not exactly plentiful to begin with. He turned his attention 80 miles away toward the Dallas-Fort Worth area. Toward the end of World War II, he landed a job with General Dynamics in Fort Worth. Later, he sold the country's first water-based paint. If the jobs were selling, Templeton was good at it, be it paint or guns. Covering his sales territory often had him gone days at a time, but he would return to Frost on weekends.

So, in a way, young Robert Lincoln Templeton, named after his grandfather there in Frost, became the weekday man of the house just as he was growing into a teenager.

There was school, extra-curricular activities and chores. The first daily ritual was feeding and caring for the bird dogs in his dad's absence. His first job was picking cotton.

At age 15, Robert graduated to the summer job of working on a hay press. It was daylight to dusk where he was a tie-out man. The hay press bundled hay. The hay would make its way to Templeton where he tied the bales.

"You had to be quick," he said, "and I got strong in the arms. It was tough work for a kid."

At Frost High School, Robert discovered girls, but he also discovered a lot of things. He was managing editor of the school newspaper, which included collecting advertising from merchants. He went to the Navarro County championship in typing where he may have been the fastest typist with two fingers. He played tennis. He played basketball but not well.

"I could shoot, but I just couldn't dribble," he said.

Football, though, was his forte despite his 5-foot-8, 135-pound size. Like in most Texas towns, it was the sport for the appropriately named Frost Polar Bears. It was a way to impress the girls for one. And it was a way to be involved with his buddies in something that galvanized the community.

Templeton, cracked the starting lineup as a halfback and defensive back. As a senior, he was the quarterback and captain in the Polar Bears' Single Wing offense.

They had modest success in his senior season, finishing with a 4-6 record. Frost lost to rival Blooming Grove, 7-6. The Polar Bears thought they had pulled out a win in that game when Billy Bonnett, the passer in the Single Wing, found Templeton open in the flat. He caught the pass and dashed 45 yards for a touchdown, but, alas, a clipping penalty wiped out the score and that proved crucial in the loss. Kerens was the powerhouse in those days, and led by Red Earl, who would play at SMU, routed Frost, 60-12.

"He (Earl) knocked me down like a piece of straw," Templeton said, "but contact sports gave me confidence."

It also gave him an unfortunate nickname that he picked up in football practice as a freshman. The Polar Bears barely had enough to scrimmage with an offense and defense. So here was Templeton, about the stature of Barney Fife, at linebacker.

A handoff went to a senior, a big 6-foot-2 fullback with the intimidating name of Earl Frank Neal. He barreled through the line, and not surprisingly, he didn't even see Templeton.

"I was down low," he said. "I had my arms out and caught him on both of his legs. He fell like a tree. He got up and said, 'My God, what happened?'

"He looked down and saw me and said, 'My God, he's just like a gopher rat.' And the name 'Gopher' stuck. I lived with that name all through high school. Hated that name. Hated it. I was ready to fight anyone who called me that, but I couldn't fight everyone. That's one reason I wasn't sad about leaving."

As for the classroom, it was easy for Templeton, but he's not sure how much he learned. He read some Dickens in English class. The head football coach taught plane geometry. Math was easy for him, so much so that, in effect, he ended up teaching the class.

Templeton's high marks were noted in the Senior Class Poem, the Senior Class Will and the Senior Class Prophecy in the Frost yearbook, "The Bear's Den." In the class poem: *"Football Captain, first name Bobby, Sports with him are quite a hobby. He also like to study books. I know from the way his grade card looks."*

In the will, Templeton willed his brains to Billy Ray Vest and in the prophecy: *Bobby Templeton devoted most of his life to studying, gaining knowledge, and going far in the educational field."*

Robert, finished as the valedictorian in the Class of 1949. Joyce Omberg was the salutatorian. Being the valedictorian meant giving the valedictorian address at graduation. But Frost had as its superintendent, Mr. William V. Harrison. A smart man as Robert recalled, Harrison wrote the speech. Templeton simply read it.

"I can still remember the first words of his speech: 'We are living in a fast and dangerous time,'" Robert said. "He talked about the whole world situation, the growing threat of Communism and all that. No one else was interested in it except William Harrison."

In small towns like Frost, boys often had to make their own fun between sports and jobs. And making your own fun usually meant getting into a bit of trouble, using poor teenage judgement – or both.

Billy Bonnett was a good friend. Fletcher Bonnett, his dad, owned the Frost grocery store. On this particular summer day while the two were still in high school, Fletcher Bonnett had a special chore for his son. He was to get in his dad's GMC truck and drive 47 miles southeast to the town of Mexia to buy a load of watermelons to sell at the grocery store.

Billy talked Robert into going with him, which truthfully wasn't too difficult. They in turn got a friend Charles Ellis to go with them. It was a dangerous thing in that they not only had money that Billy's dad gave them for the watermelons, but a few dollars of their own.

They got the watermelons just fine. While in Mexia, they ran into a man who agreed to buy these minors a case of beer for a tip. Jax beer was about $2 a case. It was cheap and somewhat foul tasting, but it was beer. They bought themselves a case.

"Terrible tasting beer," Robert said, "but it was beer."

They began making their wobbly way back to Frost. Charles drank maybe one beer, and Billy and Robert began downing the rest.

"Billy really started drinking the beer, so Charles got behind the wheel and he drove," Robert said. "Billy would take a can, guzzle it and throw it out the window. On the drive back, Billy was drunk and I wasn't too far behind."

They arrived in Corsicana, which was about halfway between Mexia and Frost. They needed gas, and on the south end of Beaton Street, the main street in Corsicana, was a gas station. While filling up with gas, Billy decided they had too many watermelons.

Looking to the north down Beaton Street was a long downhill slope. Billy picked up a watermelon and started rolling it down the street. He liked it so much that he did the same thing with five more watermelons, all of them busting at some point and the three of them staring at the five watermelons while in various stages

Robert's grandparents, R.L. Templeton and Doche.

Robert at Frost

Robert, graduation from Frost High School, 1949.

After the storm at Frost, Texas.

Tom (far left), Ben, Ted (little girl), Chicken Bill.
They were Bob's father, aunts and uncle.

1949 Senior Class play, Mumbo-Jumbo. Bob is top row, second from right.

Bobby Templeton, Senior

Billy Bonnett, Senior

1949 Football team. Back row, far left is Bobby Templeton

of intoxication.

As they got in the truck, a mostly sober Ellis continued to drive, probably the only good idea of the trip. The three had 20 more miles to drive on Highway 22. They arrived in Blooming Grove, their big rival, and about 5 miles from Frost.

Robert and Billy knew they had to sober up before they got to Frost, so they got out and begin to run toward home while Charles drove slowly alongside. They finally got to Frost, tired and still mostly drunk. Charles went home, and Robert took an inebriated Billy to his home to sleep it off.

"Fletcher somehow or another knew we had got into town," Robert said. "He came to the house and got Billy and it was almost like you see in the movies where a kid is pulled by the ear out of the house."

But it was not over. The next day was Saturday. Fletcher had another assignment for Billy and his good buddy. Those watermelons that didn't roll down Beaton Street didn't go to the grocery store. No, it was their job to head out into the country and around town and sell every one of those watermelons, and not come back until they did.

That's life in a small town. And it was a life, Robert Templeton knew, was about to end. He graduated from Frost High School in 1949 at age 17. Frost was a good town, a good place for a teenager to come of age, but he was anxious to shake the Frost black soil from his feet and see what was out there.

Two things were for sure. Whatever he was going to do in the future, it sure wasn't going to be selling watermelons door to door. And no one was going to know him as Gopher.

CHAPTER

4

Baylor And The Indifferent Law Student

Robert Templeton had never really given much thought about what he would do after high school. No one took SAT exams in those days. Counselors didn't assess the interests and aptitude of students.

High school graduates did one of three things – went to work somewhere full time, joined the military or went to college. Templeton didn't really know what he wanted to do.

As a kid, he thought about being an architect. His mother thought he'd make a good doctor. His father saw his oldest son as a lawyer. Any of those three, however, required going to college. Baylor University was just 60 miles away.

"It was just a place to go," he said. "I was glad to get out of Frost."

So Baylor it was. There was a little bit of money saved up for college, and with part-time jobs, Templeton and his parents believed they could do it.

Robert and his dad were on the crowded steps of Waco Hall in May of 1949 with hundreds of students who were registering for summer classes. In the mass of students, one caught his eye – Murray Watson from the small town of Mart, Texas.

"I'm walking up these long steps and I see this chunky kid in overalls. I had on these old blue jeans, a shirt my mother made and $2 blue suede shoes. I look up up there and thought, 'Golly, there's a guy more country than I am,'" Templeton said. "We became good friends."

They would room together their second year at Brooks Hall, and four years later shared an apartment where they rode out the 1953 Waco tornado.

While Bob was at Baylor, Tommy and Mary Templeton moved to Lubbock. After they did, Watson's father, who owned a feed store in Mart, took Robert under his wing. Often on weekends, Murray and Robert headed to Mart, just 22 miles away, for the weekend.

"Mrs. Watson would fix Sunday dinner," Templeton said. "Nobody made Sunday meals like her. I ate like crazy."

Murray was an accounting major. They were in two accounting classes at Baylor, and thanks to Murray, both made As. Murray would graduate six months after Robert and both were in Baylor Law School. What separated Murray from others was not his mind in the classroom, but in business. He was instinctive. His business mind was exceptional.

Just two years after graduating from Baylor Law in 1954, at the ripe age of 24, Watson was elected to the state House of Representatives. He served in the House until 1963, and then was elected to the State Senate where he served for the next 10 years. His legislation while in the Senate established the Texas State Technical College system.

After his political life, Watson pursued another passion – education. He was the key organizer and the CEO of the Brazos Higher Education Authority and Brazos Higher Education Service Authority in the 1970s. The two nonprofit organizations have provided more than $12 billion in student loans.

"In a race, I was the hare and he was the tortoise, and he beat me in every race," Templeton said. "Murray had attention to detail, and I was ADD. Think about a country boy from Mart, Texas – he just kept getting better as he got older."

In 2017, one year before he died, Watson was named Baylor Lawyer of the Year. He invited his college roommate to give a speech on his behalf at the ceremony in Waco.

"Murray and I never had a harsh word or disagreement of any kind," Templeton said. "He became one of those father figures that everyone respected."

But in 1949, Murray Watson was a country kid in overalls that Templeton took a liking to in that first year at Baylor. His first roommate at Kokernot Hall was Jack Anderson, also of Mart, who happened to be the valedictorian. Of the two small-town valedictorians, one from Frost, one from Mart, one didn't study much.

Classes always came fairly easy to Templeton, but there was an exception here and there. Robert actually began classes in the summer of 1949. He took an English test to assess his knowledge. A score of 160 set apart the brighter students from the average. Templeton scored a 162.

"I don't know how I made it," he said. "I got in a class that summer where the rest were valedictorians and salutatorians from bigger schools."

The teacher was Lois Douglass. The first day, she asked the class to write a theme. Robert had just one question before he started – what was a theme? He was told it was a story about something. So he gave it a shot, which apparently wasn't much of one. Douglass returned his paper with a B-/F.

Robert bought a grammar book and started studying the King's English. Anything to help in writing themes. They gradually got better, emphasis on gradually. He started making Ds, then some Cs, and finally crept up into the Bs. At the end of the semester was a paper that would count quite a bit toward the final grade. On this one, Templeton wrote on skeet shooting since his dad was one of the best skeet shooters in the country. The grade on that one was an A/A-. Douglass gave him an A as his final grade.

The next year, Douglass, whose husband had died in a car wreck, had a couple of upstairs rooms in her home that she was renting. Anderson, his freshman dorm roommate, and Robert decided they'd take them. In an abrupt twist from the year before, Templeton spent some time grading English papers for her.

"I took anything I could with Lois Douglass," he said. "Letting me grade her papers stayed with me all these years. She was really a mentor to me, believed in me. She was just a cheery wonderful lady."

Before that, however, that freshman year was an adventure to be sure. That fall of 1949 was Templeton's first real exposure to Southwest Conference football. Baylor, Texas A&M, and Texas were basically a triangle. It was 92 miles to College Station and 102 to Austin. Some bad blood boiled between the three close rivals.

The week of the A&M game, some Aggies drove to Waco in the early morning hours, climbed the flag pole in front of Harrington Hall and flew a flag that read, "Beat The Hell Out of Baylor." Then they greased the flag pole before high-tailin' it back to College Station. Several tried to climb the pole the next day to take down the offending banner, but didn't make it very far before sliding down.

"I thought I could make it up, so I gave it a shot," Robert said. "I got the flag down and you would have thought I was some kind of hero. It wasn't a big deal to me."

Kokernot Hall was a lively place to be. It wasn't much of a place to study, but it was entertaining. It was a toxic mixture of testosterone when most boys were away from parents for the first time.

Robert and Anderson were on the second floor of Kokernot, which was a new dorm. Each wing had a lavatory with showers and toilet. Their room was right next to the bathroom. That's good if you wake up in the middle of the night and need to go. That's bad if someone down the hall gets a wild hair and wanted to flood the dorm.

"That happened more than once," Robert said. "I'd wake up in the middle of the night and see my shoes floating."

One course of action was to tell the Resident Assistant. The other course of action was revenge. He chose revenge.

He told Anderson about his plan, and to put up everything that might float. One late night, he quietly made his way to the bathroom. He carried with him a big board. The board was to place inside the two handles on the double doors that opened inside the bathroom.

With the bathroom doors secured, he turned on all the faucets and showers, and plugged the drains. But the caper was not complete. He opened the second-floor window and lowered himself to where he held on to the ledge with his hands. He then dropped about eight feet to the ground. He walked back to his room and waited.

The only thing missing the next morning was two animals of each sex lined up. It was a flood of Biblical proportions.

"A day or two later, the RA told me, 'I know you did it, Bob. I know you did it,'" Templeton said. "I said, 'I don't know what you're talking about.' He told me he was giving me 14 demerits and if I got one more, I was out of the dorm and maybe kicked out of school."

The next incident was demerit-less, only because it was anonymous. Had Robert's cover been blown, he might have been booted out of Baylor if not killed first. There were two basketball players who roomed together, Billy Hickman and Lonnie Quillen, a big 6-foot-5 center.

"Quillen used to pick on boys about my size. It wasn't to hurt them, but it would be like a cat playing with a mouse," Templeton said. "There was one especially he just went on and on with it. It was almost sadistic. I thought, 'you SOB..."

Templeton got a sock and put a hole in it. Then, he got – well, let's just call it poo, human poo – and filled the sock. Then while Quillen and Hickman were on a road trip playing basketball, Templeton was able to get into their room without anyone knowing. Then, at random and carefully, he began to sling the sock around their room. He did so until the sock was empty. Then, watching where he stepped, he climbed out of their room.

"They never figured out who did it," Robert said. "I might have told Jack, but that was it. I left an anonymous note too. After that, Quillen left the kid alone. They never knew who did it. To hell with them. I hated bullies."

It's probably fortunate for Templeton and his Kokernot wing mates that he didn't have more free time. Who knows what would have happened? In 1950, college wasn't as expensive as it would be 70 years later, but a private school still wasn't cheap. Templeton needed to make some money while he went to school.

One of the first things he did at Baylor was join the Air Force ROTC. It wasn't that he was especially fond of the military, though

Bob (left) in the Air Force ROTC with good friend Murray Watson in Baylor's Brooks Hall.

Bob at Baylor

at one time, he thought he might want to be a pilot. Mainly, he liked the sharp-looking uniform, and the fact he got $75 a quarter.

A lot were joining the ROTC program. World War II had been over for five years, but the Korean War was about a year from erupting. Templeton showed a flair for leadership. He had an air of confidence about him that caught the eye of the commanding officer. But when Templeton was offered a regular commission with a chance to be a pilot, that didn't really appeal to him.

"I was asked if I wanted to make the Air Force my career, and I did not," he said. "It was something to do."

He had a chance to be cadet colonel his senior year, but when he declined the regular commission, the post went to someone else. Templeton finished his ROTC career as a Master Sergeant and in his last year as a Squadron Commander.

A considerably more interesting job was at Memorial dining hall, a girls dormitory. Templeton was shy around girls, at least until that point in his life, but he landed a job waiting tables at Memorial. Not a bad gig.

He was responsible for four tables, eight girls to a table, 32 in all. He'd kick open the kitchen door and carry out trays. He worked two meals a day. Robert would see girls, he said, without makeup and in curlers, but also saw them dressed to the hilt.

"Best job I ever had," he said. But it was also a job he got fired from.

He met a girl on his waiter job at Memorial – Anita Madden. It was his first love interest. She also worked in the dining hall.

"I was crazy about her," he said, "and I thought she was crazy about me."

That summer, Templeton left for ROTC Camp at Luke Air Force Base in Phoenix. Before he left Texas, he went up to Vernon, Anita's home town, and spent a few days with her and her family.

"Best I could figure out," Robert said, "her dad didn't like me."

Templeton had not been at Luke very long when he got a letter from his girlfriend. He tore into it, but unfortunately, it was a Dear John letter. She was ending the courtship.

Que sera sera. It hurt for a little bit, but time marches on. Robert returned to Baylor that fall, and back to his job serving the girls at Memorial. Anita too was there, working at Memorial. She saw Robert, and left crying.

"Mrs. Black, the dietician, told me I was fired," Templeton said. "What did I do? She wouldn't tell me, but I think we all knew. The rest of the girls knew what was going on. It was too upsetting for her (Madden) for me to be around."

With hindsight as 20-20 vision, it would be the best Dear John letter and firing Templeton would ever have. It would be two years later before he would know it.

Robert was never one to let moss grow under his feet. He always seemed to be in a hurry, and that included graduating. He went to summer school, and taking large loads of classes each quarter, he was able to condense three years of undergrad classes into two. In six quarters at Baylor, he was on the Dean's List in five of them.

What now? Templeton had no burning desire to be a lawyer. The thought of being one did not consume him like it may have others. But Tommy, his dad, insisted he should be one. No one looked up to his dad like his oldest son. So Robert decided to give it a shot. If it didn't work out, he could always find something else to do.

Baylor Law School was in a wartime building on campus next to the old main library. If he could get into law school, continuing at Baylor seemed to make sense. So he took the law school aptitude test and scored a 92, highest among applicants. He was accepted and entered Baylor Law at age 19 in September 1951.

In the beginning, it was easy. But just to be sure, he was studying two hours a day outside class, which, for Templeton, was more than he'd ever done. One of his first classes, in Torts, he aced.

"When the grades came out, I set the curve in that class by 10 points," he said. "All these people wanted to know who this Templeton guy was."

Baylor Law School suited him. It was a combination of practicing lawyers and professors. Abner McCall, later the renowned Baylor president but then the dean of the law school, taught him in an evidence course.

Templeton's custom was to go to class, to read ahead on cases, and study just enough to get by. He'd much rather shoot pool, play poker or drink beer. That didn't always endear him to his law school instructors.

One of them was Angus McSwain, a young redheaded Scotsman. He was a graduate of Texas A&M and would later become dean of the Baylor Law School. He was only 28 at the time. McSwain would go over cases in class, analyze them, discuss the findings, the fact and the reason. But he would do so in a flat voice and would drone on. That was tedious to Templeton, who had a somewhat short attention span anyway.

In one class, Bob Sheehy and Templeton tried to break the monotony by playing tic-tac-toe. Students sat on wooden chairs behind wooden benches, which made playing tic-tac-toe rather easy. Robert was talking as McSwain was talking. Shortly, McSwain quit talking, but Robert did not. He looked up and there wasn't a sound. And just about all eyes were on him.

"Angus was bald with this red hair on the side," Templeton said. "And when Angus got mad, you could see the red come up in that bald head. He would get as red as a man could get.

"He said, 'Mr. Templeton, I had so hoped you would not be in my class again this fall. You seem to disrupt any kind of organized proceedings. You get up, and get out of your chair.' There was a chair in the corner of the room, like a dunce chair. He said, 'Get up, go sit over there, and I don't want to hear another word.'"

So Templeton did as he was told, minus the dunce cap. He would later make a B in the course, and later made an A in a senior course McSwain taught in Texas Land Practice.

"He was a good teacher," Templeton said. "And he liked me. He really did."

Robert also tried the patience of law professor Frank Wilson, a perpetually sour man who constantly chewed on Tums. He was an old-time defense lawyer who held his classes at 8 a.m., and then went off to court and represented insurance companies. He had the practice at the end of each quarter to bring in students one-on-one to talk about their ambitions and desires.

"He was a crusty sucker. He called me in, and he knew me pretty well by then. I didn't know what he thought about me," Templeton said. "I know he never gave me good grades. He said, 'Mr. Templeton, what are you doing in this law school?' I said, 'Mr. Wilson, I have no idea.' He said, 'Huh? Goodbye.' That was it."

Wilson taught practice court, a meaty course over two quarters that taught rules of civil procedure and actual practice of law. At one point, students were assigned actual or fictitious cases. Students were either to defend or prosecute.

"He never answered a question in his teaching," Robert said. "He always asked you questions. He never answered yours. He tried to make us think."

He got Templeton to creatively think in practice court. The case Templeton was assigned was a real one – City of Waco v. Rook. It was a three-party case. A power line, owned by the city of Waco, came loose and electrocuted a man. The family sued the city of Waco which owned the power line and also a paving contractor who used some dynamite nearby to clear out the area to build a road. It was alleged the blast may have caused the power line to snap. Templeton was assigned to defend the highway contractor.

Each student was supposed to work with a specific set of facts. But Templeton knew if he did, he would lose the case. Templeton decided he would take depositions – a made up, creative deposition. The circus was in Waco, Templeton said, and Clyde Beatty was a lion tamer whose lion escaped the night of the fearful rain storm. Beatty went out in the storm looking for his lion.

"You were out there when the weather was bad, when it was raining and lightning?" Templeton told the class in reenacting the deposition.

"Yes, yes."

"And you came upon this area of the power line?

"Yes."

"And do you remember the number of the power line pole and

where it was located?"

"Yes."

"Then what happened? He said, 'Lightning struck and knocked down the power line. I witnessed it.'

Now that meant it was an act of God. Nobody was to blame for that. Certainly not the highway contractor. Then I asked him, 'Did you find your lion?'"

"Yes, I finally found her. My star lion was a female named Sheba."

"I then asked where he found her. He said she was shivering and cowering under a tree. Then what happened?"

"I called to her. I said, 'Come back, little Sheba!'"

"This was the same time as the movie, 'Come Back Little Sheba.' (a 1953 movie starring Burt Lancaster). When I read that line, the class laughed. Frank Wilson exploded and dismissed the class. For years after that, when I'd see Frank, he'd say, 'Come back, little Sheba.'"

Templeton made friends with another student, Ebb Grindstaff, whose father was a lawyer in Ballinger. For one thing, Grindstaff took detailed notes. Robert did not.

"I took lousy notes," he said, "but I could look at my notes and remember everything. So I might as well remember everything from good notes. I was a quick study. I was always a quick study. They say that's what really good trial lawyers are. I could grasp it quickly. In trial work, you can prepare and prepare but you got to be ready to react to something new."

But Templeton's time in law school was not marked with just classes and some perplexed law professors. Two events stood the test of time – a striking beauty named Martha Williams and a killer tornado that's still the worst the state has ever seen.

A good portion of those who lived in Waco thought the city was protected from tornadoes because it was in a valley. The outlying area was vulnerable. Frost, Templeton's hometown, was nearly destroyed by a monster storm in 1930. But as for Waco itself, it seemed there was a protective bubble over and around the city. Then came May 11, 1953.

Thunderstorm watches were issued for Waco and surrounding area that morning, but no one thought much of it. On this Monday, about 4 p.m., the sky darkened. It began to rain and parts of Waco got large baseball-sized hail.

About that time, Robert was making his way from law school classes back to the low slung stucco apartment he shared with Murray Watson at 9th Avenue and Clay Street. Living in those same apartments was a student named Ann Willis.

She was from Waco High School, and at Baylor on a debate scholarship. She often debated loudly with her boyfriend as Robert and Murray heard their fights and noise often. Ann Willis would later become Ann Richards and later become the governor of Texas from 1991 to 1995.

But on this stormy afternoon, the apartments were quiet as Templeton drove up to them in his green four-door 1946 Chevy that his dad had got for him.

At 4:30 p.m., about the time he arrived at the apartment, unknown to Robert, the massive F5 tornado formed in the valley and touched down in the southwest part of Waco and began to tear through neighborhoods. It began to rain pretty heavily on Templeton as he got out of the car. But the rain was warm and felt good on him.

"Boy, Murray, there's a pretty good rain coming down," he told his roommate. "Feels pretty good. I think I'll put on my swim suit and go outside and just let it come down on me."

When Templeton quickly changed and went outside, he saw a tree limb fly by. Maybe this wasn't such a good idea. He went inside, and as he grabbed the screen door, the wind took the door off its hinges.

"Murray, raise the window!" he said. "There's got to be tornado coming!"

An uncomfortable distance away, the tornado was chewing up Waco as it headed for downtown. It was 1/3 of a mile wide with winds at an estimated 260 mph.

There was a lull in the wind. Neither saw the tornado, but they could feel it. They didn't know if it was headed directly at them, but it was close enough. With no ready shelter to seek, they both

1953 Waco tornado

scrambled under the chrome kitchen table among the deafening noise.

Shortly after, the tornado roared into downtown Waco with frightening fury. Most buildings were not constructed to withstand the force. The R.T. Dennis home furnishing building collapsed, killing 30 inside. Templeton had a former philosophy professor and his wife killed when they sat in their car next to the Dennis building. A total of 196 buildings were destroyed, and 600 homes were demolished in east Waco as it left the city heading northeast. It dissipated near the town of Axtell, ending 23 miles of death and destruction.

After the storm subsided, Robert and Murray gingerly made their way outside to look around. Robert looked to his left one block away and saw an open area. Just moments before, there had been a row of houses. Now, nothing but foundations. The only thing standing around them was a stucco church right across the street and their sets of stucco apartments. About 200 feet in another direction and Templeton's law career would have been over before it started.

The tornado, still the deadliest in Texas history, killed 114 on that afternoon, injuring 597 and causing an estimated $51 million in damage, about $500 million in today's dollars. Some survivors waited more than 14 hours to be rescued.

Robert and Murray didn't know how bad it was. They started walking among the debris toward the downtown area, but didn't get very far. Murray's father drove from Mart, 20 miles away, to see about their safety. He found them walking. Shaken, they got in the truck and went to Mart for three days.

It was there that night that Robert made an important call to the Baylor campus. The university was largely untouched and still had some phone service. The phone call was to Martha. She was fine.

Martha Williams grew up in Austin. She was the youngest of two daughters. Her father, a captain in World War I, was the tax accessor of Travis County. She also happened to be the suitemate of Mary Tom Templeton, who eventually followed her older brother to Baylor.

Robert hadn't dated since Anita Madden mailed him a Dear John letter. But in his second year of law school, Mary Tom had an idea for her big brother. She set up the two on a blind date. Martha had a car. Robert didn't have much at all in the way of money. So their first date was to sneak into a drive-in movie. They just talked, got to know each other. Mainly Robert talked, but Martha proved to be a good listener.

"I thought at the time that this was a sweet gal and I could do worse," Robert said.

They continued to date, though it did have its moments. Martha had a sorority dance and, of course, invited Robert. He said he couldn't go, and gave some cockamamie story as to why. It might have even involved studying. Instead, Robert went to shoot pool. At some point, Martha thought it all sounded fishy. On a

Martha Williams

Martha and parents, J.R. (Bob) Williams & Grace Helen.

Bride, Bridegroom and some of the wedding party.

pretty accurate hunch, she called the pool hall that her boyfriend frequented and found out that he was right there.

"She was madder than hell at me," Robert said. "For years, she said I should have known then I shouldn't have married you. She threw that at me forever. But I didn't want to go to the dad-gum dance. But how many would have put up with that? What a woman."

Over the months, Robert thought Martha was the sweetest girl he'd ever met. But they were both headstrong. She didn't have any problem telling him what she thought, including the route to take in the car, or what she thought if he took a wrong one. They were honest enough and felt comfortable enough to argue with each other, more than most dating couples would. But the arguing didn't bother Robert. Maybe it was the lawyer in him.

Eventually, in December 1953, he asked Martha to marry him. Her response? "I'll think about it," she said.

"A few days later, someone asked me if we were engaged," Robert said. "I said, 'Who told you we were engaged?' She said that Martha did. I thought, 'I guess we are going to get married.'

In the lead up to their wedding, they met with the pastor of Austin Avenue Methodist church in Martha's hometown of Austin. It was some customary pre-marital counseling. While in the pastor's office, Robert and Martha got into a discussion which led into a somewhat pointed discussion.

"It sounded like a real argument to the preacher, but to us, we were just talking like we usually did," Templeton said. "He never said much to us, but finally, his only comment was, 'I believe you two are going to have a very interesting marriage.' And he was right."

Sixty-four years of marriage began on June 12, 1954. Murray Watson was the best man. Tommy Templeton, Robert's father, gave him $200 for the honeymoon. It was a quick honeymoon.

Baylor was in the rear-view mirror. Ohio beckoned. He had been called up to the Air Force as a second lieutenant. And as far as Robert Templeton was concerned, it would be a wasted two years at Wright-Patterson Air Force Base.

CHAPTER

5

An Uncertain Return Home

Wright-Patterson Air Force Base in Ohio was not exactly where Robert Templeton would have chosen to spend two years after graduation from Baylor Law School. In fact, it may have been one of the last places he would have picked.

Not that he had any say in the matter.

He was in the Air Force ROTC at Baylor, which included a stint as squadron commander. As such, he had two years he owed Uncle Sam as a commissioned officer in the Air Force.

Robert graduated from Baylor Law School in early March 1954. He was ordered to report to Wright-Patterson Air Force Base just northeast of Dayton, Ohio on March 28, 1954.

He left behind Martha, his fiancée, in Texas with their impending wedding 2 ½ months away. He was anxious to hang a shingle somewhere as a lawyer too, but that was on hold.

Wright-Patterson was one of the largest air bases in the country. About 10 years earlier, at the peak of World War II, about 50,000 were on the huge base. It was originally a World War I installation and the Wright in the name was for the original Wilbur Wright Field. Wilbur, of course, with brother Orville, invented and flew the first airplane. Dayton was their hometown.

Wright-Patterson in the late 1950s became the home of the U.S. Material Air Commandand and the Air Force Material Command.

In 1952, the base began some classified studies of UFOs. When Templeton arrived, there were 33 generals and admirals on the base.

Templeton was not one of them. But he was a Second Lieutenant. He was offered a position of Judge Advocate, which was an Air Force lawyer, and go in as a captain. Then he would have gone on to flight school. It was a three-year commitment.

"I wanted to get in and get out," Robert said. "Then I figured if I got past pilot training, they would not end up letting me go after three years."

The Air Force did put Templeton's legal background to use. He was a lawyer for the procurement committee. The B-52 was being built at Wright-Patterson from 1954-56. The procurement committee was in charge of huge purchasing and contracts, most of that on the B-52.

There were different types of contracts that the Air Force entered in with manufacturers -- supply, open and open-called contracts. The brass assigned him to write a paper on which ones were often more feasible. That even called for him to go to the Pentagon on that assignment.

"I don't know if anyone read it," Robert said, "but I wrote it. But for the most part, I sat behind a desk cleaning my fingernails and doing what I could to get in eight hours a day there."

A little more than two months at Wright-Patterson, Templeton got leave to go to Austin for the wedding with Martha in June 1954. The honeymoon, aided by $200 from Robert's father, was basically a meandering drive through the South before arriving back at Dayton.

It was a different, but not really a terrible way to begin a marriage. Martha worked for six months as a secretary and then got pregnant with their first child Linda. They socialized a little bit with some young couples about their age.

They lived in an apartment off the base for $85 a month, but were able to get a housing supplement. Robert made $275 a month. He was about $600 in debt from law school and still owed $400 on wedding rings.

Linda, their oldest daughter, was born in Dayton on Nov. 8, 1955.

Martha and Robert were in Columbus for an Ohio State-Michigan football game. Not long after they settled into their seats to watch eventual Heisman Trophy winner Hopalong Cassidy, Martha's water broke. Needless to say, Hopalong had to slice through the Wolverine defense without the Templetons in attendance.

In March 1956, Templeton's two years at Wright-Patterson were complete. He, Martha, Linda and their belongings began the trek back to Texas. To where exactly and for how long, who knew? All he knew was he was looking for his first job as a licensed lawyer in Texas. It was February 1956. It wasn't the best time to hire lawyers. That was usually in the summer.

He had a lead on an opening in Dallas with the prestigious firm of Carrington and Coleman. Paul Carrington was president of the State Bar of Texas. He was tall, regal in appearance, gracious in manners.

He and Robert talked. Carrington liked this young lawyer fresh out of the Air Force. It was mid-morning. This silk-stocking firm had 40 attorneys with some lucrative clients. For a first job, it would be hard to do better than working for Carrington and Coleman. Carrington told Templeton he was hired and to come back after lunch to talk to a couple of his other partners.

"I looked around and saw all of these guys walking around in pinstripe suits, and I just got scared," Robert said. "I mean, I just got scared. I knew I couldn't make it in that kind of firm. I didn't have enough confidence in myself. I didn't go back after lunch."

He interviewed with a couple of firms in Fort Worth, but nothing came of it. He went back to Dallas and talked with the managing partner of the Strasberger firm, which primarily defended insurance companies. But they never offered a job.

Meanwhile, Martha and the baby were staying with her parents in her hometown in Austin. While in Austin, Templeton went by to see Will Davis, a Baylor Law classmate of his. Davis was smart, diligent and graduated at the top of his class one quarter behind Robert in June 1954.

Since he didn't go into the service, Davis had a two-year head start in the job market. He landed a position working in the office of Texas Attorney General John Ben Shepperd. They both talked with Shepperd. They all hit it off, but there was just no opening.

Just after that, Tommy Templeton called his son to see if he wanted to drive up to Lubbock, where his parents now lived, and then go on up to Amarillo for a large hardware convention the city was hosting. Tommy now worked for Holt Sporting Goods in Lubbock.

Amarillo wouldn't be a bad place to work. He remembered the growing town as a young boy. Arnold Attebury, father of good boyhood friends Bill and Sam, wanted him to come here.

"I sure didn't want to go to Lubbock where my dad was because he would be telling me what to do all the time," Templeton said.

Amarillo in the 1950s was in the middle of tremendous growth. Amarillo Air Force Base and Pantex opened in 1951. Wolflin Village opened in 1953. The housing developments of Hamlet, Lawndale and Paramount Terrace added to the city's growth. In 1950, Amarillo's population was 74,000. By the end of the decade, it had increased by 85 percent to 138,000. It was in this exploding environment that Templeton searched for a job.

O.M. Calhoun was an Amarillo attorney who was president of the Amarillo Bar Association. Robert asked Calhoun about any available jobs in Amarillo. Calhoun didn't know of any openings within Amarillo firms, but for what it was worth, he'd heard of an opening in the Potter County Attorney's office. It wasn't glamourous. It didn't pay much, but it was a job.

So Robert went to talk with Potter County attorney Jerry Kolander and his assistant, Lon Moser. Kolander went to the University of Minnesota and migrated south to Texas. He worked for a while at the Amarillo Globe-News before getting his law license and getting elected to the post.

There was competition for the job. Walter Wolfram was just out of the University of Texas Law School and returned to his hometown. J.D. Helms also pursued the opening. Wolfram, like Templeton, is still practicing in Amarillo.

"Walter Wolfram, in my opinion, has long been under-recognized in Amarillo as a lawyer," Templeton said. "He is a superb lawyer. J.D. is a fine lawyer too. But Jerry called me in a day or two and said I had the job. So I accepted."

The next week, Will Davis called him to say there was now an opening in the Attorney General's office in Austin. More than that, Davis said Templeton had the job.

"That was Martha's hometown, and that's where her parents were, and truthfully, I wasn't all that excited to go there," Robert said. "In those days, Austin was not that much bigger than Amarillo. But as much as anything, I'd already accepted the job with Potter County and I wasn't going to go back on my word even though everyone probably would have understood."

Robert Templeton

Robert went back to Austin to get Martha, and took her to a place she'd never been. For a little while, they left their baby daughter with her grandparents. They stayed at the Wagon Wheel Motel on Amarillo Boulevard. They nearly froze to death in an unheated room at the back of the motel.

After about a week, they got a second-floor apartment at Astoria Park. They went back to Austin to get their belongings and 5-month-old Linda. They got back just in time for one of the worst dust storms of the 1950s to hit Amarillo.

"The place was not well insulated and dust would settle on the floor – that's how bad it was," he said.

But most of Templeton's time was spent in the Potter County attorney's office. His first job as a lawyer in 1956 paid him $325 a month. Kolander put him in charge of grunt work. He worked on foreclosures for taxes on old properties the owner had not paid that had accumulated over the years.

"They put me trying whatever they wanted to," Robert said.

The first trial in his career in front of a jury was in Justice of the Peace Court. Richard Stokes was a lawyer with the Fullingim law firm. Wayne Sturdivant, one of the firm's lawyers, defended him on a speeding violation. Sturdivant would become one of the best trial lawyers that the city has seen, but Templeton, unsure of himself, won the case.

"They were just high and mighty and haughty," Robert said. "Whoever the peace officer was, he was a good witness. Sturdivant thought they'd bull their way through the thing. They were the big fellas. I was a nobody."

Templeton came to Amarillo long on determination and ambition, but short of confidence. His stomach spent much of those early days in knots. That breezy it-will-work-out attitude at Baylor did not initially follow him to Amarillo.

"I knew nothing. I think I forgot everything I learned in law school," he said. "Two years had gone by. It was really wasted time in Ohio."

It was figuratively trial by fire, learn by doing. Kolander had him trying all the county court cases he could – misdemeanor cases, minor assault and theft cases, and a whole lot of DWI cases.

"At the time, the law required a mandatory 3-day jail sentence if you were convicted of DWI. There was no way you could get out of it," he said. "You couldn't get a blood test unless they consented. We'd get a few, but not many. Mostly we just relied on police and highway patrolmen. I had a patrolman that was the best witness you ever saw in describing a drunk. He and I never lost a case. I just turned him loose."

The year before Templeton started in Amarillo, legal history was made when Mary Lou Robinson was the first woman in the city to serve as a judge higher than justice of the peace when she became judge of the newly created Potter County Court of Law. This was a time when women couldn't even serve on juries.

Templeton tried numerous cases in her court. They became professional friends out of respect for each other. Robinson, a legal pioneer in many ways, would be appointed a U.S. District judge in the late 1970s, a position she held for 40 years. Robinson presided over one of Amarillo's most famous cases, the Oprah Winfrey beef trial in 1998.

In the late 1950s, the DWI defendants would be brought in on Monday morning. Many would plead not guilty.

"We'd be through by 10:30 in the morning," Templeton said, "and Mary Lou and I would go down to the second floor. This blind lady had a coffee shop and we'd sit there, drink coffee and talk. Mary Lou and I became fast friends.

"When I received the Temple Houston Award (in 2008), she spoke and said that Bob would always come into her court and just sigh. I sighed because it was so stressful. She also said that I wanted to take over her court. I told the group that I didn't want to take over her court. I just wanted to try my case without interference."

Judge Robinson would later earn a reputation that she was not to be trifled with. Her court was no-nonsense and attorneys better be prepared or often suffer her wrath.

"Trying cases in front of Mary Lou Robinson was not milk and honey," Templeton said. "She dominated the courtroom. She always called attorneys 'lawyers,' almost never 'attorneys.' I don't think she held lawyers in too high esteem.

"In her courtroom, it was always, 'May I,' like 'May I approach the witness?' If she liked that side, Mary Lou would say very sweetly, 'Yes, you may.' If she didn't like a side, she would say, 'Yes, you may' in pretty harsh terms. I gradually learned to study judges better – you have to."

The county attorney's office tried numerous cases in front of a jury. By Templeton's second year in 1957, the three of them tried 88 cases to a jury. Most of the cases were tried by Moser and Templeton. Kolander lost two cases. Moser lost one and Templeton lost one.

"Gradually, the butterflies subsided and I got more confidence," Robert said.

Eventually, Templeton began to represent the commissioner's court as well as the Liquor Control Board. In 1957, Kolander was appointed as a judge of the court of domestic relations. Moser ran for Potter County Attorney and won. Beginning in 1958, and for a couple of years, Moser and Templeton ran the county attorney's office. Some assistants came and went, notably Robert Carnahan, Hudson Moyer, and Stan Carter. But for the most part, it was just the two of them.

"This was when the town had an air base and a lot of things going on," Robert said. "Today, they have 15 to 17 in the county attorney's office, which is beyond my reason to understand why they need that many people there to do the job. I guess the city is bigger and a little more complicated, but my gosh."

He and Moser practiced law on the side for extra money and experience. Templeton took uncontested divorces and some collection work to supplement his $325 monthly salary. He began making as much as $1,000 a month, which was more than most young lawyers in Amarillo. But, more than anything, he was learning by doing, picking up varied and valuable experience. He represented the commissioner's court in contracts and the liquor control board on forfeitures.

"Moser was a helluva guy," Robert said. "Lon became a Christian Scientist and then got skin cancer. He never got tested or went to a doctor. But he was an able lawyer who applied himself and worked hard. He and I never had a discouraging word."

At the start of the 1960s, Moser and Templeton looked around and decided it was time to move on. Robert had been with Potter County for three years. That was three years of hectic experience. He was no longer an unknown. He did not take a vow of poverty to be a lawyer.

They decided to strike out on their own. They got Kolander to join up and they formed the law firm of Kolander, Moser and Templeton and, with one secretary, took an office on the second floor of the Fisk Building. They took whatever cases they could get.

Templeton's first personal injury case in front of a jury was on an accident at an intersection. It was a case no one really wanted, but Templeton jumped at it. His client had come to an intersection that was under construction. There was a temporary stop sign that had been spun around and was not visible to the driver. There was a collision.

Templeton's stance was his client was on the right side of the other driver at the intersection, and the traffic law stated that the right side of the driver had the right of way. So Templeton sued the driver.

The defense attorney was Albert "Snuffy" Smith. He was a crusty tough codger who chewed on a cigar all the time. Templeton believed the case was going well. There was a recess for lunch, and then Smith put on the defense. He called his first witness.

It was Templeton.

"I had no idea this was coming," Robert said. "It scared me. He could be an intimidating guy. I didn't know what he was going to do."

In the courtroom there had been a drawing on the blackboard of the intersection for the jury to see. It showed the angle of the stop sign. Smith thought the drawing had been messed with.

"Mr. Templeton," Smith said, "as we came back from lunch over the noon hour, I look up and see the sign has been changed. Did you come back in here and change the angle of this sign on the blackboard?"

"I said, 'Of course not, I hadn't,'" Templeton said. "And the jury knew I hadn't."

The ploy backfired, and the jury found in favor of Templeton's client. It was a small insurance policy, and the judgment was more than the policy.

But the case wasn't over. The Stowers Doctrine came into play. The Stowers Doctrine, established in the 1920s by the Texas Supreme Court, holds that a liability insurer in the defense of the insured has a duty to act in good faith.

Templeton knew he had given the insurance company a chance to settle for the policy amount and they had refused. So he sued in federal court. C.A. "Pete" Stein defended the insurance company. In what goes around comes around, Templeton had Snuffy Smith on the stand.

"It was fun," he said.

After that, Stein offered to settle for almost the amount of full judgment of $50,000. In 1961, that was a lot of money.

Shortly after that case, Templeton unwittingly stepped into dueling affairs between attorneys that could have been a plot from "Peyton Place," a steamy prime-time soap opera that was about two years from debuting.

Templeton was preparing for one case while trying to settle another. The common denominators were Rick Oaks and B.A. Hawkins (not their real names) from the same law firm.

Dale Cutberth was Templeton's client. He was in a neighborhood collision when he was driving down a residential street and a woman backed out of a driveway just in front of him. Cutberth claimed a back injury. Oaks defended the woman's insurance company. It was a small policy. Templeton tried to settle, but Oaks refused.

Hawkins was the defense lawyer in another trial on the horizon in which Templeton was the plaintiff's lawyer. He was working on getting a small settlement of about $3,000, but Hawkins refused.

"He was one heckuva lawyer," Robert said, "and a tough defense lawyer. After he turned me down, I got mad and cussed him. I said, "I'm going to get you.' I took it personal."

Unknown to Templeton at the time, Oaks had been sleeping with a secretary at Fullingim. Hawkins had been sleeping with her originally, but then Oaks started infringing on his territory.

"Apparently, Hawkins was madder than hell at him," Robert said.

So the Cutberth case went to trial. Templeton's best witness was Dr. Bill Stout, who testified to Cutberth's injuries and withstood Oaks' cross-examination. Templeton asked for $44,000. The jury found for Templeton, and awarded him $2,000 more than he asked. All of this was on a $10,000 insurance policy. Oaks should have settled. Templeton was almost skipping back to the Fisk building from the courthouse after the verdict.

"Here's Hawkins walking back toward the courthouse and he's smiling and just as happy as could be," Templeton said. "He came up and shook my hand and said, 'Bob, I'll settle that case with you.' He was so happy and I didn't find out until later why."

It was a bit of musical legal chairs for Templeton for a few years after that. Cleo Clayton and his son, Cleo Clayton, Jr., split off from the Fullingim firm. Clayton, Sr., was small in stature, but as far as Templeton was concerned, as good an all-around lawyer as there was in Amarillo. He approached the two of them to see if they wanted to join forces in one firm. They agreed. So the Claytons, Templeton, Kolander and Moser came together. They stayed in the Fisk Building, but moved to a more roomy office area on the east end of the fifth floor.

It wasn't long, however, before the elder Clayton fell ill. About all he could do was issue some title opinions. That left the four of them, and Templeton discovered that Cleo, Jr., was much like Kolander in that he couldn't bring in much money.

"He was probably worse than Jerry in that regard," Templeton said. "Nice fella, not dumb. I just don't know what it was with him."

Moser and Templeton were making most of the income for the firm. The money draw some months was not fun. It was peaks and valleys for the three of them. It could be a struggle, but as the mid-

1960s approached, they were starting to get more business.

"I came to Amarillo out of ignorance," he said, "and stayed out of fear."

Then came a case that took Robert Templeton's career to another level. And for that, he could thank "The Most Hated Man in America."

CHAPTER 6

The Most Hated Man In America

George Lincoln Rockwell was the closest the United States has had to an American Adolph Hitler. In 1959, after his discharge from the Navy, he founded the American Nazi Party and became a symbol of hate to many.

In 1938, at age 19, after being denied entrance to Harvard, Rockwell was accepted and enrolled at another Ivy League university, Brown. He was there just one year before he dropped out after a commission into the U.S. Navy.

Rockwell served in the Battle of the Atlantic and in the Pacific Islands during World War II. After the war, he worked as a sign painter and later founded his own advertising agency in Maine. He and wife Judith had three children.

When the Korean War broke out in 1950, Rockwell was recalled to duty as a Lieutenant Commander in the Navy. He and his family moved to San Diego where he trained pilots for the Navy and Marines.

That sounds more like the background of a wholesome straight arrow, not a devoted follower of Hitler. But something had been bubbling inside for at least 10 years, and it began to surface while in San Diego.

He became a public follower of Hitler and an advocate for Nazism. It was then that he read Hitler's biography "Mein Kampf." He was influenced by Sen. Joe McCarthy's witch hunt of Communists in Washington and Hollywood.

The flame only got hotter as the decade of the 1950s wore on. By 1955, he published a magazine that opposed integration and Communism. In 1958, he met Harold Noel Arrowsmith, Jr., a wealthy heir and, like Rockwell, an anti-Semite. They formed the National Committee to Free America From Jewish Domination.

By December 1959, his organization was renamed the American Nazi Party, and his movement began to get the attention he craved. To attract media attention, he led rallies with his small, but vocal numbers at the National Mall in Washington, D.C. and Union Square in New York. Many of them turned violent, including one where he wanted to celebrate Hitler's birthday.

Rockwell denied the Holocaust and believed Hitler was "the white savior of the 20th century." He said civil rights leader Martin Luther King, Jr., was being used by Jewish Communists wanting to rule the white community.

Blacks, Rockwell said, "were a primitive lethargic race who desired only simple pleasures and a life of irresponsibility." He advocated for a resettlement of U.S. blacks to a new African state to be funded by the U.S. government.

Rockwell tried to put on a regal dignified air. He was tall, at 6-foot-3, and usually had a corncob pipe, modeled after one of his heroes, Gen. Douglas MacArthur. He was a write-in candidate for president in the 1964 election, receiving 212 votes. He was in the Virginia governor's race in 1965, receiving 5,730 votes or 1 percent of the total.

It was in 1965 that the paths of Rockwell and Robert Lincoln Templeton would cross. If that seemed bizarre and off-the-charts unlikely, it's because it was. The two shared the same middle name, but that was the end of anything in common.

Templeton was still swimming upstream a bit as a partner with Kolander, Moser and Templeton. In the mid-1960s they worked primarily on contingency fees. If their client didn't win or if they couldn't reach a settlement, they didn't make a living. This was in a

George Lincoln Rockwell was an American Adolph Hitler. He founded the American Nazi Party in 1959

Rockwell and his corncob pipe, which he used to resemble one of his heroes, General Douglas MacArthur.

time when, because of Special Issue Submission, it was harder for a plaintiff to win.

"I was trying cases against lawyers from larger firms in town. There were three big ones in Amarillo at the time – Underwood, Gibson Oschnor, and Culton Morgan," Templeton said. "I was always trying cases against local lawyers representing insurance companies. Those law firms had stroke with these judges. I had nothing, nothing.

"I was just a little ex-assistant county attorney. If there was some discretion involved, I knew which side it would fall most of the time. Now Mary Lou Robinson was the exception. When she got on the district bench, she was the exception."

Then George Lincoln Rockwell and his American Nazi Party paid Amarillo a visit in 1965, and things changed for Templeton. The Amarillo Globe-News wrote a story on his upcoming appearance and wrote that Rockwell and his party were on the U.S. Attorney General's list of subversive organizations.

A subversive organization, at that time, was another way of identifying a Communist. Nazis were enemies of Communists, which is one reason why Hitler invaded the Soviet Union in World War II.

"Anytime you falsely call someone a Communist," Templeton said, "it is libel per se, which meant libel as a matter of law. It was pretty cut and dried."

Television station KFDA, a CBS affiliate, picked up on the Globe-News story, repeating what the newspaper had written about Rockwell and the American Nazi party being on the Attorney General's subversive list. Rockwell wasn't in Amarillo long, staying at the Herring Hotel, but was there long enough to see the KFDA report.

He didn't like it at all. He went back to Virginia and decided to file a libel suit against the television station in a "diversity of citizenship." Rockwell and the American Nazi Party were non-residents of Texas and KFDA was a local Texas corporation. Because it's a citizen of one state suing an entity of another state, the suit could be tried in federal court in Amarillo.

And so it would be. Longtime federal judge Joe Dooley would preside over the case. To add to the drama of the case, Dooley's only son, an Army captain in World War II, had been killed in Germany fighting Nazis. Dooley had a large picture of his son in his office.

Moser had done some legal work for KFDA. He didn't want to try the case, so he offered it to Templeton. No doubt, this wasn't a run-of-the-mill DWI case of the kind he had worked many times earlier. This very well could be a highly public trial.He may have gulped a couple of times, but, yes, he would take the case. He had to take the case.

"I don't know why he didn't sue the Globe-News," Robert said. "I guess he thought KFDA would be easy pickings."

Rockwell's ego wouldn't allow anyone but himself to be his lawyer. Plus, not many would rush to defend such a divisive character. There was some pre-trial discovery, but nothing to the extent that it is today. No depositions were ever taken.

In preparation, Templeton heard that Rockwell had written a book, a semi-autobiography, "This Time The World." He got a copy of the 1961 book that explained how Rockwell's beliefs on National Socialism were formed and how he came to embrace the words of Hitler. The book was dedicated to Hitler, in which in the dedication he apologized for helping wage war on Germany: *"I helped to bomb and burn millions of your brave young men. Your blue-eyed young mothers were raped and murdered by Soviet and Negro savages. The millions of little blond boys and girls you loved so well lie smoldering in acres of devastation and ruin..."*

He ends the dedication with this: ...*"Out of the mud and slime of lies, your holy red, white and black Swastika has been flung back into the skies in Virginia, United States of America, and we pledge you our lives, Adolph Hitler, that we should not flag or fail until we have utterly destroyed the forces of Marxism and darkness. HEIL HITLER! It is necessary that I should die for my people, but my spirit will rise from the grave and the world will know that I was right."*

Inflammatory words from who most would consider a psycho. Templeton didn't have time or the desire to read all of the book. But he read enough to know who and what was on the other side. As he was leafing through the book a few days before trial, the mail arrived at his law office in the Fisk building.

There was a large plain white envelope. There was no return address. As Templeton opened it up, he pulled out numerous white sheets of paper. Whoa. On them was the transcript of every phone conversation that Rockwell had while staying at the Herring Hotel. It was a half-inch thick.

"All of them were local conversations," Robert said. "No question about it, the Anti-Defamation League had tapped his phone and had sent the transcripts to me."

The question immediately came as how to use this information, and how much could he legally use. The trial began in 1965 in a packed courtroom in the federal courthouse. Among the onlookers was one Stanley Marsh 3, who was still in college.

Rockwell put on his case first. He put two witnesses on the stand, both of them his lieutenants. They were dressed in khakis, all spit and polish. One was blond, the other black haired. They look like an Aryan race recruiting poster. Their basic message was their party was simply an outspoken, but conservative group.

Then it was Rockwell's turn to play to the jury. Tall and striking, he paced in the courtroom and told his story. He went to Brown University. He was a commander in the U.S. Navy. Why, he wasn't much different than the jury or the good folks of the Texas Panhandle.

Templeton knew it was a load of crap. He knew what the transcripts said and he knew what was in Rockwell's book. Rockwell had not told the jury that he believed Hitler to be the savior of the world, that he had a shrine in his home to the ruthless Nazi dictator.

"He got up there and said, 'Oh, we're not Nazis like you think from Nazi Germany. I just utilized the name to attract attention. We're conservative, and we believe in conservative causes just like you folks. What this television station has said about us, how they've libeled us, has hurt our ability to raise funds for my party,'" Templeton said.

It was no secret the John Birch Society in Amarillo was very active. It was a fertile place for Rockwell to raise money. One of his main fundraising targets could have been the controversial J. Evetts Haley out of Canyon.

"Got to thinking about that," Templeton said. "That's why the guy came here."

Haley was an ultra-conservative political activist. A historian, he graduated from then-West Texas Normal College in 1923 after high school in Midland. He wrote the biography of Charles Goodnight and was later the field secretary of the Panhandle-Plains Historical Society.

But he was known beyond the Panhandle for his political views. He unsuccessfully ran for the 18th Congressional seat as a Republican in 1948. Eight years later, this time as a Democrat, he failed in his bid to get the nomination as governor. He vowed, if elected, that he would use the Texas Rangers to force public school segregation in the wake of the Supreme Court's ruling of Brown v. Board of Education two years earlier.

Haley organized a short-lived third party in Texas, the "Jeffersonian Democrats of Texas." A frequent critic of Franklin Roosevelt and the New Deal as well as Lyndon Johnson, Haley made waves and got the attention of radical right wingers with his book, "A Texan Looks at Lyndon." He described the president as "vain and vicious," and in 1964, he suggested Johnson was involved in the assassination of John Kennedy.

Scathing words and just the kind of vitriol that might attract Rockwell to pay him and others in the Amarillo area a visit. When it was Templeton's turn to cross examine, he was prepared. He had read enough of Rockwell's book to get a good picture of his background. While the secretly recorded transcripts were not admissible in court, it gave him an idea of why he was there and that was a crucial opening.

"I remember Stanley talking to me later – he was a fan of mine – and said I saw this little guy with a great big voice just get up there and kind of take over," Templeton said.

First, Templeton tore to shreds the idea that Rockwell was just like most conservatives in the Panhandle, that he just had a different way of going about his beliefs. He grabbed his autobiography in front of the jury and turned to a passage.

"You write that the doctrine of Adolph Hitler is the new Christianity of our times and that Hitler is the new savior," Templeton told him. "It has your name on this book. Is this you who wrote that?"

Rockwell nodded and admitted he did.

Templeton wasn't finished. He thumbed a couple of pages over to another passage. "It says here in your book," he said, "that 'I became an all-out Nazi, worshipful of the greatest mind in 2,000 years, Adolph Hitler.' And there are two exclamation points after that. It has your name on this book. Is that you who wrote that?"

Rockwell quietly said that he did write that.

One last time, Templeton opened up "This Time The World": "It says here also in this book," he said, 'today, the Nazi parties in other countries operate with front names, just as I direct our Nazis in many American cities to operate under other names until they are strong enough to survive the Jewish terror attack.' It has your name on this book. Is that you who wrote that?"

Rockwell nodded.

"I found some of the most scathing passages in the book and asked him if he believed what he wrote or was he just lying?" Templeton said. "He had to admit it. We had unmasked his deception."

But the trial really turned when Templeton pushed Rockwell on what exactly brought the leader of the American Nazi Party to Amarillo, Texas. Rockwell was suing KFDA for a considerable amount, and so Templeton asked who were his local contributors.

"I can't tell you that," Rockwell said. "That's confidential."

Templeton turned to Dooley, telling the judge that if Rockwell was suing for damages, he needed to answer the question.

"Commander," the judge said, "you need to answer the question."

Templeton asked Rockwell again the names of his local contributors, and, again, he refused to divulge names. Dooley told Rockwell that he must answer. Templeton asked again, and, for the third time, a refusal to answer.

"Commander, this is Friday," Dooley told him. "We're going to recess the case. I will give you until 10 a.m. Monday to come back and answer that question. If you don't do that, I will dismiss your case."

Over the weekend, Rockwell packed, and took a flight out of Amarillo's English Field back to Virginia. Dooley dismissed the case, and the young Templeton, at age 33, had won a huge victory for his client. The consensus was that had Rockwell returned and obeyed the judge, Templeton still would have won the case. But, boy, would there have been some naming names fireworks from the witness stand.

"The Panhandle of Texas is filled with good people, people who go to church, have good morals, work hard and take care of their families. That was very true in 1965," Templeton said. "You could say George Lincoln Rockwell got his comeuppance in Amarillo, Texas."

In moments of reflection after the case, Templeton could not help but admire Dooley, whose own son had been killed in combat fighting against the Germans in World War II.

"I never talked to him about it, but can you imagine how Judge Dooley felt?" Robert said. "He handled it as though it were simply another lawsuit. But you couldn't help wonder what was going through his mind."

What went through Templeton's mind during the trial was what he had started to hone during all those cases in the county attorney's office and what would serve him in the next six decades. A good lawyer had to rise to the occasion.

"Every lawsuit that I've tried in front of a jury I have felt stress," he said. "But the stress is like the fight-or-flight syndrome. What happens is suddenly my senses get more alert. I'm more aware of my surroundings. My memory is better, my mind quicker."

It's what led him to read Rockwell's autobiography to him to strip away the veneer of normalcy, and then to back him into a corner with the help of the recorded transcripts.

"The big problem about defending KFDA was not the thought that Rockwell would recover any money damages," Templeton said. "It was the fact that libel per se meant that Rockwell was entitled to nominal damages because calling him a Communist was libel as a matter of law.

"I didn't know how to get around this. But as things happened, Joe Dooley gave us the opportunity to walk away when he told

Commander Rockwell to divulge his contributors or he would dismiss the case. Judge Dooley allowed us to go home free."

When the trial was over, Templeton destroyed the anonymous letter and never let anyone see it.

In what would be several legal crossroads in his career, this was the first that helped further establish himself in the Amarillo legal community. He and Rockwell were two brief adversaries passing in the night.

Two years after the trial, on Aug. 25, 1967, Rockwell was shot and killed while leaving a laundromat just a few yards from his home in Arlington, Va. John Patler, who had been expelled from the Nazi Party by Rockwell a few months earlier for trying to inject Marxism into party publications, was convicted of the murder and sentenced to 20 years in prison. He was one of the lieutenants who testified on Rockwell's behalf at the trial.

— Reflection —

"It's why I got hooked on lawsuits, and am still hooked on it. You're never fully prepared or completely ready. I feel like I have a moral side of the case, and I really want to win.

"I'm not a country lawyer. I'm a country boy who became a lawyer. I became one out of necessity, but realized later it was a calling."

CHAPTER

7

Larger Than Life W.A. Maddox

W.A. Maddox was a Lubbock dentist in the 1960s. That didn't come close to telling the story of the man who could cast an imposing shadow. He was a craftsman, able to take leather and carve works of art in them. Some of his carvings were in the Cowboy Hall of Fame in Oklahoma City.

More than anything, he was a trader. He'd trade for property, trade for dental work, trade for land, trade for horses. When patients couldn't afford to pay him money, they'd work out a deal for livestock.

"He'd trade for anything," Robert Templeton said.

In the late 1940s, Maddox traded for the Natatorium on Route 66 in Amarillo, which is now Sixth Street. The man managing the business at the time was not running it to suit Maddox. He moved from Lubbock to Amarillo, took over management of The Nat and never pulled another tooth. At one time Maddox owned the Villa Inn in east Amarillo, one of at least three hotels he owned that included one in Lubbock and one in Nebraska.

In 1967, Maddox was getting up in years. He was now pushing into his mid-70s. Frances, his second wife, was considerably younger, but not really a trophy wife. They had been married more than 20 years.

Maddox also owned some ranches, one in particular in New Mexico. It was in Rio Arriba County near Chama in northern New

Mexico. The El Poso Ranch was 27,000 acres and Maddox and the New Mexico government were getting crossed. Lesson 1 about Dr. W.A. Maddox: Cross him at your own risk.

"He was just a crusty old sucker," Templeton said.

It was 1967. Templeton was not that far removed from representing KFDA in a libel suit brought against the television station by American Nazi Party leader George Lincoln Rockwell, a case that was dismissed when Rockwell abruptly left town. Templeton didn't know Maddox.

He knew of him since Maddox was a longtime client of a new law partner, Cleo Clayton, Sr. But the elder Clayton was falling ill, and Maddox needed some help. He was already familiar with Templeton from a previous condemnation case from a few years back.

The state of Texas needed land along Grand Street for the construction of I-40 that would bisect Amarillo. Maddox owned much of the contested land in that area. Clayton, Sr., before he partnered with Templeton, represented Maddox against the Texas Attorney General's office in a condemnation case.

There also was a man of not much means who operated a fruit stand on that land. Through the sufferance of Maddox, his livelihood was impacted. Templeton represented the man, who didn't even have a lease. The fruit stand was there simply on the good will of Maddox. Templeton settled with the state, and got the fruit stand operator a nice sum.

"I guess we were kind of a thorn in their side," Templeton said. "Fred Talkington, who was a lawyer for the state, decided to get me out of there. He didn't like what I was doing. It was an emotional thing for this little guy. We got a pretty good dime for him."

With Clayton falling ill, Maddox remembered the young attorney and what he did for the fruit stand owner when the New Mexico legislature encroached on Maddox's land a little later.

In 1964, three years earlier, the Congress passed the San Juan Chama project. It had two major projects.

The first was to build a dam on the San Juan River for the Navajos. The second project was much more involved, and impacted Maddox.

W.A. Maddox

W.A. Maddox and wife, Frances.

Frances Maddox died
in 2008 at age 96.

It called for the diversion of water from the west side of the Continental Divide to the east side by emptying into tributaries of the Rio Grande River. To do so meant building collecting dams on the west side of the Continental Divide in the mountain country since most of the water fell on the west side.

The water would go through miles of a large man-made tunnel through the Sangre de Cristo Mountains, a tunnel large enough that a man could ride a horse in it. The water would empty into the Willow Creek tributary of the Chama River, which was a tributary to the Rio Grande.

The San Juan Chama project would dedicate 110,000 acre feet a year to downstream users. One acre feet is 325,850 gallons. Of that, 50,000 acre feet were dedicated to the City of Albuquerque, 5,000 acre feet to the Cochiti Indians, and the remaining 55,000 acre feet were designed to go to other Indian tribes as well as the city of Santa Fe.

All of this would come from the Heron Reservoir, built where the Willow Creek emptied into the Chama. The federal government said it needed 10,000 acres for the Heron Reservoir. Of that, 6,816.5 acres were on Maddox's El Poso Ranch. It was a mixture of wheat pasture, valley land, graveled hills and mountain slopes.

"The San Juan Chama Project was hugely popular in New Mexico," Templeton said. "Most of New Mexico is an arid state with rainfall

Heron Reservoir

no more than 11 inches a year. This project took water that would have gone through to the Colorado River to California and brought it into the state of New Mexico."

New Mexico gave Maddox a low-ball offer of $110,000 for the nearly 7,000 acres. He refused, and it wasn't a polite refusal. Maddox didn't really have a filter. He said what he thought.

This was headed for trial, no doubt. Clayton was ill by that time. Maddox needed a replacement attorney. What was the name of the fellow who got a nice settlement for that fruit stand owner? Templeton?

"He called me and said that he wanted me to handle the case," said Templeton, who was only 35 at the time. It wasn't that Maddox asked if he would consider the case, but more or less telling him to take it.

"I said OK," he said. "I took the case on a contingency fee, which meant I got one-third of the amount by which you increased the original offer. If I increased that $110,000 by $30,000, I'd get $10,000. But if it didn't increase, I didn't get anything.

"I had some experience with condemnation cases, but they were all highway cases with I-40 came through Texas. I had no idea of what I was getting into. Here was my client, W.A. Maddox, a crusty old dentist and Texan, small, bald-headed. He was a classic example of a Texan that New Mexico folks disliked."

Templeton headed to Rio Arriba County in the summer of 1967 to look for witnesses, and talk with appraisers, whom Maddox paid. Chama is the largest town in the county at about 1,000 people. Tierra Amarilla is the small county seat.

"I went up there, dumb and ignorant," Templeton said.

He had no idea what he was walking into, either from history or from culture. Ownership of land in Northern New Mexico had been an intense struggle for 120 years. The controversy stemmed from rights over land grants between Latino and Indigenous communities and the U.S. government that had gone back centuries.

Much of the land in northern New Mexico had been deeded by Spain to the Spanish settlers and Indians by titles known as land grants. Most of the land was for farming and for creating necessary irrigation systems.

In the U.S.-Mexico War in the 1840s, the United States obtained much of Mexico's northern territory that included some or all of New Mexico, Arizona, Nevada, California and Colorado. The Treaty of Guadalupe Hidalgo, which ended the war in 1848, was supposed to guarantee those land grant rights in perpetuity.

But going into the 20th century, it had not. There was some 600,000 acres in dispute in the Tierra Amarilla land grant. Emotions had always run high between Latinos and Anglos, and in the 1960s, behind militant leader Reies Lopez Tijerina, it was boiling.

Moving to New Mexico from Texas in 1960, he embarked on a crusade to establish Mexican and Indian rights in what he and others believed was their rightful land stolen from them. In 1963, Tijerina formed the Alianza Federal de Mercedes, or the Federal Alliance of Land Grants.

In October 1966, hundreds of Alianza members in 150 vehicles drove into Echo Amphitheater Park on what was once a land grant of San Joaquin del Rio de Chama, but was now property of the U.S. government. In a stand-off with law enforcement, several Alianza members were arrested.

As Templeton was making trips to Rio Arriba County that summer of 1967 on behalf of Doc Maddox, he probably missed the billboard that had the face of Mexican revolutionary Emiliano Zapata with the words underneath, "Tierra o Muerte," which means, "Land or Death."

On June 5, 1967 Tijerina, who later ran for governor of New Mexico, led an attack of the Alianza group on the Rio Arriba courthouse. Their attack had a dual purpose – to free jailed Alianza members who had been arrested days earlier, as well as to make a citizen's arrest on Rio Arriba County District Attorney Antonio Sanchez. The district attorney was not at the courthouse.

In a hail of bullets, two law enforcements officers were wounded, one of whom was later killed before he was to testify against Tijerina. A reporter and a deputy were held hostage. Several Alianza members

Reies Lopez Tijerina. In 1963, Tijerina formed the Alianza Federal de Mercedes, or the Federal Alliance of Land Grants.

fled into the mountains. Nearly 50 members of the National Guard from Taos were deployed in the massive manhunt. It was in that backdrop that Templeton defended Maddox in the condemnation case.

"Like I say, I was dumb and ignorant," he said. "It was a lawless country. I didn't know how dangerous the whole thing was."

In most condemnation cases, the value of land is largely dependent on comparable sales. About the best Templeton could find – and it wasn't good – was $8 an acre.

Templeton hired a local lawyer from Albuquerque to help him when the trial began in October 1967 in federal court in Albuquerque. His assistant, who was a railroad attorney by experience, didn't know the field of condemnation, but knew a few things about local cases.

One of the witnesses was a local rancher, Bill Mundy, who spoke on the value of property. His home had previously been burned by locals. Against immense pressure, he testified. Carney Wyrick had been an Amarillo appraiser, whom Maddox had hired. In the interim, Wyrick moved to Santa Fe and began working for the

New Mexico Highway Department.

"So he was working for an arm of the government and he was supposed to be my expert witness," Templeton said. "He was compromised. He was never a strong witness and became worse when he moved to Santa Fe."

Add to that a jury that likely wasn't too sympathetic, a federal judge, H. Verle Payne, whom Templeton said thought the federal government could do no wrong, and a worthy opponent representing the U.S. government in Dick Taylor.

Taylor was also a Baylor Law School graduate, getting out a few years before Templeton. He had been one of the government's top condemnation lawyer since he got out of Baylor. Taylor was also fond of liquor, and the more he had, the better he seemed in the courtroom. This lasted a month.

"Every morning before trial, he'd get a water glass and fill it half full of vodka, drink it straight, and then go in like a mad dog and flat tear us up," Templeton said. "I mean he did a helluva job."

One day during the trial, there was a large photo of Maddox's ranch. There was a lot of sagebrush on the ranch, and Templeton did his best to describe the rustic beauty of the land and how much it would cost Maddox to lose such a prime piece of rich ranch land.

"Look at this land," Taylor told the jury. "I mean, look at it. If that's the heart of this ranch, it looks like it's got an awful bad heart."

The appraisal value of the 6,186 acres not surprisingly varied wildly. Mundy testified the value of the ranch before the taking at $1.675 million, and the value after to be $1.2 million with a difference of $443,000 in compensation. Another appraiser for Maddox put the pre-taken value of the ranch at $2.8 million, and after the taking at $2.17 million for a difference of $635,000 owed to Maddox.

Meanwhile, government appraisers threw out figures of $885,000 before the taking, $765,000 afterward for a compensation of $120,000 while another witness put the compensation value at $140,000.

Templeton was seeking $220,000, double what the New Mexico government had offered. The jury came back with an award of $155,000 – an increase of $45,000. Considering the climate of the time, it was probably best to get out of there with something and go on. But it didn't feel that way.

"I walked back with my tail between my legs to Texas," Templeton said. "So while we got a small increase, it just felt like a very bad whipping."

Maddox was livid. He wasn't accepting any $155,000. He insisted that Templeton appeal. So began likely the most stressful, tedious and ultimately rewarding four years of this young attorney's life. Since Maddox was retired, the impending appeal consumed him, and if it consumed him, it consumed Templeton.

"He'd come to my office if not daily, damn close to it," he said. "He'd start cussing those people in New Mexico. He swore he'd never have another thing to do with the state of New Mexico."

Maddox, with his money, had political connections. He was a major donor to Texas senator John Tower, a Republican. He got Templeton an audience in the Washington office of Tower. He was ushered into Tower's office where the diminutive 5-foot-5 Tower, who towered over no one, sat behind his desk with an assistant standing at his side. Templeton poured out the facts of the case, told him he could use his influence to help his client and Tower's donor.

"He never said a word," Templeton said. "Never said one word. He just let me have an audience and after I gave my pitch, stood up and said, 'Thank you very much,' and that was it."

Tower was of no help. But an Amarillo lawyer by the name of J. Hadley Edgar was. Edgar was a friend of Templeton's and a defense lawyer for the Gibson Oschnor firm. He had Edgar help him on the appeal.

"He was great," Templeton said.

Templeton gave him all the factual information and Edgar dictated the appeal which was headed to the U.S 10th Circuit in Denver. They appealed on 10 points. The major point was that in federal condemnation cases, unlike the state of Texas, the question for a jury is the value of the whole ranch before the taking and the value of the ranch after the taking.

"So, in a case like this", Templeton said, "where they put on evidence that this reservoir was going to enhance the value of the remainder of the ranch, you could try a case like that and come out with the remainder of the 21,000 acres being worth more than the 27,000 before the reservoir, which made sense."

In May 1969, the 10th Circuit ruled favorably for the appellant on 9 of the 10 points. Said the 10th Circuit: *"When the sovereign appropriates part of a particular parcel of land, the owner's compensation includes not only the value of the land taken, but also the diminution in value of the remaining part resulting there from...The benefits that arise in these situations have been characterized by the courts as "direct," "indirect," "general," and "special" being allowed as a set off...Accordingly, the enhancement in value resulting from frontage on a wider and more desirable street or the proximity to a body of water contemplated by a public project is the type of benefit that has been recognized as direct and special."*

"In the instant case the Government attempted to show that special benefits to the remainder would result from its demand for use as cabin sites, recreational uses and the like. To the end, the Government's valuation experts testified that the market value of the remainder was enhanced. Their conclusion was said to be based upon sales of land adjoining other reservoirs. There apparently were no comparable sales with regard to this particular reservoir.

"The expert, Darrow, testified that his evaluation was based upon the assumption that the adjoining would enjoy unlimited access to the reservoir. This is clearly an unwarranted assumption in this situation in which the United States condemned the fee interest. Having appropriated sufficient acreage to ensure that the water level will at all times be well without the bounds of Government land, the United States as an owner in fee will have the legal right to fence the reservoir or otherwise prevent access to the water.

"The landowners will have no greater right than the general public. Thus, the right of access in itself will not be a special benefit, and the lack of access will affect the value of the special benefit arising by reason of the lakeside property's potential for homesite development. Clearly, the demand for lakefront property will be lessened when it is known that the principal advantage in such property may well be the scenic view it commands. The expert, having relied upon an erroneous assumption as to the abutting owners right of access, his valuation will be set aside and the case remanded for new

findings. United States v. Honolulu Plantation Co., 182 F.2d (9th Cir. 1950)

"Perhaps more significantly, however, we conclude that the testimony of both Governments experts as to the value of special benefits is too speculative to be meaningful. In connection with the reservoir project, the United States allocated $400,000 to provide for the construction of recreational facilities consisting of picnic tables, sewage, water, electricity and a boat launching ramp. This concrete ramp, essential for launching boats in the reservoir, will be several miles for the appellant's land and will be the only one constructed since the Government has full title and has provided for no other.

"Thus, the only recreational facilities are to be located off the appellant's land at a place where no roads of any kind directly connect those facilities and the El Poso Ranch. It also appears from the record that because of the nature of the rugged terrain, very little of appellant's land will be blessed with a view of the water. Moreover, it is undisputed that from the date of the taking on July 21, 1965, until the completion of the dam in the spring of 1971, some six years will have elapsed before the reservoir can be flooded.

"From the time the flooding begins, it is possible that as many as 10 years might elapse before the water reaches the level necessary to enjoy the Government recreational facilities. In view of these facts, it would seem difficult to conclude that the value of the lakeside land will be enhanced. The land will have a restricted view, no unique access to the water, no direct access to the recreational facilities, and a number of years to wait even for that.

"Against the background of uncontradicted physical fact, the Government expert merely indicated in unexplained total dollar figures, their opinion as to the value enhancement. In such circumstances, their testimony is of little value. To have probative value, expert opinion must be "founded upon substantial data, not mere conjecture, speculation or unwarranted assumption. It must have rational foundation." United States v. Sowards, 370 F.2d 87, 92 (10th Cir. 1966).

"Here the Government experts relied on erroneous legal assumptions, made no attempt to specify the kind of benefit contemplated or to limit the amount of acreage felt to be benefitted. Surely the entire 26,000 remaining acres will not be useful for lakeshore development and will not be benefitted. Yet the Government experts did not explain their gross valuation or denominate the extent of the benefit in any way. Obviously such "speculative and remote possibilities cannot become a guide for the ascertainment of value in judicial ascertainment of the truth." Wilson v. United States, 350 nf.2d 901, 909 (10th Cir. 1965); United States v. 2,635.04 Acres of Land, 336 F. 2d 646 (6th Cir. 1964).

"Numerous other alleged errors have been raised by the appellant. However, in view of the fact that the case is to be remanded, it is necessary only to comment briefly on some of the issues raised."

"Never had a ruling out of appellate court that I could remember been so favorable to the land owner," Templeton said. "My favorite quote was a footnote to the 10th Circuit's opinion that said: 'The Government experts did not attempt to indicate the dollar value placed upon special benefits. They merely stated aggregate 'before and after' values and indicated that the 'after' value was reduced by a certain unidentified amount for special benefits. Such a lackadaisical presentation, not unlike embodied in the appellate brief, hardly deserves commendation."

The case of 6,816.5 acres of land in Rio Arriba County in New Mexico [411 F. 2d 834, 10th Cir. 1969] has been cited favorably numerous times and is so cited to this day.

The 10th Circuit's opinion reversed the original verdict and ordered a new trial. Templeton could exhale – at least for a little bit. He tried again for a settlement, but didn't get anywhere. So, once again, Templeton and the U.S. government were in federal court in Albuquerque, this time in October 1971.

"I made up my mind I was going to see this suit through and finally get the trust of W.A. Maddox, who never trusted anybody – or else," Templeton said.

Things were a little bit different at this trial. First, New Mexico appraisers were hired that would help with the jury. Mundy, the rancher who testified in the first trial and had his house set on fire again, refused to testify again.

Templeton hired Robert Teichert from an Albuquerque firm. Teichert, in turn, suggested another attorney, Henry Birdseye, would be a help. The federal government not only wanted the surface land, but the minerals, and Teichert worked on putting a value on the minerals.

H. Verle Payne remained the judge, but he was bound by the 10th Circuit's opinion. Richard Taylor still represented the U.S. government in the case. But in four years, he had quit drinking.

He was cold sober.

"He was a different man," Templeton said, "and not as good in the courtroom."

The jury, Templeton knew, wanted to hear from Maddox. But that would be a disaster if he got on the witness stand. He had no filter, and Templeton knew he would probably start cussing the state of New Mexico and anyone else. He would cost both of them money with every word he yelled.

At one point in the trial, Maddox began cleaning his fingernails with a pocketknife. Where upon Payne admonished him in front of the jury: "Dr. Maddox, are you carving on my table?"

Maddox, it was clear to Templeton, would undo any goodwill, any progress made if he testified.

"So I had to find a reason not to put him on," he said. "And we had the burden of proof. In a federal condemnation case, you have the burden to show the damages. So we put our case on first."

Templeton had an idea. Frances Maddox was W.A. Maddox's second wife, whom he called "my black-headed heifer." She dyed her hair black. Frances could be a witness and maybe explain away why her husband could not testify.

"Is this your husband?" Templeton said, pointing to W.A.

"Yes."

"How is the doctor's health?"

"It's not so bad, but he has trouble understanding people."

"If I were to get him up here, would he be able to understand my questions?"

"No. He would not be able to do that."

So Templeton believed he'd established why the crusty Maddox could not testify. Now he had to establish that Frances, who was at least 20 years younger, was no trophy wife.

"I asked her how long she and the doctor had been married," he said. "She said, '24 years,' and the jury just smiled. Dick Taylor objected, and it was sustained. But that told the jury two things – what she got out of this, she earned, and she wasn't like a brand new second wife. They liked Frances."

This new jury also liked the New Mexico appraisers, who did a commendable job of selling the value of the El Poso Ranch. Maddox didn't get anything for the minerals, but only for the land. But the jury came back with a verdict of $384,000. It was more than double the original verdict of four years earlier. The government didn't appeal.

"Maddox always said he'd never have another thing do with the state of New Mexico," Templeton said. "The ink was not dry on the settlement, when he used the money he received to buy a 50,000-acre ranch near Hobbs (N.M.) He was something else."

Eventually, an attorney friend of Maddox's negotiated with a nearby Apache tribe in Rio Arriba County on the remaining 21,000 acres of the El Poso. The Jicarilla Apaches had some good oil and gas production, and bought the remaining ranch in the mid-1970s for $9.5 million. Maddox used the money to set up a trust to benefit several charities, including a children's home and most especially, to Lubbock Christian University.

Maddox had a home in the 2500 block of South Grand, a historical home that remains south of a Walmart. He died at age 89 in 1982, while Frances died in 2008 at age 97.

As for Templeton, the saga of W.A. Maddox and the El Poso Ranch was an example of that which will not kill me will make me stronger. Maddox's overbearing personality and the pressure that Templeton felt had him at a career crossroads as he neared his 40s.

"I had made up my mind, and I said this a dozen times after that, but if I didn't win that case, I was going to try to do something else instead of a lawyer," he said. "This was make or break. All that time and effort and not getting anything out of it, I don't know if I could have handled that.

"I don't know if really would have quit, but I said it. It was that kind of case."

CHAPTER
8

A Family Feud

As the 1970s approached, Robert Templeton had begun to establish himself in Amarillo after more than a dozen years in his childhood hometown. He and Martha had five in the family. Linda, born in Ohio in 1955 when Templeton was assigned to Wright-Patterson Air Force Base, was in high school. Tom, born in 1960, was 10 years old. Luanne, born in 1964, was starting to school.

They lived at 1510 Rusk, a house the Templetons bought in 1967. They paid $40,000 for their third home in Amarillo, and they loved the place.

His law firm, as it would during his career, began to shift. Lon Moser told Templeton he was leaving, and he understood. Moser was a good attorney, and would do well in almost any place. Templeton went to partner Cleo Clayton, Jr., and told him that maybe this was a good time to break up partners.

The two Claytons left and formed a partnership with Lyman Stubblefield. Jerry Kolander and Templeton stayed together, moving a few floors up to the ninth floor of the Fisk Building. Templeton was determined to show Kolander how to make more money.

They soon accepted another partner. It was Robert Carl Hamilton, better known as a R.C. He was a Baylor Law School graduate too. When the 31-story Texas American Bank building was completed in 1971 – "Amarillo's finger to the world," Templeton joked – Kolander, Templeton and Hamilton moved to the 18th floor. The offices were nice. There was a common library. Business was good.

One case, in particular, was good to the firm.

Burl Brister was a client of Tom Morris, who referred Brister to Templeton. Brister, a tough-minded, hard-working man, was successful in the pipeline construction business. He built pipeline for Santa Fe Energy.

Williams Brothers out of Tulsa was the general contractor, and Brister was the main sub-contractor. In its contract with Brister, Williams Brothers had the right to supervise him.

"But they were the worst nit-pickers you ever saw," Templeton said. "They made it very difficult for him to perform, but he did perform very well."

Through the ordeal, Brister took detailed and voluminous notes of all the confrontations and tedious action from Williams Brothers, one that he said cost him a lot of money. Templeton sued both Santa Fe Energy and Williams Brothers for Brister.

"It was a case where the lawyer really fit the case. Hamilton did a wonderful job," Templeton said.

Templeton settled with Santa Fe before trial. Williams Brothers wouldn't settle. It went to trial with U.S. District Court Judge Halbert O. Woodward presiding. Templeton cited "torturous interference" against Williams Brothers. Brister made for a superb witness, who held up again and again in cross examination.

The jury sided with the plaintiff, and gave Brister a large amount of money in damages. Williams Brothers filed a motion to reduce the amount. Woodward granted the motion, cutting the amount greatly to $120,000.

Hamilton was devastated and Templeton didn't feel much better. He filed a motion to reinstate the monetary damages. He convinced Woodward to reinstate the original amount of $364,000. It was affirmed on appeal.

"I showed the judge he had made a mistake and we were entitled to the whole thing," Templeton said. "He did just that. That was Hal

Woodward – he was that kind of man. Hardly any judge would have done that.

"It has been cited again and again on the principles of 'torturous interference.' It was a case of the little guy being stomped by the big guy."

The three partners reputation was enhanced by that case. They had all the work they could handle. They were helped by another attorney in the firm, John Judge. John Smithee, a University of Texas Law School student from Amarillo, started doing some summer work for Templeton in 1974, a rather innocent beginning to what would be more than 40 years of work together between the two.

"R.C. Hamilton was a very smart fellow, very smart, but he was very temperamental," Templeton said. "He was wound up tight."

Hamilton also liked to speculate in the commodity market. In the spring of 1975, he speculated heavily on pork bellies. He hit the jackpot. In what seemed like little time at all, Hamilton had made close to $500,000. Templeton was in his office one day when Hamilton came in with a stack of his files.

"I quit," he said, laying the files on his partner's desk. He had all the money he needed because of the commodity market.

Six weeks later, all that money that Hamilton had made was gone when pork bellies went south. He reappeared in Templeton's office, hat in hand, asking for his old job back.

"R.C., I'm not going to do it," Templeton said. "You're my friend and a good lawyer, but I'm not going to do it and be left in the lurch again. You'll do it again."

Hamilton went on to practice by himself. About a year later, Templeton began to hear from a Lubbock attorney, Bob Garner, who was noted for his defense of insurance companies. They talked on the phone, played a little golf together, and all the while, Garner appealed to Templeton to let him join his firm.

It was a double-edged sword with Garner. If Templeton took him on, he was taking the entire package.

"He was very good at what he did. He was a good trial lawyer,"

Templeton said. "But he made more enemies in Lubbock than you could possibly imagine."

Garner lost his Martindale-Hubbell rating in Lubbock, the gold standard of peer and client reviews of attorneys. Templeton knew there were problems in Lubbock, but thought a change of scenery 120 miles to the north would do him good. It was a way to wipe the slate clean.

So began in 1975 an up-and-down business relationship for the next 13 years. Sometimes it was tumultuous, and sometimes it was smooth. But it was always eventful.

"I don't know what it was about Bob," Templeton said, "but I always had some control of Bob."

Things seemed to spin around Garner. Coincidence or not, Jerry Kolander, who Templeton had worked alongside since he came to Amarillo in the late 1950s, soon left and began practicing with Hamilton. It wasn't long before Judge left to work in Austin.

Garner proved to be a good rainmaker. He brought in good cases to the firm. He also brought in some attorneys to the firm. Nancy Stone, from Houston, came to Amarillo. Garner brought in Sam Stein and Paul McGuffey, as well as investigator Jim LaFavers, who would prove to be indispensable over the years. Meanwhile, John Lovell joined the firm, and later, so too did his brother, Joe.

Soon there were eight lawyers, and the firm became Templeton and Garner. They moved to the 13th floor to bigger offices.

"I saw how Garner was, and I thought, 'OK, the only way this is going to work is for you and me to have a partnership, and so I'll go 50-50 with you,'" Templeton said. "He jumped at that."

They had not been together long when Templeton took on Amarillo royalty in rancher M.T. Johnson. The Johnson family was old money. At Amarillo High, he quarterbacked the Sandies to the 1940 state championship.

Johnson initially went to play football at the University of Oklahoma. When World War II erupted in December 1941, he left OU for the Naval Academy where he graduated. But he made his mark as a land owner and developer. He organized the Johnson

Land and Cattle farm and ranch operation in the Texas Panhandle and Central Oklahoma.

Johnson cut an imposing figure in Amarillo. He managed the Amarillo Livestock Auction and founded Tascosa National Bank. Soon after that, he developed Sunset Center, Amarillo's first indoor shopping mall, to great acclaim in the 1950s.

He was elected to the Amarillo ISD school board at the young age of 32 in 1954 where he served for the next five years. He was also president of Amarillo Country Club where Templeton was also a member. On the golf course at ACC, Johnson was a 5-handicapper.

His love of golf and his reputation had him on the executive committee of the United States Golf Association where he served a time as executive secretary of the prestigious organization. Johnson was also a member of the Royal and Ancient Golf Club of St. Andrew's in Scotland.

"That family, they were the top of the line socially and in many other ways," Templeton said. "M.T. was sort of an imperious-looking fellow."

M.T. Johnson

Johnson cast a large shadow over Amarillo. That didn't stop Templeton from representing Johnson's two sisters and other family members in a lawsuit against him in 1983. The Johnson partnership owned a section of land on the edge of Borger on which Phillips 66 Refinery sat. The Johnsons leased the land to Phillips in perpetuity for a modest sum.

Johnson got word through a Phillips official the company was interested in purchasing the land. No more lease. It would be for a tidy sum of several million dollars, possibly as much as $10 million. The only thing was that Johnson didn't disclose that information to the rest of the shared owners in the family. What he did disclose is that he and his cousin Bob Johnson would like to buy them out.

They took Johnson up on his offer. Negotiations began in December 1980. They had documents drawn up in January 1981. Johnson paid them in June. Ninety days later, he sold the land for a whopping $10 million. Whoa, Nellie. What's going on? The rest of the family believed they had been played.

They reached out to Templeton when his friend Bill Attebury recommended Templeton to other family members. They believed a deal had been made between Johnson and Phillips 66 on the land sale, one that he had been dishonest with the remaining owners about why he wanted to buy them out. They filed suit to recover as much of the $10 million as they could. Johnson hired the Jenkins Gilchrist firm out of Dallas. David Hunt, a big bully of a man, was the lead partner.

The important question was when did Johnson's duty as managing partner end? Was it in January 1981 when they signed up or did it continue? Johnson produced the best partnership lawyer in Texas to testify that his duty ended when he signed up.

Templeton believed he had to prove that Johnson knew that Phillips was going to buy the land before he had the family sign up. Templeton said he had some evidence of that, but he needed more. Then in Midland, he got it.

It was in the deposition and discovery phase that Templeton, to his surprise, uncovered a key document in the case. Johnson needed about $6 million to buy out his family in the Johnson partnership.

Templeton learned that Johnson got the loan from First National Bank in Midland. Individual bankers had great authority in Midland, and Templeton and Garner discovered who had authorized the loan.

Templeton was convinced that the Jenkins Gilchrist firm had gone into the bank the week before the deposition in an attempt to clean out any kind of records concerning Johnson's loan.

"They had delayed us and delayed us on the thing," Templeton said. "The Jenkins firm (representing Johnson) had gone in the bank the week before the deposition and I know they tried to clean out the record of any kind on the loan."

Templeton and Garner made their way down to Midland to take the deposition of a loan officer there. The two were in his office, quizzing him about the loan.

"He had this cadenza right behind him. I said, 'Well, do you have any records of the loan transaction, how Mr. Johnson got the loan, things like that?'" Templeton said.

The banker said, as a matter of fact, he did, he kept a personal copy of the loan records, and they were in his credenza. He pulled out a copy of the loan and Templeton marked it as an exhibit. What they'd really like to have was the loan application. That might shed more light than anything, but that's probably nowhere to be seen.

"Garner is sitting right next to me," Templeton said. "I'm questioning the banker, and it's getting kind of dramatic. Bob keeps nudging me and elbowing me. I said, 'Bob, I'm trying to question this witness.' He said, 'Look over here.' And right there was the application."

If there were such a thing as a smoking gun, this was it. The application was in Johnson's handwriting. It said he needed the money to buy out the other owners, and that he expected to sell the land for a price between $15 and $20 million. The date of the application was also at a time when Johnson's siblings wouldn't have known his intentions.

"Sometimes in a case, you see a turning point and this was it,"

Templeton said. "This was Exhibit 58."

The trial was in Judge George Dowlen's 181st District Court. Dowlen was known as the "Cowboy Judge," but his reputation among local attorneys was not that of a legal scholar. Johnson, in essence, told the jury that all he was doing was attempting to buy out his family, and take on that obligation. He was not aware that Phillips was interested in purchasing the land.

Then it was Templeton's turn to cross-exam. He passed around about 16 copies of Exhibit 58, a copy of the loan application. Each member of the jury received one.

"You talk about a turning point," he said. "That turned the case. The application showed that he knew he was going to sell to Phillips. It was a helluva lawsuit."

Templeton was facing another battle during the Johnson trial. Of all things, toward the end of the trial, he developed a knot on his left testicle. He went to see Dr. Virgil Pate, who said it could be cancerous.

"I'm toward the end of the trial," he said. "I get to question M.T. Johnson on Monday afternoon. I have just got to finish this trial. I said, 'What would you do, Virgil? Couldn't we do it Tuesday morning?'"

Pate agreed, and Templeton got his time with Johnson. In addition to Exhibit 58 of the loan application, the two did have one exchange that Templeton recalled nearly 40 years later.

"I said, 'M.T., we've been acquainted before. We've known each other out at the country club, haven't we?'" Templeton said.

"I've seen your face," Johnson said.

On that Tuesday, Templeton had his surgery while the trial wound down. Garner and Wayne Sturdivant, widely considered perhaps the best trial lawyer in Amarillo, were co-counsels. Those two barely tolerated each other.

"They were absolutely at war," Templeton said.

Templeton assigned Garner the task of cross-examining the point person with Phillips. Sturdivant grumbled to Templeton he thought Garner did a miserable job.

"But the jury, after it was over, thought the guy from Phillips was in on the whole thing," Templeton said. "That's the kind of thing Garner could do that people didn't appreciate."

Templeton returned to the trial two days later on a Thursday. The evidence had closed and the sides argued into the wee hours on the court's charge.

"The judge's obligation is to submit a good fair charge," Templeton said. "The jury went with us on 49 of 51 issues."

But it certainly took a while. The jury stayed out for a week, an interminable amount of time. Finally, they reached a verdict in favor of the family.

"They had one holdout," Templeton said. "One idiot holdout."

Johnson appealed the verdict. Sturdivant worked the appeal. The two sides reached a settlement of $6.5 million awarded to the other family owners.

"We became friends after that," Templeton said of Johnson, who died a few days before Christmas in 1999. "When he got sick, I sent him flowers."

— Reflections —

"When I get a lawsuit, that's what you think about — how can I win this? What is it I got to work with, and what do I need to do? I dream and sleep lawsuits. I've done that all my life. I can't turn anything off when I go to bed. I don't know what is in that subconscious, but I come up with a lot of answers the next morning and a lot of them are good.

"I'm sure it didn't start out this way. You've got to think about winning and how to win. If you let fear conquer you in litigation or get the upper hand, you're going to lose. I don't know how to say it. You got to be aware of your obstacles, and you have to have a real concern of how to meet those. But if you let real fear dominate your thinking, you're going to lose. But if you think about how you can win then usually solutions come to you.

"With experience, like today, I can take one look at a lawsuit, even as old as I am, and know what the key is, how to succeed with it, and what to do. But that didn't come automatically. I started out as dumb as a man can be."

CHAPTER

9

When White Oil Wasn't Oil

As far as being a geologist or petroleum engineer, Robert Templeton made a good lawyer. He did not live in the world of specific oil gravity, casing head gas or the heating content of gas. But in the early 1980s, he would -- simply because if he were to be a good attorney for his client, he had no choice.

"I did what I've always had to do," Templeton said. "If it was a complicated case in a different field – whether it was medical, negligence or whatever – you better learn the language, meaning of the terms, and learn the facts of the case. Then the truth comes out."

Templeton was thrust into a case in the early 1980s to represent Dorchester, an oil and gas company that wasn't quite to the level of the country's major oil and gas producers, but wasn't small either. On the other side was a group of independent oil producers in the Texas Panhandle.

And in the middle was something called White Oil, and Templeton's charge was to prove these independents were illegally taking gas out of the rich Hugoton field.

Sixty years earlier, in the 1920s, Don Harrington, Stanley Marsh and Lawrence Hagy were the most renowned of the early oil pioneers in the Texas Panhandle. They both arrived within a few months of each other just prior to the oil boom near Borger in 1926.

Marsh and Harrington were Midwesterners, originally from Ohio and Illinois. Marsh had been at the Burkburnett oil boom near Wichita Falls before heading to the Panhandle. Harrington and Hagy came from Oklahoma.

They proved to be a formidable team. Harrington was a trained land man and engineer with a talent for finding rich deposits of oil and gas. Marsh was a salesman, legendary for a down-home ability to charm skeptical farmers and ranchers to obtain leases on their land. As for Hagy, who got a geology degree from the University of Oklahoma?

"I don't think I ever did much," Hagy told *Texas Monthly* in 1988. "I just had a lot of friends."

Harrington died in 1974. Before that, with wife Sybil, they became the most philanthropic family in Panhandle history. The Harrington name heads a Boy Scout camp, a discovery center, and a renowned cancer center to highlight just a few of their endeavors. Marsh, who died in 1946, may be more noted by his eccentric and controversial grandson, Stanley Marsh 3. Hagy would become Amarillo mayor just after World War II and would live far longer than the other two. He died in 1993 at age 94.

All three became very wealthy, and much of that came later from the rich gas reserves in the Hugoton Field. The massive Hugoton was named for the town in Kansas near where the first well was drilled.

Natural gas in the Hugoton area was first discovered in 1922 in Seward County, two miles west of Liberal, Kan. The well was drilled in 1919 to a depth of 2,919 feet, but was shut in for three years because it did not find oil. In 1922, the well was completed as a gas well, but there was little demand for natural gas in the area and it was five years before another gas well was drilled in the field, according to Larry Skelton, author of "Hugoton's Rich History."

In 1927, gas was discovered at about 2,600 feet southwest of Hugoton. This is considered the center of the Hugoton Field. By the end of 1928, five wells had been drilled in the field and the first pipeline transported gas to local markets. In 1929, Argus Pipe Line Co. started construction of a pipeline to furnish gas to Dodge City,

Kan. Construction of major pipelines in the 1930s encouraged further drilling in the area.

The field, with one of the world's largest known gas reserves, was 8,500 square miles and 1.4 million net acres. The heart of the field was in Kansas, but it cut a swath through the Oklahoma Panhandle and into neighboring Texas with a rich part of the Hugoton near Borger and Pampa.

"While these folks were good partners, and had a good partnership for years, they eventually split up," Templeton said. "Harrington and Marsh kept the natural gas rights, or 'dry gas' as they called it. They let Hagy have the rights to the oil and all the casing head gas on all the sections owned by the partnership."

The geologic makeup of the Hugoton is a stratigraphic trap overlying a monocline with the primary pay found in the Krider Dolemite of Permian age, according to L. Pippin, author of the paper, "The Hugoton-Panhandle Field, The First 50 Years." This dolomite and the overlying Herington dolomite make up the Wolfcampian carbonates.

A quick and simple, but what would prove to be a very crucial geology lesson: Within much of the Hugoton in the Texas Panhandle was that dolomite formation. With a few exceptions, it was not productive for oil in that formation, but it was for gas.

Below the dolomite was the Granite Wash, another formation, which was more likely to produce oil. There was some oil production in the dolomite where it dropped off in eastern Hutchinson County, but primarily, the production was natural gas.

In the late 1970s, some mostly local independent oil producers obtained leases from Hagy to drill for his oil and casing head gas rights on some sections near White Deer. These were sections where there was an existing gas well and dry gas was produced. Nearly all those leases were limited to one well a section.

Prior to that, Dorchester, an oil and gas production company, obtained some of the natural gas rights in that same area. In all, it was about 50 sections.

"As the years went on, the gas got richer with heavier

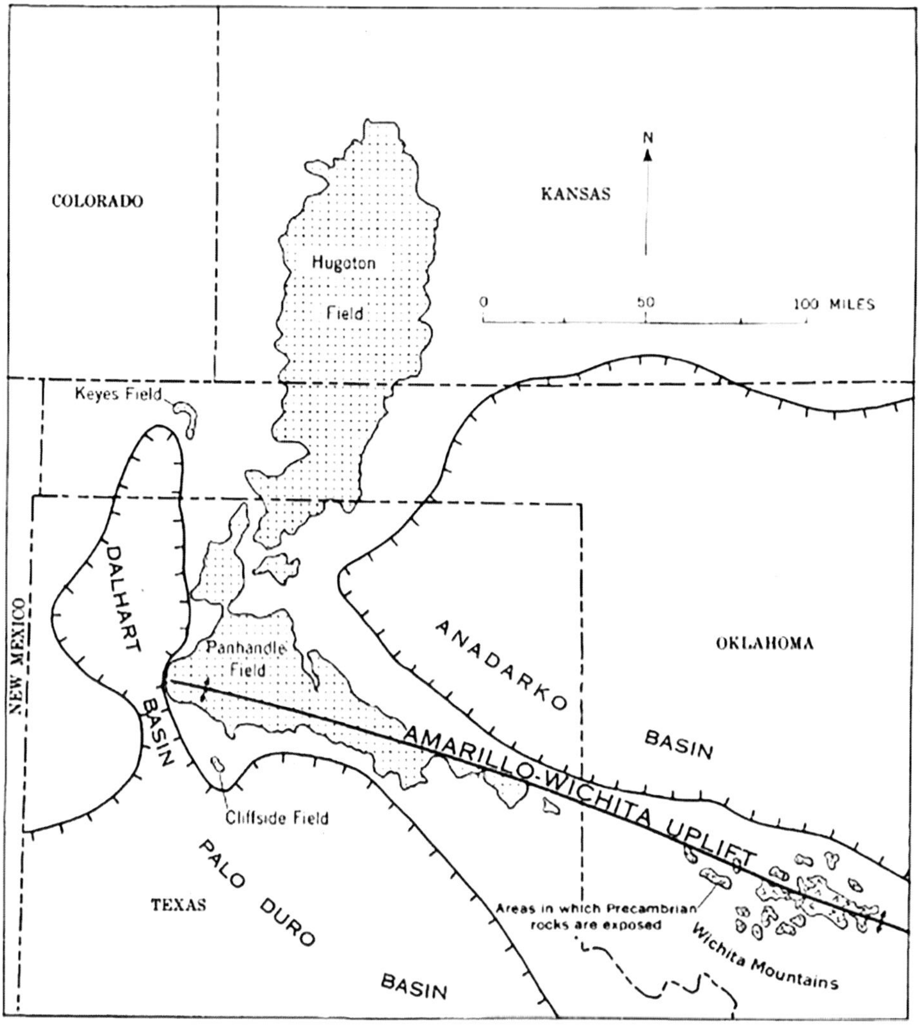

The Hugoton Field.

hydrocarbons," Templeton said. "Methane is the natural gas typically burned in homes. The typical BTU, that is, burning capacity or heating capacity, of methane is standardized at 1,000 mcf. The gas over the years increased in BTU to around 1,250 mcf. To put it simply, people in Amarillo using gas from the Hugoton had a very hot fire to cook with for awhile."

Methane is the main component in natural gas, followed by ethane, propane and butane. Natural gas also carries a smaller composition of carbon dioxide, oxygen, nitrogen, hydrogen sulfide and rare gases. The gas in that part of the Hugoton was so rich from the gas wells that at the surface it could be refrigerated and the heavier hydrocarbons would turn into liquids.

"That's where the term 'white oil' came from because those liquids were white," Templeton said. "The condensed hydrocarbons that were refrigerated into liquids were white, were clear."

The question became what kind of well was it? The Texas Railroad Commission, which regulates the production of oil and gas in the state, had established a set of rules for production in the Hugoton Field. There had to be a ratio of 100,000 mcf to five barrels of oil to be classified as an oil well.

"In other words," Templeton said, "if the producing well was producing five barrels of oil to 100,000 mcf, it would be classified as an oil well."

A light bulb went on in the minds of a few independents. If they drilled for oil and casing head gas – as their contract allowed – they could perforate the rich gas zone in the dolomite, then refrigerate the gas, and produce five barrels of liquid. If the Railroad Commission would approve that well as an oil well, it would not infringe on the rights of Dorchester, the gas lessee, or so the thinking went.

That is what happened. They got a letter from the Railroad Commission that stated this classified the "white oil" as an oil well.

"Of course, they took this as gospel," Templeton said. "What they were doing is reporting they had perforated below the dolomite, when, in fact, they had not. They drilled below it, but they didn't perforate. They came up and perforated in a dolomite zone to take the gas."

The independents took the Railroad Commission letter to local banks as they looked to borrow money to drill more wells. Their selling point was some of these early wells were producing "white oil" at a lucrative rate, and it's all legal. It's an oil well.

"The banks went to their lawyers and asked them if these were legal oil wells," Templeton said. "The local lawyers in Amarillo and elsewhere said, 'Yes, it was.' So the independents borrow money from the banks to start drilling and it just caught on. A wild estimate would be the independents had drilled well over 200 – quote – 'oil wells' – unquote."

It wasn't long before Dorchester started scratching their heads. Those gas wells of theirs which had been doing so well were now performing poorly. They couldn't understand. Then they started doing some digging – literally and figuratively – and they began to understand.

They weren't amused. Dorchester believed their gas in the dolomite in the Hugoton was being stolen by the independents with this nebulous "white oil" claim. No, this wasn't going to work.

"Dorchester said, 'No, you're not doing that. You're producing our gas and we've checked this. You perforated in our zone. You're not entitled to produce that because it's not an oil well,'" Templeton said.

Dorchester, encouraged by major oil companies, wanted to put a legal stop to what the company believed was a taking of its gas. But where to go? Most of the major law firms in Amarillo had given opinions that the oil wells were legal. Dorchester went to see Tol Ware, chairman of Amarillo National Bank.

"He said, 'Go hire Templeton,'" Templeton said. "Tol and I had always been great friends. And they did."

The Templeton and Garner firm came to a quick agreement, and filed a lawsuit against a number of independents in 1981. But the independents weren't just sitting on their hands. They hired some Austin lawyers to represent them. They needed a small producer for judicial precedence. They got one in Bill Harlow who had two oil wells – or, rather, two "oil wells," – on a lease.

So the independents sued to take the offense and get the Harlow wells individually classified as "oil wells".

The independents were trying to expedite the Harlow lawsuit. Before Templeton knew it, he got a surprise that the Harlow v. Dorchester trial would be 30 days out in the Gray County Courthouse in Pampa. It was the home of many independents. Bob Garner, who had the job of defending the Harlow lawsuit, had not done any discovery yet on the case and the clock was already ticking.

"Garner was nowhere to be seen," Templeton said. "So I had to go over to Pampa and file a motion for continuance with the judge."

The Gray County Courthouse, with its one big courtroom, was packed mostly with independents. Judge Don Cain denied the motion.

"I drove back to Amarillo and began to think of what a terrible mistake we had made as lawyers in failing to stay up with the case," Templeton said. "They were ready with experts, with everything to show that Harlow was producing oil, and we didn't really have anything at all."

Templeton was at a what-to-do crossroads. He had been there many times in his career where he had to pull something – if not a white rabbit, a bit of strategy on the fly – out of his hat. It often came to him at night, or in the morning when his subconscious had a chance to kick it in gear. This idea came to him the next day.

He had a secretary type an order of recusal to present to Cain. He knew and liked Cain. He hand-delivered the order the next day in Pampa to Cain and then laid it on thick.

"I told him, 'Judge, I saw the incredible pressure they put on you last night. I know there are two camps in Pampa on this, one for the White Oilers, and one against them. You don't need this kind of pressure. I'm asking you to take a look at this and see if you'd like to recuse,'" Templeton said. "I left it with him and he said, 'OK, Bob, I'll think about it.'"

The next day, Cain called Templeton and said he was removing himself from the case. Templeton had made an ex parte decision, meaning he had done so without requiring parties on both sides of the question to be present. The White Oilers didn't like that in the least, but there was nothing they could do.

Score one for Templeton.

"I had done something I should not have done," he said. "I owed a duty to let the other side know. But I didn't really worry about that because I thought the other side was a bunch of outlaws."

Then a new judge was appointed, Robert Montgomery, State District Judge of the 100th Judicial Court in Memphis. Montgomery was a native of Kermit, graduated from Texas Tech in 1948, and – how convenient – was a classmate of Templeton's at Baylor Law School in the class of 1953. He was editor of the Baylor Law Review.

"What a break," Templeton said. "Bob was a very bright man, bright lawyer, but he was the kind of judge who never made up his mind until he was absolutely forced to."

Score a second one for Templeton.

But another big issue remained before the trial began. Having the trial in Pampa was about like a Democrat running for a local seat in West Texas. This did not look like an even playing field at all to Templeton. Many of the independents lived in Pampa, and the question of a fair trial was an obvious one.

"I didn't think I could win the case in Gray County," he said.

Templeton filed for a change of venue. A change of venue in a civil case was seldom made at that time. The White Oil lawyers obviously wanted the home field advantage and so they trotted out a lot of locals who said that Dorchester could certainly get a fair trial. Templeton had Danny Conklin, a knowledgeable oil and gas man, as a witness. But the locals were bearing down on Templeton.

"How could I combat that?" he said. "It was really a simple thought. Some things seem impossible until you find a solution that is usually always there."

Late in the venue hearing, Templeton got up to cross exam yet another of the Pampa citizenry when the solution to him was obvious, and it became obvious based on his questions:

"Mr. Johnson, you're a longtime resident of Pampa, Texas, is that correct?"

"Yes, sir."

"And you like this town, do you?"

"Oh, it's a great town, a great place to live."

"You understand what Dorchester is trying to do?"

"I'm not sure."

"Well, Dorchester is trying to shut down all these independent oil men. Are these independents important to the economy of Pampa, Texas?"

"Oh, yes, I'm sure they are."

"Would you want to do anything to hurt the economy of Pampa, Texas?"

"No, sir, I sure wouldn't."

"Then I have to ask, Mr. Johnson, could you be a fair and impartial juror in this case?"

"Well, sir, I guess I couldn't be."

This went on for three more witnesses with similar answers. The Austin lawyers for the independents could read the writing on the wall. Montgomery granted the motion and moved the case to Lubbock.

Score a third one for Templeton.

So, in a short period of time, Templeton was able to get a longtime Pampa judge off the trial, got a break when an old friend from Memphis was appointed, and got the trial moved 150 miles away to Lubbock.

His outlook started to change, but it didn't last long. During pretrial discovery, Templeton had requested they be allowed to sample the oil out of the two Harlow wells. The plaintiffs kept resisting. Templeton kept requesting and the independents counsel kept delaying.

The trial was set for August, and it was getting into July. Finally, Templeton was allowed to test the oil in the wells to see if, in fact, it was oil. Phil Moses, with a testing company in Fort Worth, pulled some oil and tested it.

"Mr. Templeton," Moses told him over the phone, "we're in trouble. I'm sorry, this is real oil."

"Phil, are you sure?"

"I'm sure."

The entire case seemed to be hanging on this phone call. If this were truly oil, there wasn't much that could be done. But in speaking with geologists and petroleum engineers prior to trial, Templeton had a grasp of the components of oil.

"I said, 'Phil, what is the specific gravity of the oil? Did you test that?'" Templeton said. "Phil said he hadn't. I asked him to test it. He said he would."

Specific gravity is an index used to measure the density of a liquid. Liquids with a density lower than water, which includes most crude oil grades and petroleum products, will have a specific gravity between 0.0 and 1.0.

In the oil industry, specific gravity is a common quality specification for finished products. Specific gravity for Texas crude oil is 0.876.

In a few days, Moses called back: "Mr. Templeton, it's not virgin oil. It's refined oil."

"They had salted the wells with refined oil," Templeton said. "Refined oil has a different specific gravity than raw oil. 'Raw oil' is a term I coined for people to understand. They salted the well and we caught them."

The trial began with a Lubbock jury, a group not familiar with oil production in an area of agriculture. No ax to grind, Templeton said. But the independents traveled well and they filled up the Lubbock courtroom. Undaunted, Templeton believed he had the evidence on his side.

He tried to keep it simple and bore in on a couple of major points. The first was what was casing head gas, which was allowed by the lease contract, and what was natural gas, which was not. The Harlow wells had a BTU of around 1,200. True casing head gas has a BTU of approximately 1,550 to 1,750.

Typical Natural Gas Composition

Component	Typical Analysis (mole %)	Range (mole %)
Methane	95.0	87.0 - 97.0
Ethane	3.2	1.5 - 7.0
Propane	0.2	0.1 - 1.5
iso - Butane	0.03	0.01 - 0.3
normal - Butane	0.03	0.01 - 0.3
iso - Pentane	0.01	trace - 0.04
normal - Pentane	0.01	trace - 0.04
Hexanes plus	0.01	trace - 0.06
Nitrogen	1.0	0.2 - 5.5
Carbon Dioxide	0.5	0.1 - 1.0
Oxygen	0.02	0.01 - 0.1
Hydrogen	trace	trace - 0.02
Gross Heating Value (MJ/m^3), dry basis *	38	36.0 - 40.2

"The best proof we had was the fingerprint, so to speak, of what the gas was," Templeton said. "A fingerprint is a simple analysis of what that portion of the hydrocarbon gas is composed of.

"We tested the gas out of one of the Harlow wells. The fingerprints on what they called casing head gas and the fingerprints of the dry gas produced by Dorchester out of that section were identical. Now that simply couldn't be if they were producing casing head gas.

"That alone tells the jury that Harlow and the other independents had not perforated the Granite Wash that is below the dolomite and sometimes is productive for oil. They had lied about it to the Railroad Commission and perforated in the gas formation of the dolomite."

To get the jury to understand what casing head gas actually was when contained in the oil when produced, Templeton thought it better to show than tell.

"I did it with a simple Coke bottle," he said. "The Coca-Cola was carbonated and had gas contained in the Coke. When you would shake it, it would bubble up. I would shake it to demonstrate how the gas was contained in the liquid, the fizzing up would be the gas. It was a simple illustration they could understand."

Templeton also had corrected records of perforations to show the independents were producing from the dolomite and that Dorchester was hurt by this because the natural gas was coming out of their sections.

Templeton did have a formidable foe representing the independents. Broadus Spivey actually went to the tiny Goodnight public schools – when there was one – near Clarendon. He graduated from the University of Texas and the UT Law School in 1962. He practiced with Huff and Splawn, considered the best plaintiff firm in Lubbock, before moving to practice in Austin. Spivey would later be president of the Texas Bar Association.

"He was just a natural," Templeton said. "He was the kind of person that people instantly liked. More than that, he was a really smart lawyer and superb salesman. If I would have been against him in an ordinary lawsuit, I would not have had much of a chance, but we had overwhelming evidence."

Spivey knew the evidence deck was stacked against him. He tried every tactic he could devise. He wasn't going to be outdone by Templeton and his soft drink bottles. One day he brought about a half-dozen bottles with him to the courtroom to make a point in a cross examination with Moses, but more than anything, to distract and confuse.

"Broadus was saying, 'What about this? What about where it does it here?' and then he took one of those Coke bottles and started shaking it up," Templeton said. "He said, 'OK, what am I doing with this, Mr. Moses?' Moses said, 'Well, I don't know, but it looks like you're trying to spray Mr. Templeton.' The jury broke down laughing.

"Broadus did everything he could. As good a lawyer as he was, you couldn't beat those facts, but he was a helluva lawyer."

The trial lasted about 2 ½ weeks. Aside from some near-spewed Coca-Cola, there were a couple of twists. Templeton was now lead counsel. Garner was responsible for questioning one of the Dorchester executives at the end of one day. It did not go well.

"He had done nothing to prepare for that, absolutely nothing," Templeton said. "He was unprepared and did a terrible job, and I got Judge Montgomery to recess for the day. I got hold of both after that and cussed Garner bad. I said, 'You are not going to lose this lawsuit. You sit down and get the questions ready – 1-2-3-4 – this is what you need to do and you do it right. I'm not going to let you lose this lawsuit.

"Garner got him on the stand again the next day and did a very good job. Garner's achilles heel was his lack of preparation because he was a really good trial lawyer. But he thought he could take a witness and twist and turn him without any preparation to either discredit him or build him up. He was good at it. But this wasn't that kind of case."

At another point in the trial, Garner did neutralize the testimony of one of the independents on cross examination. The oil man out of White Deer said that they were producing real oil – not gas -- because they found a racoon which had drowned in an oil tank.

"This was classic Garner," Templeton said. "He said, 'What do you reckon that racoon was doing? Hunting for a lube job?' The jury laughed. He had in one question ridiculed the plaintiff's evidence."

The other twist was right before trial Dorchester was bought out. After that, the Scott Douglass and McConnico firm from Austin was hired to help Templeton. Frank Douglass, a major partner in the firm, could have taken a bigger role in the case, but declined. Templeton believed it was because he was well into the case by then and Douglass wasn't sure Templeton was going to win and didn't want the mark on his firm's reputation. Douglass examined one witness just to officially say the firm had some part in the case.

The jury didn't deliberate long considering the length of the trial.

They returned a verdict in favor of Dorchester, a verdict that would reverberate around the state. It was one worth millions of dollars and that doesn't even consider how many millions in the future would have come into play.

There was a legal aspect that had to be considered. Once the jury found that Harlow had converted the natural gas, and in effect, stole it from Dorchester, Templeton believed they had to show how much was converted and how much the Dorchester loss was.

"Frank said no," Templeton said. "Once you've proven you've converted it, then the burden of proof falls on the person who converted it to show how little they converted. Otherwise, it's presumed they converted a whole lot. He was firmly convinced once you prove the theft, the burden is on the thief to prove what he stole. That was the instruction we finally got from Judge Montgomery."

The case, with so much at stake, got its share of publicity. There had been bumper stickers for the independents. There was a buzz for 2 ½ weeks. It was covered heavily by the media, both in Lubbock and Amarillo.

"Old dumb Bob wanted to help Garner. Lubbock was his hometown that he had to abandon," Templeton said. "I gave full credit to Bob. I let him do the interviews and I didn't do a thing. They all thought it was Garner who won the case. I wasn't really dumb. I was generous. I always thought it was a good idea to boost my partner."

The verdict was affirmed on appeal. The independents were shut down by the Federal Energy Regulatory Commission. Some made deals with the majors. It became a popular case for seminars in the 1980s. To think, Templeton was hired almost by a process of elimination since most Amarillo firms had already prejudiced themselves.

"It was a huge victory for the majors," Templeton said. "Me, personally, I won a case I knew we were right on. That doesn't always happen. I had to learn cold turkey about the whole thing, but once I got into it, it wasn't that difficult to understand. We started out behind the 8 ball."

— Reflections —

"There are people who make these rules on how to try lawsuits — 'never ask a question you don't know the answer to,' or don't ever ask a 'why' question, or make sure you have control of the witness.'

"There is one rule — there are no rules. Every one of these rules at some point in time should be broken in a given case with a given witness in a given circumstance, whether that's in deposition or in front of a jury. Every one of them. It's your instincts that should guide you."

CHAPTER

10

The Battle With Boone

The divorce, as most are, was an ugly one for Boone Pickens and Amarillo. It was already teetering that way in the 1980s, but the fight with Mesa Petroleum, where Pickens garnered national media attention as its founder and chairman, and the City of Amarillo over gas prices, sent it over the edge.

The case had a little bit of everything – hardball tactics, listening devices in meetings, back and forth negotiations and a billionaire ultimately leaving his hometown for Dallas.

"We were, I guess you'd describe it, 'acquaintances.' We knew each other and were cordial," Robert Templeton said of Pickens. "But when I came along in the lawsuit and for the rest of his life, I was the enemy. But that's the way it was with him."

Templeton was a little late to this skirmish, but once he arrived, he made an impact until a settlement he deemed unfair caused him to resign. But by then, it was virtually over – except for a sweeping out of the city commission the next year.

A history lesson is necessary to understand the roots of the rift between Mesa and City of Amarillo. Going back to the 1920s when gas was discovered north of Amarillo, Amarillo Oil Co. supplied gas to the city for decades.

The West Panhandle gas field, which Amarillo Oil Co. owned, had much more gas than what supplied Amarillo. Being profit-driven, they sold the field to Colorado Interstate Gas Co.

There was a contract provision, known as the "B Contract." The contract read that Amarillo Oil Co. had the right to take all the gas from that West Panhandle field to serve Amarillo and its environs around the city. Amarillo Oil Co. had to only pay for the cost of production, which was very little.

"So Amarillo's gas utility got gas at really no cost other than the cost of production," said former Amarillo city manager John Ward. "So we had the cheapest gas in the world for sure."

Colorado Interstate installed a gas transmission pipeline to take gas back to Colorado. This arrangement continued for decades. Amarillo Oil Co. eventually became Pioneer Natural Gas Co., which still provided the city gas at their cost of production under the terms of the B Contract.

In 1980, Amarillo consumers were paying approximately 30 to 40 cents per mcf, or per 1,000 cubic feet. It was, Ward said, well below market value. But about that time came the first legal shot across the bow.

Mid-America Pipeline Co., better known as MAPCO, sued Pioneer. MAPCO had a contract with Pioneer and owned the rights to the liquids in the gas. MAPCO alleged Pioneer was taking liquids out of the gas at the Fain processing plant north of Amarillo.

Natural gas produced from the Panhandle field is composed of a number of hydrocarbons such as pentane and propane. All but methane are classified as liquids, which means that these heavier hydrocarbons could be easily reduced to liquids by processing. These liquids were valuable then as they are today.

The City of Amarillo intervened because gas customers were not receiving the same heating capacity because of a reduction in heavier hydrocarbons. Putting it simply, the gas didn't burn as hot and therefore not heat as well.

When MAPCO sued Pioneer, the City of Amarillo and Colorado Interstate intervened as voluntary plaintiffs. The city intervened because gas customers were having to use more gas to receive the same heating.

Pioneer filed for a summary judgment in Bryan Poff's 47th

Judicial District Court. Summary judgment is a judgment by a court for one party against another without a trial. The motion for summary judgment was denied.

So in the summer of 1982, Merrill Nunn, City of Amarillo attorney, was asked to join Pioneer lawyers and staff in Colorado Springs and meet with an attorney for Colorado Interstate. The meeting had Nunn perplexed.

"I never could figure out what the purpose of the meeting was," he said. "We just talked about the lawsuit. We didn't decide anything."

At one point, Nunn went back to the law library at the firm where the meeting was held and pulled out a volume on Anti-Trust. He read the group a statute, which prohibits combinations in restraint of trade. After that, Nunn said, a big silence came over the room, and he was told not to mention that to MAPCO.

"It occurred to me after the meeting," Nunn said, "that some kind of side deal had been worked out with Colorado Interstate and Pioneer.

"I immediately smelled a rat. So I told (Amarillo mayor) Rick Klein that we're about to get 'had' here. If you stacked all of it up, if Pioneer and Colorado Interstate had some kind of side agreement, the only ones to lose in this settlement would be the City of Amarillo. They would cut us out of any claims we had in the pending lawsuit."

But the legal fight about the quality of gas was just a portion of what was to come, and what was to come dwarfed the initial squabble. This would be on the price of gas to the city of Amarillo, and it would eventually put Amarillo and Pickens squarely at odds.

The price increase in Amarillo started slowly, however. Around 1980, Pioneer created Energas, which would be the utility to serve Amarillo. Energas then bought gas from Pioneer. Energas was not technically a party to the B Contract. Pioneer told the City of Amarillo that Energas would continue to provide the same gas.

"They said we're no longer going to be a utility, but this is going to be great deal," Ward said. "But the kicker was, if Pioneer were no longer the utility, they could charge what they wanted for the gas because they weren't regulated by the Railroad Commission."

Energas filed an application with the Texas Railroad Commission for a gate rate as the utility didn't have one. A gate rate is the price paid for gas when it crosses into the city limits. Legally, the City of Amarillo had to be informed of the application notice.

"When they did, I took the notice to intervene in that proceeding before the Railroad Commission which we had the absolute right to do," Nunn said.

After Energas was notified of the city's intention, the company sent a representative to talk with city manager John Stiff. Stiff was told this was really just a formality, standard procedure and no reason for the city to get involved.

Just a couple of years prior, on a previous commission, mayor Jerry Hodge and Southwestern Public Service had waged an intense fight over electricity charges from the Harrington Station. This could be another battle looming with a utility.

"John Stiff approached the city commission during a work session about this and had been assured it was just a formality and there was no reason to get involved in the litigation. But did the city commission want to do that?" Nunn said.

"They recalled the bitterness of the fight with SPS and they said not to get involved. So they instructed me to withdraw our intervention."

Meanwhile, the cost of gas to Amarillo had already been inching up. Gas prices to city residents began to escalate from 29 cents per mcf to close to $1 per mcf and still going up.

"So we started wondering why is the gas going up?" said Ward, city manager from 1983 to 2004. "We started getting complaints and Energas said that's the contract we have, and that's just the way it is."

City officials began to scratch their head. This didn't make sense. They took a look at Energas' gate rate meeting with the Railroad Commission, the one that Energas convinced Stiff that it was just a formality and no need to intervene.

"We did discovery, got a copy of their contract, and there it was in black and white," Ward said. "Of course, we pitched a fit about it. The Railroad Commission had not approved their rate increase. They may have approved some increase, but it was substantially less than what they were asking for."

"In the transcript of the proceedings, the Railroad Commission asks them point blank, 'What does the City of Amarillo have to say about this?' " Nunn said. "And an Energas official said, 'Oh, they withdrew their intervention so there's no ax to grind.' So the Railroad Commission, being an uncontested case, passed it."

City officials were incensed. The city appealed to the Railroad Commission, but because it was for an application for a rate increase, the city was told it couldn't be contested because the rate had already been set and it could not be re-litigated. By the time it had reached $2 per mcf, MAPCO had filed its lawsuit on the quality of gas and had brought the city in as an involuntary plaintiff.

"I called the guys at Pioneer and told them I was going to change my position in the lawsuit from involuntary to voluntary plaintiff if they didn't do something about the gate rate," Nunn said. "So they shut it down at $2."

On the day that Klein agreed with Nunn that the city should intervene in the lawsuit, Pioneer was acquired by Pickens' Mesa, which now controlled all the gas to Amarillo. Pickens' one successful takeover was an acquisition of Pioneer in a stock exchange. He approved "golden parachutes" for Pioneer executives, which compensates, often lavishly, an executive in an acquisition of the company.

And so fireworks between now the City of Amarillo and Mesa immediately ensued? Not really. "Then, it just rocked along for quite a while with nothing going on," Nunn said.

The intervention in that lawsuit was like on old book that sat quietly on a bookshelf for six years. It never got removed, but it never got read either. It was just there collecting a bit of dust – until 1988.

That's when Ward, who succeeded Stiff as city manager, got a call from Pickens. It seems the City of Amarillo still had this lawsuit for a number of years that was now directed to Mesa, Pickens told him, and it's just meaningless. It's headed to court unless the City of Amarillo does the sensible thing and dismiss the suit.

"Boone," Ward said, "I don't think we can do that."

Pickens then contacted the city commission individually – mayor Glen Parkey, commissioners John Chandler, Don Chrysler, Keith Adams and Dave Taylor. Their response? What lawsuit? It had never been explained to them the history of the lawsuit. So Ward presented the history and reason for the lawsuit and why it had never been dismissed.

"Glen Parkey was adamant that we dismiss it," Ward said. "He said that we don't have any business being involved in this. Chandler and Chrysler agreed with him."

Fine, Ward said. He'll get Mesa to draw up a settlement. It will be on the agenda at the next city commission meeting and it can be approved on then.

"They didn't want it on the agenda," Ward said. "I said that you can't have it both ways."

Ward and Nunn were instructed to negotiate with Mesa on a settlement that would dismiss the suit. Mesa wasn't budging. The best offer was one of $6 million in rate relief. After that, Mesa wanted a gas price of $2.65 per mcf with future prices on the average rate price of gas of three downstate cities – Fort Worth, Austin and San Antonio. Those rates were much higher because there was no gas near them, and had much more in the way of distribution costs.

"It was a tricky way to put it to Amarillo consumers," Templeton said.

The settlement was put on the agenda for approval. But Chrysler, who would prove to be a key figure, had a change of heart. He joined Adams and Taylor and it was a 3-2 vote against the settlement.

Nunn was asked by the commission if he wanted to try the case. No, he told them. He was not a litigator. So the three who voted against the settlement set out to hire local counsel to go after the gas rates and Mesa.

They hired Bob Templeton.

Before there was the possibility of a trial, there was a looming question of where a trial would occur. Mesa, no how and no way, wanted the trial in Amarillo. If there were to be one, its attorneys wanted it in Ysleta County in El Paso, the only county in Texas that did not have petroleum production. With a local jury likely made up of Amarillo gas customers who had their rates greatly increased, Mesa attorney Harlow Sprouse argued, how fair could a trial in the city be?

But really it was likely more than that. For the first half of the 1980s, Boone Pickens was Amarillo's Favorite Son. He graduated from Amarillo High School in the late 1940s, graduated from Oklahoma A&M (now Oklahoma State), and in the 1950s, returned to Amarillo where he eventually founded Mesa Petroleum Co.

By 1981, he had grown Mesa into one of the largest independent oil producers in the world, primarily with the takeover of the Hugoton Production Company, 30 times bigger than Mesa. By the mid-1980s, he displayed the character in business that Amarillo thought was symbolic of the area – bold, aggressive, feisty – when he came to be known nationally as a "corporate raider."

Using Mesa as his financial vehicle, Pickens launched takeover bids for much larger oil companies, including Gulf Oil, Phillips Petroleum, and Unocal. None of these attempts succeed, but Pickens called attention to their business tactics. He still managed to extract hundreds of millions of dollars in profits by getting these companies to buy back their shares from him at a premium in exchange for promises that he would just go away.

He would land on the cover of *Time* Magazine in 1985. It showed Pickens in a poker game, holding four cards with one hand and reaching for chips with another. "The Takeover Game: Corporate Raider T. Boone Pickens."

To the public, he seemed to do that with a folksy charm that belied Wall Street. It brought Amarillo some unexpected national attention. "You go, Boone," most seemed to say.

But the crown on his do-no-wrong head would soon get knocked sideways. As president of the board of regents of West Texas State, he was instrumental in bringing in controversial president Dr. Ed

T. Boone Pickens

Keith Adams

John Ward

Time Magazine, 1985

Roach. Roach lost favor with the faculty. A new president's home was in the spotlight because of huge cost overruns. Pickens defended both man and home.

The public was starting to see what most who crossed paths with Pickens knew for a long time – he didn't get to where he was by being a nice guy. He could be ruthless and cold and hold grudges. Mesa employees knew any day could be the day when there would be a cardboard box on their desk and a security guard next to it. They were fired.

Then there was the odd public feud with the Amarillo Globe-News. The newspaper, for the most part, had given Pickens almost fawning coverage his entire career. But the Globe-News became his foil in late 1986 for what he decried as negative coverage of him, the city and West Texas State.

On Dec. 8, 1986, in an interview with KFDA, Pickens hinted he would move Mesa to Dallas if the company was not treated better by the newspaper. In hindsight, it looked to be like the Globe-News was just cover to move to Dallas. He, and especially Bea, the second of his five wives, felt the company had outgrown the city. It would look as if he were just too big for his corporate britches to Amarillo if he simply left, but if the newspaper was just too darn negative, well, who could blame him?

At a company Christmas party in 1986, Pickens urged his 400 employees to cancel their subscriptions in protest of "negative reporting." That did not appear to be a suggestion, so Mesa en masse canceled subscriptions.

The sniping would continue for most of 1987. In May, Billy Morris, chairman of Morris Communications, parent company of the Globe-News, flew in from corporate headquarters in Augusta, Ga., for a meeting with Pickens. It was brief and blunt as the two traded insults and Morris parted. Ironically, years later, Pickens and Morris would be members of the Augusta National Golf Club, which hosts the Masters golf tournament.

That fall, a group, Panhandle Citizens For A Better Amarillo Newspaper, was formed. Led by Cactus Feeders owner Paul Engler, a friend of Pickens, the group mounted a flashy campaign helped by a hired organizer from Washington. It included a bumper sticker, "I Canceled."

The group accused the Globe-News of hindering efforts to recruit business. It also had seven "demands" that included an apology to the residents of Hereford for coverage of migrant workers and their conditions there, as well as a promise of "a dedicated and honest commitment to journalistic excellence."

Less public but no less important, Pickens wanted editor Jerry

Huff ousted. The feud had become personal between the two.

In November, just before Thanksgiving, PCBAN group held an unusual rally at the Civic Center that attracted a crowd of about 1,000. It was a paper tiger of a crowd, mainly filled with Mesa employees, Pickens cronies and those who worked for them, the curious, and several fraternities from West Texas State which were paid to attend. The fraternity which made the most noise earned even more cash.

For their part, someone at the Globe-News had buttons made that read, "The Attila of Amarilla." They became a collector's item.

The spat came to a public end around the time of the rally as Huff did leave. It was announced he would coordinate Morris Communications' presidential coverage, a move the company said had been in the works for months. Many, including those at the Globe-News, were skeptical.

On one of the last days before Huff left Amarillo, a huge yellow banner greeted those who came into downtown Amarillo. It hung from the south side of Mesa's 10-story building at 320 S. Polk Street. It read:

GOODBYE JERRY.

It might have been a way for Pickens to give the middle finger to Huff and the Globe-News and it might have been good for a few laughs. But to many, who thought the feud with the newspaper was trumped up and silly, it backfired. Pickens had the look of a vindictive bully.

And it was just a few months later that Pickens and the City of Amarillo were in the cross hairs over gas rates. No, he didn't start it, but inherited it. But he wasn't about to back down either. In standing firm, the swashbuckling corporate raider, the one-time toast of the town, didn't think he could get a fair trial in Amarillo.

A venue hearing was set for late July 1988 in Judge David Gleason's 47th state District Court. It was a marathon session. Mesa, with Sprouse as lead counsel, pulled out all stops to convince Gleason a fair trial was not possible in Amarillo.

V. Hale Starr, a communications consultant from Des Moines,

Iowa, hired by Mesa, testified that a survey to determine whether Mesa and Energas could get a fair trial in Amarillo showed bias against the defendants.

Starr told Gleason that 56 percent of 300 respondents to a survey in Potter County favored the city over Mesa, and 63 percent sided with Amarillo against Energas. Starr said a 40 percent bias rate is sufficient to prove an unbiased trial could not be expected.

Templeton called the random selection as "trial by computer," and in cross examination of Starr, tried to show bias in the questionnaire based on method, wording and order of questioning conditioned specific responses.

Both Amarillo Globe-News executive editor Garet von Netzer and KVII news director and prime time news anchor John McKissack testified. Because of Pickens' controversial stance with West Texas State and the fight with the newspaper, and now, the city's gas rate, they both said that it hindered chances for an impartial trial by Potter and Randall county jurors.

"I would say that my perception of what people say is that Energas does not have a good image," Von Netzer said in the hearing. "Being in the community for 19 years, you can't help but pick things up."

The hearing went well into the night. At the end, Templeton had as witnesses two long-time Amarillo residents. The first was an older man who worked at a service station at 10th Avenue and Buchanan Street.

"I remember he told Bob that he talked to people every day and knew of nobody who had ill feelings one way or another in his opinion on Pickens," Nunn said.

It was how the trial ended that was classic Bob Templeton. He called up a man who worked for the Santa Fe Railroad. He was the kind of man a stranger couldn't help but like.

"I said, 'Do you understand what this is about, this is Mesa Petroleum saying they can't get a fair trial in Amarillo, Texas, so what do you have to say about that? Can they get a fair trial?'" Templeton said.

"He said, 'Sure – lessen' they's guilty.' That brought down the house. It just about clinched it."

Mesa's change of venue was denied by Gleason. The trial, absent a settlement, would be in Amarillo. "That really took the wind out of their sails on that aspect of the case," Templeton said.

Before and after the venue hearing, there were a number of meetings between the city commission, Templeton, Ward, Nunn and Mesa, and primarily its attorney, William Patterson. The goal was a settlement both sides could live with and avoid a trial.

"Pickens never came over to show his face. He just sent Patterson," Templeton said. "I was doing a pretty good job on trying to negotiate the price down so that we had a firm contract at a fixed price that was not exorbitant and had some relationship to what gas was being sold in the market.

"I'd get Patterson committed to this and that. Every time we'd have a meeting, it would end with Patterson saying, 'OK, that's fine. We're going to do that.' He'd go back to Pickens, and Pickens would cuss him out and say that we're not going to do that. And he'd come back to have another meeting. It was just meetings after meetings."

Although Pickens wasn't at the meetings physically, in a sense, he was there. He set up one meeting in the basement conference room at the Mesa building. Like most of the offices at Mesa, the conference room was bugged. This was confirmed by multiple parties.

"We had quite a discussion with the commission while we were there," Templeton said. "Pickens heard it all. Shortly after that meeting, Parkey, on his own and without counsel, had a meeting with Pickens."

Ironically, the Mesa building at 320 S. Polk has long been the domain of Maxor National Pharmacy Services and its chairman and founder, Jerry Hodge. Hodge was no friend of Pickens. The firm of Templeton, Smithee, Hayes, Heinrich and Russell has officed on the 10th floor of the Maxor building since 1997.

"It's no longer bugged," Templeton quipped.

Mesa continued to negotiate over the average cost of gas of Fort Worth, Austin and San Antonio. None had gas in its backyard like

Amarillo, and none had anything like the B contract with its utility either.

"Pickens never budged – never budged an inch," Templeton said. "We got Patterson committed three times to a reasonable settlement, and he'd go to Pickens and Pickens would raise hell with him and tell him, no, we're not about to do that. I liked Patterson. He was a decent fellow and good lawyer, and very loyal to Pickens."

At one point, Patterson told the city if it would agree to the new gas contract, Pickens guaranteed he would bring in 600 new jobs to Amarillo.

"I told the city commission and Merrill that was an improper inducement to enter into a contract," Templeton said. "That would not be enforceable."

Ultimately, this would fall on the city commission, the divided city commission. This was going to fall one of two ways. The commission was either going to approve a settlement hammered out between the two sides, or it was going to vote to go to trial.

The key figure was commissioner Don Chrysler. He was looked as the swing vote on the 5-person commission. Parkey and Chandler were aligned with Mesa. Adams and Taylor were in the city's corner.

Chrysler, who was in the home health care business, was a sincere man. He was a product of north Amarillo. He felt a kinship with the economically disadvantaged in town. Both sides knew his vote was crucial.

"I'd try to talk to him. I'd think I had him, and he'd slip loose again," Templeton said. "I kept trying to work on that man. He would vacillate and then come back and say, 'Bob, I'm with you.' Next time he was back in the other camp."

Templeton believed Parkey relayed to Pickens the importance of Chrysler's vote. Pickens called in a favor with Horace Scott, a longtime real estate developer. Scott was, as Templeton called him, "a disciple of Pickens." He was the point person to schmooze Chrysler.

Chrysler attended a meeting at Lake Tanglewood. After that he told Templeton that while it was a difficult decision, he was going to vote to accept the settlement presented and dismiss the lawsuit.

In September 1988, the city commission voted 3-2 to accept a settlement that looked to be clearly in Mesa's favor. Nunn said he was not part of the agreement, indicating the commission went around its city attorney.

The city of Amarillo's gas rate would be the average of the higher prices of Fort Worth, San Antonio and Austin – higher because of transportation costs. Mesa would incur $6 million in rate relief, meaning that its utility company Energas would keep the rate at the previous level until $6 million in difference had been met. At that point, the new rate would begin.

"It was not a whole lot," Ward said, "but that was all they were willing to offer. The settlement we ended up with was essentially the same we started with."

"That $6 million didn't last but a few months," Templeton said. "Boone Pickens put it to Amarillo, Texas. He achieved in politics what he couldn't in the courts."

When that settlement was approved 3-2 by the city commission, Templeton washed his hands of it. At a hearing to dismiss the lawsuit and accept the settlement, Templeton appeared in Gleason's court. Gleason asked if the city were prepared to go forward.

"I was in a real dilemma," Templeton said. "I don't believe I ever quit on a client in my career, but I could not stand the settlement. I made a decision and then kept it to myself. I told Judge Gleason that this is a bad settlement for Amarillo. I can't stomach this. I can't be a part of it, and I resign as counsel."

That suppressed the settlement agreement for a bit. Ed Morris from the Whittenburg firm replaced Templeton, and the settlement was eventually approved in 1989.

The contract was for a period of years. The cost of gas in 1988 was well below $2. The distribution cost to Amarillo consumers was almost negligible. So even at $2, Energas, a subsidiary of Mesa, was making a huge profit. At $2.65, the gross profit was eye-opening.

"Pickens and Mesa profited greatly from the takeover of Pioneer and the new gas contract," Templeton said.

For Templeton and others, it was a hollow feeling. The city commission had bent to Pickens. He would have relished a reckoning in court, even though it would not have been an easy case.

"If we'd had gone to trial, Templeton said, "we had a strong jury verdict in our favor. The more difficult question was whether we were on sound enough legal footing as third-party beneficiaries. But do I regret not going to trial? My gosh, yes."

"The whole argument," Ward said, "was whether the gas customers in Amarillo were harmed or not, whether they had any right to relief that was based on the B contract that Amarillo Oil Co. had years ago (starting in 1928). So the argument from those who didn't want to settle and try it in court was the gas customers in Amarillo had beneficiary rights to that contract, third-party beneficiary rights."

Citizens didn't seem quite as divided down the middle on the gas rate increase as the city commission. But there was division. One side didn't want to anger Pickens, believing he and Mesa were too important to Amarillo and there was fear he would move. The other side simply didn't want to pay much higher gas prices.

"I wouldn't describe it as two schools of thoughts, but two attitudes," Templeton said. "Why argue over gas prices? Mesa was one of the top companies in this part of the country, and it was important to have them here. These were people on the so-called 'rich end of town.' The rest of the city that knew anything about it knew it was in Amarillo's best interest to keep gas prices low. The cost of living was important in attracting industry."

There was a P.S. to this legal squabble that would not unfold until eight months later. It was the city election in May 1989. Pickens recruited and funded a slate of five for the commission spots. For the first time, beyond voting, Templeton got involved in local politics when he helped recruit a group to run against Pickens' slate. Pickens' slate was defeated.

Adams won over Parkey in his bid to become mayor by nearly 5,000 votes – 14,231 to 9,460. Chandler and Chrysler were defeated in their bid for re-election. Taylor chose not to run. On the commission were Kel Seliger, who would eventually become mayor for eight years and has been State Senator for District 31 for 16 years, John McKissack, J.L. Skeen and Dianne Bosch, the second woman ever on the commission.

Later that year, Mesa Petroleum Company packed up and went to Dallas. The move surprised no one. And Chrysler later confided to both Nunn and Templeton that he had made a mistake, that he should not have voted to dismiss the lawsuit and accept the settlement.

As for Pickens, he sold Mesa in 1996 when the company was in deep financial trouble to financier Richard Rainwater. Darla Moore, his wife, soon fired Pickens, ending 40 years with the company he founded.

In the following years, Pickens founded BP Capital Management which ran two successful hedge funds. In 2006, Pickens earned $990 million from equity in two hedge funds. He also turned to wind energy and water, but buying water rights and selling them to cities never really got the traction he wanted.

Pickens could be complicated. He operated in shades of gray. He made millions but also gave away millions. In his life, he gave away $700 million to charity, of which nearly $500 million went to his alma mater, Oklahoma State.

Pickens health deteriorated with a series of strokes starting in 2015. Perhaps to make amends with his hometown, he hosted a fundraiser for the Texas Tech veterinarian school in Amarillo.

His 65,000-acre ranch and mansion in Roberts County near Pampa went for sale for $250 million in the last years of his life. It remained unsold at his death on Sept. 11, 2019 at age 91.

"In his mind, I was his enemy to his last days," Templeton said. "He called me 'Pemberton.' He said I called him 'Prickens' but I never did."

Templeton likely read Pickens about as well as anyone.

"I had a lot of respect for his initiatives and aggressiveness," he said. "He was very intelligent. Whatever his critics said about him, Boone was a natural leader. He accomplished many things and was generous with his money to many charities."

In a very real way, Mesa's and Energas' battle with the City of Amarillo more than 30 years ago is still felt today. As the attorney who was in the middle of that in the late 1980s noted, current gas production has increased greatly in Texas. With an average gas price hovering near $1.50, Amarillo consumers are paying an exorbitant price, presently around $3.84 per 1,000 cubic feet with a BTU of about 900.

"The question remains, what could be done about it now?" Templeton said. "I don't have those answers, but city fathers do. In fact, the cost of gas in San Antonio, Austin and Fort Worth has diminished greatly because of the Barnett Shale findings and reduced price of gas.

"So what's to be done about it? That answer lies with the present city council and their attorney. But something should be done."

CHAPTER

II

Firm Foundation

John Smithee was not yet out of Texas Tech Law School in the summer of 1974. But he showed up at the office of Robert Templeton, per his instruction, on a Monday morning. As Smithee told the receptionist, he was ready to go to work.

"And who are you again?" she asked.

It was a rather inauspicious start for a promising attorney who would have the longest stint working with Templeton. It's 46 years and counting. Smithee is better known as a Republican state representative from the Texas Panhandle. He currently serves District 86 in this his 17th consecutive term.

But serving in the Texas House pays Smithee $7,200 a year. For a salary to live on, he's been connected with Templeton since the mid-1970s, and has been a partner with Templeton since 1980.

"John Smithee, anytime he gets into a lawsuit, he digs thoroughly and deeply," Templeton said. "He knows how to try a lawsuit very very well. He's a man who understands the law. I don't know of a more effective lawyer when he gets into it."

All Templeton knew the first time he met Smithee was he was a pretty good tennis player. They first met opposite the net at a summer tournament at the T-Bar-M racquet club in Amarillo in that summer of 1974. Smithee, who played tennis at Tascosa High School and Amarillo College, was paired against Templeton in a singles match.

"They paired me to play against this old man, or who I thought was old at the time. He was about 40," Smithee said. "Bob wasn't a great tennis player, but he was as scrappy as he could be. It was a long match that I finally won. He was mad and I thought he was mad at me because I'd won. But he was just so determined to win."

They had some small talk after the match. Smithee told Templeton he was between years at law school at Tech. Templeton told him he was an attorney, which Smithee knew. Templeton then asked what he was doing the rest of the summer. Before he could answer, Templeton invited him to work the rest of the summer with him and the other two attorneys, Jerry Kolander and R.C. Hamilton.

"I told him that I got some things for you to do, and we'll keep you busy the rest of the summer," Templeton said. "Come by Monday."

"That's great," Smithee said.

Templeton, though, would be out of the city that Monday, but just come to the office, he told Smithee. Someone would get him set up.

The confused receptionist called in Kolander, who asked Smithee the same two questions – who in the world are you and why are you here?

"I told Jerry that Mr. Templeton told me to come down here and come to work today," Smithee said. "So he sent me to the library and tried to find me some work to do. The next day Bob got back and he got it all fixed."

For an attorney who worked for more than 60 years in one city, those who Templeton has practiced with is surprisingly small. He never worked in one of Amarillo's largest firms. He's always liked a modestly sized work environment.

Maybe for that reason, Templeton can fairly easily recite the lawyers he's worked alongside from the 1950s to 2020. From the earliest – Kolander and Lon Mosier, who he started with in the Potter County attorney's office -- to the latest – David Russell, who joined the firm as a partner in 2001. Alphabetically, it's from Cleo Clayton, Sr., to Coleman Young.

It's 21 in all, but none had the start, has stayed the longest or has more name recognition than Smithee, one of the most even-handed and respected lawmakers out of Austin for parts of five decades.

"Bob gave me a wonderful opportunity that summer," Smithee said. "He let me do some meaningful work on some meaningful cases. To this day, I appreciate that. You always appreciate anybody who gives you a break to start. At the end of the summer, he paid me a bonus. He said that if you have some time during the school year, we'll have some work for you to do."

Smithee worked for Templeton the next two summers between law school semesters, and continued to work on some important cases. After graduation, he eventually started to hang around the office. They couldn't get rid of him. So he was hired full time.

"Bob has never paid me a salary except when I was a clerk," he said. "I told him at the start that I'd just rather be on a deal where I got a part of what the firm made because I didn't want the pressure of having to produce, and Bob worry about whether I was here at any given time. My hours were irregular. And that's the way it's always been."

Before Smithee received his law degree, Templeton was busy with eminent domain cases. It's likely no attorney in Amarillo represented more landowners, especially in the eastern Texas Panhandle, than Templeton when I-40 was built through existing farm land and ranch land in the 1970s. It was a long list.

"Most of those cases were not very big," Smithee said. "Bob asked me if I wanted to go over there and try some of those. There wasn't that much money in them, but, frankly, I wanted the trial experience. We'd try several in a day. If we had a big win, I might get $800. But for a young lawyer, it was one of the best things that could happen to me."

Most of the time, Smithee tried the cases alone. The lawyer on the opposing side was with the Texas Attorney General's office in Austin. Most of the time it was a disinterested lawyer who wasn't even sure what county he was in.

"I had sympathy from the jury," Smithee said, "so it was a good position to be in. We tried a lot of these cases in Pampa, and they were upset because I-40 didn't go through Pampa. McLean was upset because they thought it would bypass McLean and kill all the local business. We had favorable juries."

It didn't hurt that the state would make obvious low-ball offers. Often an appraiser from Odessa was used. He had a flamboyant air, and often wore expensive tailored clothes. He charged as much for the appraisal as the property he put a value on.

At the level of law Templeton was practicing in the mid-1970s, it was not profitable for him to try those cases when there were others who needed his attention.

"The experience was invaluable," Smithee said. "My friends in law school weren't even getting in the courtroom yet."

It was while Smithee was getting his legal feet wet in the courtroom that the face of the Templeton firm began to change. It began when he agreed to partner with Bob Garner, who had a checkered past with his practice in Lubbock. He could be excellent in the courtroom, but outside of it, he had a habit of rubbing people the wrong way.

Kolander soon left to open his own practice. John Judge left for Austin. In their place, Garner brought in John Lovell, Nancy Stone from Houston, and Sam Stein.

"Garner started bringing in this one, bringing in that one," Templeton said. "But John Lovell, when he got a case, he never let go of it. He worked hard. I later hired Joe, his brother, and he hit the ground running."

But maybe the best hire than can be tied to Garner wasn't an attorney. Jim LaFavers, an investigator, proved his worth many times over in the next 30 years. He was like Paul Drake to lawyer Perry Mason in the fictional TV series.

"He saved us on so many cases," Templeton said. "Jim was just so good at what he did. He was the reason we won a number of cases."

Maybe it was a fluke, maybe it was fate, or maybe just life in how LaFavers became part of the Templeton firm. He left the Amarillo police department as a homicide detective in 1981. The following year, he was dating a woman whose younger brother attended Texas Tech. The brother was driving to Houston when he was caught in a blinding snowstorm near Buffalo, Texas, 105 miles south of Dallas. A semi-truck blew his Chevy Manza off the road, and then a second truck collided with the car, killing the student instantly. LaFavers' girlfriend asked that he look into it.

The next day, LaFavers was at the scene of the accident. There was still much evidence left of the accident. With the snow melting, tire marks were visible, and LaFavers started to get a picture of what happened.

A young DPS officer worked the scene the previous day. It was his first major accident. He was reluctant to speak because his partner was with a woman at the time, leaving the investigation to him. The officer admitted he was very inexperienced in accident investigations.

LaFavers walked him through the evidence. The first truck blew him off the road. The second truck hit him. Both trucks belonged to the same company.

"He agreed with what I showed him, but he told me that he had already turned in his report that the driver of the car just lost control," LaFavers said. "He said, 'What should I do?' I told him to just amend your report to show these facts occurred, simply make a supplement to your report."

All hell broke loose. The officer's partner said the report was not changing. Lesson: Don't challenge Jim LaFavers when he knows he's right. He got a camera and tape measure to get the physical facts. He discovered there were four others who were involved in the chain reaction of the accident who required medical attention. They were never interviewed, but were right behind the accident. LaFavers got affidavits from them.

"It got into this big controversy," he said. "I even went to Austin and met with the head of the DPS. He basically told me to take a flying leap. So I dug in my heels."

LaFavers prepared a 200-page report. He was advised to take the report to Bob Garner in Amarillo. Garner filed a lawsuit in federal court, the U.S. District Court of the Western District of Texas in Waco. Lucius Bunton was the judge. A jury was impaneled.

"In the midst of this, the judge called Garner and the defense attorney to the bench and said you gentlemen had better resolve this for your own good," LaFavers said. "And they did. Before we left Waco, Garner asked me if I'd come to Amarillo to work with him. I said that I might. And then he offered me more money than I'd ever made before."

It didn't take long for LaFavers to make an impact on the firm. Very few could have done what he did.

A local man was working construction on a steel building in Amarillo. He was on a ladder using a ratchet. The ratchet slipped, causing the man to fall. When he landed, he hit his head and was a paraplegic.

What caused the ratchet to slip? The man's family claimed it was the tool, specifically, the pawl, the gears inside a ratchet, that were faulty. The man had mentioned purchasing the ratchet, but could not remember where.

LaFavers was also a certified forensic hypnotist, one of just two at the time in the state. He hypnotized the man to determine where he bought the ratchet.

"One of the big issues was how would we prove that he was the purchaser, proved that he owned it, and how could we prove the misrepresentation of the warranties?" LaFavers said.

Through hypnotism, LaFavers was able to track down the purchase to a small store in Houston. The lawsuit was settled for $4.5 million.

"That started me here," LaFavers said, "and Bob started drifting toward me."

LaFavers' probing questions, his camera, his nose for facts, are over some of the biggest cases in a 30-year period. The Key Well blowout, the Pampa fire, the Emma Jean Oliver drug case, those were just a few examples where LaFavers played a key role.

"I don't think when I first came on that Bob Templeton wanted me," LaFavers said. "He has since said – how do I put this? – that I was the best mistake Bob Garner ever made, or words to that effect."

Templeton remembers it a little differently: "Jim and I hit it off from the word 'go.' Jim took to investigating our cases like a duck to water."

LaFavers had a front row seat to the two partners, Templeton and Garner. It didn't necessarily take an investigator to see that it was more of an arrangement than a partnership.

"Garner and Templeton together, it was such a dichotomy," LaFavers said. "They were two different people living in the same world. There was a lot of tension forming in the law firm between the two Bobs."

The two Bobs had somehow stayed together through nearly all of the 1980s. Garner could be very effective in the courtroom and a good rainmaker, but he was unpredictable. He could be a lightning rod – for good and for bad.

"I never let him have what I thought was control of the law firm," Templeton said. "He could just be wild. I'd come in and see a receptionist working and I'd never seen her before, or a lawyer I'd never seen before. Garner had them do this, promise that."

As the 1980s were ending, the tipping point was nearing in this difficult working partnership. It wasn't going to take much for it to fall. Templeton was upset with him in general, believing he wasn't working as hard as he should and spending too much time at his Spearman farm.

Then there was a bizarre incident of some missing briefcases that Garner was convinced were stolen. It got to be a bit of a joke with Templeton making reference to Humphrey Bogart investigating who stole the frozen strawberries in "The Caine Mutiny."

But the tipping point was the aftermath of the Toni Banks divorce case. Banks was the Templeton firm's client, but they sued her because she had not paid the firm for their extensive work. Templeton was adamant they get their money. Garner did not share that much enthusiasm.

"I need her to pay that fee because by gosh I've worked for it," Templeton told Garner. "She owes us $250,000."

Banks hired an attorney from Dallas and countersued. Both sides took depositions. Susan McKissack had worked on the case as a paralegal. She was deposed at length.

"It was 'What did you charge for this? What did you charge for that? Did you charge for going to the bathroom?' It was ridiculous," Templeton said.

By this time, Templeton had about had it. Then he went looking for his law partner. He found out Garner was in New York with his wife on a vacation.

"I told my wife that I was done. I'm splitting up. She said that I didn't have the guts to do it," Templeton said. So he comes back, and I sat down with him, and said, 'Bob, I'm your friend and I'll always be your friend, but I'm not going to practice law with you any longer.'"

The firm was splitting. Templeton had to leave for Iowa for depositions in a case involving John Deere and a hay baler where a man had been killed. Before he left, he received two propositions.

"John Lovell talked to me and said, 'Bob, why don't we office together? We won't be partners and you will have your separate deals,'" Templeton said. "I just said that I don't think I want to do that. Then Bob came in too and said that we don't need to split up, that we're good together. I said, 'No, Bob, I'm not going to do that. I'm just not going to practice law with you any longer.'"

When Templeton returned from Iowa, some of the lawyers were going, some staying. The Lovells – John and Joe – went with Garner. So too did Sam Stein and Nancy Stone. Smithee, LaFavers and Paul McGuffey stayed with Templeton.

"I was working in the yard and got a call from Bob telling me that he was splitting the firm," LaFavers said. "He told me that he had talked to Martha and made the decision. He asked me if I knew what I was going to do. I told him, 'When the train pulls out, I want to be on your track.'"

The firm as it's currently constructed began to take shape. Joe Hayes was with the Culton Morgan firm. Templeton wanted him to practice with him for a while, but it just didn't fit. Then Garner left.

"I rode up the elevator with Bob Garner one day, and he said, 'I guess you know Bob and I are getting a divorce" Hayes said. "I said,

'Really?' He said, 'Yeah.' I said, 'Here let me get off with you.'

"I walked into Bob Templeton's office. I said, 'I hear Bob Garner's leaving. You got room?' Bob said, 'Yeah, come on.' And that's what we did. It was about that quick."

Templeton believed he was getting the finest oil and gas attorney in the Panhandle. And as he would discover when the firm defended Don Storseth in a Pampa fire lawsuit, an effective trial lawyer as well.

"He approaches a trial in an intellectual way," Templeton said.

Hayes would soon join Templeton and Smithee as a partner. In due time, Brian Heinrich and David Russell would join them. Templeton was like a good head coach who was made to look even better by surrounding himself with quality assistant coaches.

Heinrich joined the firm in 1998 from working with the Barry Peterson firm. Prior to that, he practiced in Midland. Templeton had worked a case with Heinrich and remembered his work.

"I can recognize legal talent pretty quick," Templeton said of Heinrich, who has served as president of the board of directors of the Amarillo Economic Development Corporation. "I didn't really teach Brian much at all. He hit the ground running. He's never had a dissatisfied client. He's an excellent, excellent trial lawyer."

David Russell completed the firm, joining as a partner in 2001. Like Templeton, he's a graduate of Baylor. Unlike Templeton, he was at a large Amarillo firm – Culton Morgan Britain and White. They merged with the Hinkle Cox firm in the mid-1990s.

"You just have to see this fellow work a jury," Templeton said. "Oh my gosh, he never lost a case as a defense lawyer. He never lost a case until he got here on the plaintiff side of the docket and found out you can't win all of them. But he hasn't lost many over here. Great Christian, great person. "

As the 21st century swung open, Templeton hit the home stretch of his career heading a law firm he felt at peace with from not only a professional side, but a personal side as well. Long gone were some of the in-house worries of the past.

"I've had to juggle more balls than a human being ought to juggle," Templeton said, "but these guys are self-starters and self-finishers."

Robert Templeton (center, front row) has worked with or partnered with more than 25 attorneys in his more than 60 years of law practice in Amarillo. The latest are (left, front row) David Russell and John Smithee, and (back row, from left) Joe Hayes, Brian Heinrich and Cole Young.

Sometimes a major case starts with simply buying a car. Smithee bought a new vehicle in 1994. As he looked over the list of charges, there was an item that struck him as odd.

A vehicle inventory tax? Never heard of it.

Smithee called the sales manager at the dealership, who didn't know Smithee was in the legislature. Smithee was told that was just another tax the crazy legislature had put on them.

"My first thought was, 'Oh my goodness, I hope the legislature didn't vote for that,'" Smithee said. "I went back and looked and didn't find anything."

He talked with officials with the Texas Automobile Dealers Association to confirm what he already knew. There was no inventory vehicle tax other than that's what the TADA conspired to put on vehicles.

"I was kind of busy with other things," Smithee said, "but I mentioned it to Bob and he ran with the ball."

Property is taxed and assessed each January 1 according to the state constitution as an ad valorem tax. The TADA, in conjunction with new car dealers, decided to add a "vehicle inventory tax" and put that language in the sales contract.

"They entered into an agreement that if someone didn't want to pay that tax, they wouldn't sell them a car," Templeton said. "It was a huge conspiracy, just a huge conspiracy and they thought they could get away with it."

Templeton filed a class action lawsuit against 700 car dealers across Texas. The firm partnered with renowned East Texas attorney Franklin Jones. He was well connected and respected and held sway in that part of the state. The case was filed in the small East Texas town of Jefferson, county seat of Marion County.

Smithee prepared the briefings and Templeton took the depositions. They filed a deceptive trade practice in state court with Judge Lauren Parrish. An anti-trust violation was filed in federal court with Judge Richard Shell in Beaumont.

In both cases, the judges certified the class. Before a class action lawsuit can proceed, the class must be certified. This process ensures that the plaintiffs have enough similarities to proceed with litigation against the named defendant as part of one larger case.

On the state level, the case went to the court of appeals and to the Texas Supreme Court where the court affirmed the certification of class. On the federal level, the Fifth Circuit Court of Appeals reversed the claim for damages, but allowed the claim for mandamus.

What was left was a deceptive trade practice. The case wasn't settled until 2006. It turned out to be a lucrative case for the firm, and it changed the language in a sales contract.

"You see the inventory tax language in all sales contracts which says this is a charge the dealer applies toward payment of their ad valorem tax," Templeton said. "You're not obligated to pay for it if you don't want to."

Sometimes the opposition is as broad and far-reaching as car dealerships across the state. Most of the time, in a plaintiff case, it's specific and direct. In 1994, it was the Olsen Manor Nursing Home.

Winston Trostle was 88 years old when he was admitted to the nursing home. Inexplicably, he died shortly after he was admitted on July 7. It didn't make sense at the time, and further investigation into his death, made even less sense.

Ten months later, in May 1995, Inez Trostle, the widow, filed a wrongful death lawsuit against Olsen Manor. The claim was that Winston Trostle was given insulin while under the care of the nursing home. Trostle was not diabetic, and the insulin killed him.

Templeton represented Inez Trostle. Steve McConnico, a formidable Austin attorney, was hired to defend Olsen Manor. McConnico tried to talk the insurance company of Olsen Manor into settling with Trostle, but they refused to do so.

The case slowly wound its way toward trial. Smithee prepared the case. It did not go to trial until November 1998. Give Smithee that long to prepare – even with time in Austin with the legislature – and no rock will be left unturned. Circumstantial evidence pointed to a charge nurse with the wrongdoing.

"Here was the problem we had – we didn't have any direct evidence the nurse gave him insulin," Smithee said. "All we had was that she was the charge nurse. We also knew that when Trostle got to the hospital, he had this incredibly low blood sugar."

The charge nurse could not be located for a deposition. She had vanished.

But some damning circumstantial evidence was piling up. At previous places of medical employment, the nurse had been called "Angel of Death" because she told others that should couldn't stand to see some patients suffer. A thorough background check revealed she had been fired three times.

So while there was no direct evidence the charge nurse had given Trostle insulin, she definitely had access to him. The autopsy also showed insulin in the blood stream. But not only was there no direct evidence, another problem was looming.

Discovery showed that when Trostle was transported by ambulance to the hospital, he was given a "finger stick," a procedure where the finger is lanced and capillary blood taken for testing. The results showed a high sugar level that was above normal.

"He wasn't diabetic, and a person who's not diabetic would not have high blood sugar if he'd already been given insulin," Smithee said. "So it was a real puzzler why that would be on the initial stick with the high blood sugar if he'd already been given insulin. Insulin is fast-acting."

The defense would likely argue that Trostle was given insulin while in the ambulance. That didn't make much sense, but it might be enough to affect the verdict. So Templeton and Smithee sought a medical opinion that might explain this. They found one with a nurse at the Texas Tech Health Sciences Center in Amarillo.

She said a finger stick can provide a false reading if alcohol is put on the skin before the stick and not properly wiped. If a finger stick is done and alcohol gets into the test, alcohol is high in sugar.

"So they get a sugar level from the alcohol and not the blood," Smithee said. "That was the only explanation."

That was established at trial. The handwriting was on the wall. McConnico, who had wanted to settle, tried to mitigate the monetary damages. Templeton asked for $12.5 million.

"One of the things that weighed in our favor was how many problems this nursing home had in the past," Smithee said. "Their inspections were a disaster. They had so many violations that one retired inspector said it was the worst one in the region, the worst one he'd ever seen."

The defense had a nursing home administrator from El Paso testify that Olsen Manor was actually running an efficient and healthy nursing home. Prior to him testifying, Smithee got the history of the El Paso nursing home that showed at least five violations.

"When I questioned him, I put these stack of violations in front of him and asked if he knew what these were," Smithee said. "When he said no, I told him these were your violations from the Department of Protective Services against your nursing home when you were the administrator there. That was a visual the jury understood. He lost all credibility at that point."

The jury awarded widow Inez Trostle and son Earl Trostle approximately $13 million in actual and punitive damages. It was the largest malpractice monetary verdict in Potter County history. The two parties settled after the verdict with the two Trostles receiving $6.5 million in damages.

McConnico, like Templeton, was a Baylor Law School graduate. He was the 2011 Baylor Lawyer of the Year. In trying more than 200 cases to jury verdict, this was a rare defeat in his career.

"Steve called me after that and was very gracious," Templeton said. "He was always a gentleman. He said, 'Bob, that's the first malpractice case I've lost in my life.'"

There was a P.S. to the Trostle case. When the lawsuit was pending, Smithee called Joe Trostle, who was an estranged son from the family. He informed Trostle of the lawsuit and asked if he wanted to join the other two in seeking damages.

"He got angry. He said, 'I know what you're trying to do. You're trying to hijack a nursing home for money. It was an accident. I know how you lawyers work,'" Smithee said. "I told him, 'I just want to be clear. You have no interest in the suit?' He told me not only did he not have any interest, but that if we used his name in any way in that suit, he'd sue us. I never understood why he was that angry."

After the verdict, the Houston Chronicle picked up an Associated Press story on the trial. Trostle called the Templeton firm wanting to know when he would get his share of the money. Smithee told him he wasn't getting a dime, that he made it clear in a previous call he'd sue if his name were mentioned in any way on that suit.

Joe Trostle sued Inez Trostle in an attempt to get some of the monetary damages. The Court of Appeals in Amarillo threw out the suit.

There was no doubt that Templeton had found a comfort zone with the last of his four partners in Smithee, Hayes, Heinrich and Russell. But he would also discover something about himself and Bob Garner.

Sometimes good friends can't be roommates in college. Sometimes

Bob Garner had an oversized personality. He and Templeton remained friends, but split up the partnership.

good friends can't be law partners and work together. In the last years of his life, Garner and Templeton long put aside any work friction and looked at each other through a different lens.

"We actually became fast friends at the end," Templeton said.

Garner later hired Templeton to represent his daughter in a legal matter. Templeton had a hand in helping Garner receive the Temple Houston Award in 2003, an award for career achievement given by the Panhandle Trial Lawyers Association.

In early 2005, they drove to Lubbock for a Texas Tech basketball game. Garner, a longtime smoker, confided to his former partner that he had some serious health issues. He died at age 67 a few months later.

"I liked Bob personally. You could not help but like the man,"

Templeton said. "At his funeral, I said that we were like Abbott and Costello. It was magic."

One of the last things Garner did before he died was leave a message on Templeton's phone. It's one Templeton couldn't initially erase. He kept that one for a long time.

"Bob, I love you."

CHAPTER

12

A Cigar For His Troubles

A fire in the dead of night at the home of John Bryan Vernon and wife Martha Vernon in Pampa in 1991 sent trucks screaming to the blaze. Fire engulfed the house. Neighbors got as close as they could to see tragedy unfold between the flames and the smoke.

Margaret Vernon staggered out to the yard where she was treated by firefighters. But her husband, John, and the couple's teenage son, Stuart Jacob Long, were not so fortunate. They were both asleep and died of carbon monoxide poisoning before they could escape.

The aftermath would involve the fire marshal and investigators, the Boy Scouts of America, and insurance companies. The likelihood that it would involve Robert Templeton in a contentious trial seemed remote, but it eventually did.

The reason was Don Storseth asked him for a favor. Storseth was a longtime friend dating back to when they were kids in the early 1940s.

"He was just a really really good friend," Templeton said, "and when he asked me to represent him, there was no way I could refuse."

It would be one of the few times that Templeton represented a defendant, but a client like this was personal. Storseth owned M&L Storage, and Margaret Vernon blamed the company's cardboard boxes for the cause of the fire and sued Storseth for several million dollars.

"Look, a lawyer's a lawyer," Templeton said. "If you're a lawyer, you should take on just about any case. As a matter of fact, the few cases where I represented the defendant, I took those with more zeal, effort and fun because I was getting paid all the time."

The Vernons were in the process of moving. John Vernon worked for Fluor Daniel, a high-level construction company. They were leaving Pampa.

The day before the fire, M&L employees had been at the house, packing up belongings and preparing to move bigger items. Boxes from M&L were left around the house that evening. Some boxes, the plaintiff contended, had been left on top of a floor furnace. When the furnace came on in the middle of the night, it caused the boxes to ignite.

Quite simply, that was believed to be the source of the fire. The Pampa fire marshal concurred. So too did the state fire marshal as well as a retired fire marshal from Missouri. It seemed like a rather open and shut case.

Well, maybe. Templeton has said often that investigator Jim LaFavers saved many of his cases. He could get just about anyone to feel at ease with him and trust him. A former homicide detective for the Amarillo police department, he could see what others couldn't. His instincts seldom led him in the wrong direction. He was dogged in his pursuit of evidence.

Templeton called LaFavers on a Friday to drive the 60 miles to Pampa over the weekend and take a detailed look at the house. When he got there, the house, of course, was cordoned off with tape by order of the fire marshal.

So LaFavers drove to the office of Tommy Adams, the Pampa fire marshal. LaFavers saw him the previous night on KVII, the Amarillo ABC affiliate. It was an interview where he said the living room boxes were too close to the furnace, which was adjacent to the stairs. He preferred Templeton's investigator not enter the house.

"I asked him if he took any pictures, and he said no one had,"

LaFavers said. "I told him that I had a camera, and if he'd like, we could go over to the house together. He said, 'I don't know about that.'

"Then I reminded him that he said it was the worst fire he'd ever seen in Pampa, and it would seem to me that people are going to wonder what the scene looked like and I'd be glad to share any and all pictures."

Adams finally agreed. When they entered the house, even in the daylight, it was dark. But that didn't stop LaFavers from taking what he called "wonderful pictures."

What he saw disturbed him, and in his mind, cast doubt on the original story of the boxes and furnace being the source of the blaze. LaFavers saw tell-tale signs of flammable liquid running down the wall and liquid under the baseboards.

"It was obvious to me that flammable liquid started the fire," he said.

He took photos of the furnace, but noticed no debris underneath the furnace, which he thought was odd. He thought if the fire started there, it would be covered in debris. Then LaFavers saw some evidence that stopped him in his tracks. A dark "V" was apparent on the walls.

"Anytime you have a 'V,' the bottom of the 'V' is the ignition source," LaFavers said. "I saw more than one 'V' on the walls and living room area. We use that as the 'point of origin.'

To give things a bit more juice, Templeton discovered Margaret Vernon had a bit of a past. She had not been married long, having been divorced less than a year. She had plead guilty to solicitation of murder in South Carolina of a previous husband and was on probation. Vernon also had a history of mental issues and had also spent some time in the psychiatric Pavilion in Amarillo.

These were the battle lines that were being drawn as the lawsuit was making its way toward trial. Templeton twice offered to settle, once for $350,000 before the trial began, and then sweetened that to $600,000 later, but both offers were refused. The other side had grander designs by as much as $3 to $4 million.

The other side was represented by Pampa attorney Jon Warner, active in his church and Pampa community. Templeton was joined by Joe Hayes, who was recently hired from the Culton Morgan firm. Hayes was regarded as one of the top oil and gas attorneys in the Panhandle.

A native of the Phillips – the famous Panhandle oil town turned ghost town – who had previously practiced in Canadian, Hayes was not yet a partner with the Templeton firm, but that would eventually change. His work in the Pampa fire case only sped that along.

"I had known Joe for 15 years," Templeton said. "I knew he was a good lawyer, but he was even better than I thought."

The trial at the Gray County courthouse pitted two opposites and almost got more attention for some of the antics rather than what was ultimately at stake. It was Templeton at his shoot-from-the-hip best. Part of it was courtroom performance, part of it was quick study, and another part was looking for that Achilles heel, which he was able to find in the strait-laced, buttoned-down Warner.

The two mixed like Pampa oil and Amarillo water.

It started in voir dire where the two sides went through the jury panel to select the 12 jurors. Lee Waters was a young judge for the 223rd District Court. He presided over the case.

"He turned out to be a terrific judge," Hayes said, "but as all new judges do, he let Warner go on and on in voir dire."

Warner was a member of the American Trial Lawyers Association, and must have pulled out every page on voir dire strategies. Not only was he expressly by the book, but he started at 10 a.m. and didn't finish until 4:20 p.m.

What little time remained belonged to Templeton, who acted like someone woke him up. He told the panel that this was usually the position he was in during a voir dire – 20 minutes or so, but he wanted to tell them a story. It was vintage Templeton because jury selection in a trial like this was crucial.

He said there were a few things Mr. Warner didn't tell them, but he would – that the plaintiff had plead guilty to solicitation of murder of a previous husband 18 months prior to the fire, that one month before the fire she took out a $1 million life insurance policy on her husband, John, and that in the 10 months they had lived in Pampa, she spent six of them in the psychiatric Pavilion in Amarillo.

Then he began to slyly – or maybe not so slyly – play some mind games with the panel and plant a few seeds.

"Bob pointed to one guy who wasn't in the first 24, which meant he wasn't going to be on the jury," Hayes said, "and said, 'Mr. Cowboy' back there, you don't need to worry about being on this jury because Mr. Warner doesn't want anyone like you. You already told him you believe people are responsible for themselves and should take reasonable measures to protect themselves. You don't have to worry about being on this jury.

"That was a significant statement. I'm thinking, 'Damn, we're going to get a mistrial out of this.' But no objection, and the judge didn't say anything."

Both sides tried gamesmanship from a "don't touch me" episode between lawyers to an ill-fated motion for a mistrial based on what was believed a bogus Eagle Scout award.

Templeton, if he could, looked for what he called an Achilles heel in the opposing side. It was a weakness, maybe a character flaw, and if he found one, he would exploit it.

In a previous trial, he represented the family of a woman who died of cancer. The family alleged she died because a physician misread a crucial X-ray. He did not get a second opinion or a specialist to read it too. Templeton believed the doctor didn't because of his ego. No one was smarter than he.

During the trial, Templeton brought an old telephone to the courthouse. He kept it at the table for several days. When it was Templeton's turn to cross exam the doctor, he grabbed the telephone.

"My point was the doctor did not or could not properly read the X-ray," Templeton said. "He tried to be the expert. When I had had him on the stand, I said, 'Doctor, all you needed to do was pick up a phone. Just pick up the phone and ask an expert to read the X-ray and you never did that. Why?'

"He didn't have a good answer. And the jury found him negligent."

With the Pampa trial, it was nothing nearly as dramatic. In fact, it was kind of silly, but the jury remembered it. It was Templeton playing games a bit, trying to find that Achilles heel of opposing counsel, Warner. Templeton thought he could take advantage of the emotional Warner's sensitivity.

The courtroom in Pampa was set up differently than most. There was a bench, and a long table for the opposing attorneys. The jury box was to the left of the table. One side would be closer to the jury. It was thought to be an advantageous position. The plaintiff attorney, in this case, Warner, customarily took the left side closest to the jury.

"We got there first and took the spot near the jury box," Hayes said. "Warner came in and threw a fit. And Bob made a deal with him. While he's putting on his case, he can sit there and we'll move to that spot when we put on our case. We'll just trade."

One morning early in the trial, Warner was putting on his case and so Templeton was on the far right side away from the jury. He got up and began making his way to the jury to make a point. He purposely made his way behind everyone seated at the table rather than in the front. All had their back to him, including Warner. When Templeton passed by Warner, he laid his hand heavily on his shoulder.

"There's a rail right behind the chairs, and not a lot of room to get by," Hayes said. "Bob was kind of holding his balance."

No, it wasn't really that way, Templeton said. He did it all on purpose to see if he could get a rise out of Warner. He did.

"Don't touch me!" Warner said. "Judge, make him quit! Make him quit!"

All heads turned to the outburst. It was Templeton's hope that Warner would look excitable and somewhat nervous, and the defendant's attorney in control. Subconsciously, maybe the 12 would identify with the Templeton.

"The jury, oh my God, they took umbrage in the way he acted,"

Templeton said. "The next morning we were just getting to the courthouse. We were all outside, and no one had really said anything yet. This one juror, just an old country boy, looked at us and says, 'Don't touch me! Don't touch me!'"

Indeed, the Gray County courthouse had its share of characters in the trial. Bobby Baker, the court reporter, would be at the top of any list. No attorney who tried a case in Pampa wasn't aware of Baker. He was left-handed, and one of the few court reporters who still took testimony by shorthand. He didn't mind telling a lawyer, "OK, I didn't get this," or "speak up."

"Oh, he was one helluva court reporter," Templeton said.

He was a court reporter who didn't mind taking control. At one point in the trial, a Friday, Warner asked Baker for a transcription of some earlier testimony that was going to take a lot of work to produce over the weekend. Baker got upset about the request, but did it anyway.

"The next week, we were all sitting in the courtroom and the judge was still in chambers," Hayes said. "The jury is seated in the box. Baker has his back turned to the jury and he starts talking loudly how weak the plaintiff's case was. The jury is listening. They can't help it. That's the way Baker got even with Warner for making him work over the weekend, which was not unusual for him. He was a character."

But ultimately, the verdict was not going to be determined by a lawyer touching another on the shoulder, or a court reporter sounding off about the case. It would have to turn on testimony and evidence.

It turned in an unexpected way with the plaintiff's expert witness, a retired former fire marshal from St. Louis. His conclusion was the fire started over the furnace from the boxes. Warner skillfully led the witness through much of that morning, building a case for the plaintiff question by question.

"He was excellent and compelling," Hayes said of the witness. "He was the last to testify that morning. He was a likable guy."

The courtroom recessed for lunch and it was not a care-free meal. No doubt damage was done by the morning testimony. Templeton would have his turn that afternoon on cross examination, but he had an uphill fight.

"I asked Bob what he was going to do with this guy," Hayes said. "He said, 'I don't know, but I'll figure it out as I go.'"

Shortly after, Templeton offered the plaintiff $600,000 to settle. It was refused. Onward to the cross examination then. Being able to think on your feet, to adapt to change, to be a quick study – all the things that Templeton could often do – had to be summoned as he was about to question the witness.

"You have to understand who the witness is," he said. "I had a feeling he was an honest expert, and the best ones are honest. So when you're dealing with an honest person and if you see a little opening, you have to take it."

The fire marshal's hypothesis had always been that the ash on top of the furnace grate indicated the boxes had burned at that point and was the fire's ignition. Templeton began by tossing a few softball questions, similar to those asked by Warner in the morning's examination. Then they gradually got more pointed.

"What's the first thing these firemen did when they entered the house to knock the top off the fire?" Templeton asked.

"They would have turned on high-pressure hoses at the fire," he said.

"And what would have happened then?"

Before the fire marshal answered, Templeton threw out a likely answer: "Would it have thrown the ash at the bottom of the furnace up in the air? Couldn't that be the answer on why the ash was on top of the grate?"

Hayes said it was if the light bulb was going off in the witness' head.

"I never thought about that," he said, "but it's a plausible explanation."

Score a major hit for the defense.

They moved on to the irregularity of burns on the rug, going into detail about the ramping effect and signs of flammable liquid.

"Sir, what was more likely to have caused those irregular burns? Templeton asked. "He said, 'flammable liquid.' He really hadn't looked at those rugs in that portion of the room. He had not studied that. He just told the truth, and the greater weight of evidence was flammable liquid. He ended up what I thought was a favorable witness to us."

"I don't know how pretty that cross exam was," Hayes said, "but it was as an effective cross as I've ever seen – ever. He was such a credible witness, but, gosh, when Bob turned him, he was his witness."

The jury deliberated only two hours and returned a verdict of no liability against M&L Storage. But that wasn't the end of things, not in this odd trial that always seemed to have something simmering on the back burner.

In closing arguments, Warner at one point tried to appeal to the jury that he was one of them, that he was a Boy Scout and an Eagle Scout growing up.

"And an Eagle Scout doesn't lie, that kind of thing," Templeton said.

Templeton interrupted: "Judge, I got to object to this. I was an Eagle Scout, but I'm not parading that in front of the jury.' It was a backhanded way of telling the jury I had been an Eagle Scout too."

No one thought much about that until after the verdict. Warner filed a motion for a new trial. On what grounds? That Templeton had told a blatant lie. Warner had checked with the Amarillo office of the Boy Scouts of America and there was no record of a Robert Lincoln Templeton ever receiving an Eagle Scout award.

"We didn't think it was sufficient ground even if it were true," Hayes said. "It was pretty cheesy."

In the hearing, Warner testified about the grounds for the new trial, that Templeton had lied to the jury on receiving the Boy Scouts' highest honor.

Templeton was not there, so Hayes took the honors of cross examination. He did so while holding what looked like an 8 ½ by 11-inch white paper in his hand.

"How did you come to the conclusion that Mr. Templeton was not an Eagle Scout?" Hayes asked.

Bob Templeton and Don Storseth

Bob Templeton's Eagle Scout certificate

"I looked up his bio and it said he was born in Amarillo, and that he's practiced in Amarillo all his career," Warner said.

"Does that mean he lived there all his life, or was that something you assumed?"

Before Warner could fully state that's what he assumed, Hayes handed him what was a certificate.

"I said, 'Do you know what that is?'" Hayes said. "He just stared at it. He couldn't talk. I said, 'You got one just like it, don't you?'"

It was an Eagle Scout certificate, one that even today hangs in Templeton's office. It says: Robert Templeton, Dec. 12, 1946, Troop 239, Frost, Texas."

Templeton moved from Amarillo when he was 10 years old in 1942. Two years later, the family arrived in his dad's home town of Frost where he spent the next six years before leaving for Baylor. It was during that time that Templeton got his Eagle Scout award at a fairly young age for such an accomplishment.

Oh.

"Jon was very emotional, and cried a lot during trials," Hayes said. "He started crying and saying, 'Judge, I didn't know. I didn't know he was an Eagle Scout.'"

Waters let out a sigh. There would be no new trial.

But there would be something else, something that was even further vindication for Templeton and Hayes and M&L Storage. To the surprise of most everyone, the jury handed down a supplemental verdict against Margaret Vernon. It was an unusual step.

"I'm paraphrasing here, but it was a message to the judge along the lines of the jury believed she intentionally caused the death of two people and believed the matter should be referred to a grand jury," Hayes said.

Eleven signed a document agreeing to the supplemental verdict. One did not. The matter went to a Gray County grand jury to determine if charges should be filed against Vernon. The state fire marshal came to Pampa again, this time speaking to the grand jury and relaying his original theory that it was the furnace and boxes that started the blaze.

Vernon was no-billed. That testimony of the state fire marshal was believed to have swung what was thought to be a close call. Templeton didn't believe Vernon started the fire. LaFavers and Hayes did.

"I really felt sorry for the woman," Templeton said. "She was a psychological mess. I was never convinced she set the fire. And the reason I was never convinced was her 16-year-old boy died in the fire."

But the bottom line was that Templeton averted liability of several million dollars for his friend Don Storseth and M&L Storage. In his career, Templeton never had a client that was as good a friend as Storseth.

"It was tremendously satisfying," he said. "Don was my great friend. We drove back and forth to Pampa every day of the trial. If he thought I did well that day, he gave me a cigar. Most of the time, I got a cigar."

For Hayes, who's remained a partner with Templeton into 2020, that was his first real up-close view of him during a trial.

"Bob, to me, is one of the two best trial lawyers in the area over the last 45 years," Hayes said. "He's unconventional, but not in a bad way. It's something to do with left-brain/right-brain. Bob is left-handed and very much like that.

"His mind works very quickly. It's a lot of instinct on his part. I've never seen anyone like him in the way he goes about things. He's a ham. He's entertaining, but not in a way that's unsavory or would make a judge mad. The courtroom is a stage for him. He gets to perform, but he's mindful of his client and what's in their best interest."

— Reflection —

"I've seen opponents not my equal, some my equal, and some more than my equal. If a fellow is more than my equal, you got to work harder. Every person — lawyer or not — always has an Achilles Heel. If I can, I'm going to find that and make use of it. Not in a mean way at all, but in a way that touches a nerve.

CHAPTER

13

Women Needing Help

Emma Jean Oliver and Felicity Lopez. Two women of meager means in the 1990s who needed help, two women – one black, one Hispanic -- with nowhere else to turn but the legal system.

One was a single mom of four who made a mistake and was looking at her life possibly ripped apart. The other was a minor who was sexually assaulted and impregnated at work with the corporation trying to sweep it under the rug.

In May 1993, a huge drug bust in Amarillo resulted in the arrests of 21 who were charged with selling and transporting narcotics. The bust cast a wide web. Attorneys were court-appointed for the defendants. In a rare instance, Templeton was appointed to represent Emma Jean Oliver, girlfriend of the alleged kingpin.

She was a drug mule, meaning she drove hidden drugs from one location to the next for money. Oliver, in her mid-30s, had four children. Working in a laundry in Wichita Falls had her under the poverty line. Transporting drugs was just too tempting. She was also arrested for possession of narcotics in her attic.

"She was really a nice person," Templeton said. "She had a 14-year-old boy who was terribly handicapped. Like everything Jimmy (LaFavers) and I did, we took it to heart. We wanted to help Emma Jean. I said, 'OK, Jimmy, let's see what we can do.'"

In the first meeting with Oliver, she said her boyfriend, the drug kingpin, would be helpful. He was in the Potter County jail. Templeton and LaFavers went to the jail to speak with him. LaFavers brought a tape recorder. Oliver's boyfriend absolved her of most criminal activity, and minimized her role in the enterprise. He said Oliver had no knowledge of the drugs in her attic, that she didn't put the drugs there.

The drug kingpin told his lawyer about the recording. That information eventually made its way to federal prosecutor Sharon Kimball.

"She went nuts," LaFavers said.

Probably for good reason. She wanted the recording

"In a federal criminal case, it's different than state law," Templeton said. "If the defense requests that and receives the government file, then the defense has to give the prosecution corresponding discovery of what you have. But we never requested information from the prosecution because there were 21 other defendants and we knew everything we needed to know from one or two of them. So we never requested the government's information in this case and the government couldn't get the recording of the kingpin. It was driving her up the wall."

The offense Oliver was charged with occurred in Wichita Falls. Templeton wanted to separate her from the others in an Amarillo trial. He filed a motion to transfer the trial in front of U.S. District court judge Mary Lou Robinson. The hearing was on the Friday before the trial was scheduled to start on Monday.

Robinson asked Kimball if moving the trial to Wichita Falls would negatively impact her. She said it would not. Robinson said she was inclined not to grant the motion transfer, but she was going to go ahead and grant the transfer since Kimball said it would not negatively affect the trial.

"Mary Lou kinda liked me," Templeton said, "though not a lot of people knew it. So Emma Jean getting transferred from this big trial where she surely would have been found guilty was huge."

But even before the venue hearing, Templeton was a thorn in the side of the prosecution. He had learned of a crucial government witness who was being sequestered.

"Another reason Kimball was upset and a little fearful was that our defense would mess up her big trial was our attempt to locate her key witness," Templeton said. "That was Stephanie Lozipone."

Lozipone was a woman from the Wichita Falls area. She was also charged in the drug bust, but she was granted immunity by the federal prosecutor for her testimony against more important figures.

She had worked as a dancer at a strip club in Wichita Falls, but was hidden in South Texas until trial. Templeton felt it important to reach her to show the favor this woman had with Kimball compared to his client who worked in a laundry and had young children.

Templeton and LaFavers drove to the strip club in Wichita Falls to get a lead on Lozipone's whereabouts. It was a tough job, but someone had to do it.

The two slipped into the club early one evening where Lozipone used to work. The dancers, when not on stage, must have sensed an easy mark. Templeton and LaFavers quickly sat down and were welcomed to the club. Templeton started working the women like they were on a jury.

"That's the first time I realized Bob Templeton had something going on," LaFavers said. "These young women must have thought he was cute. They were eating out of his hand."

This was going to be delicate to eventually get to the point with the dancers on their real reason for being there. Somehow it had to go from small-talk chit-chat to asking about Lozipone.

Templeton had a plan. One of the dancers left the table to dance on the stage. Before she left, Templeton gave her $20 and told her to come back after she finished. She nodded. The thought then was when she returned, Templeton would casually slip in a question about Stephanie, that he had met her at the club a while back and wondered where she was.

"So I'm starting to ease in to where I could find Stephanie, and Jimmy's sitting in his chair turned around backward, kind of aggressive-looking," Templeton said. "He says, 'See here, Miss,

Robert Templeton is a lawyer and he's representing Emma Jean Oliver on a big case. We want to find out how to get in touch with Stephanie Lozipone. I'm an investigator.'"

LaFavers got into his old homicide detective mode. No more tap dancing. It was time to get serious – except that it backfired.

"I made a critical mistake, no question about it," LaFavers said. "I told her who we were, that we were representing Emma Jean Oliver, and we needed to locate Stephanie Lozipone.

"My God, that woman went berserk."She jumps up and starts yelling out that these guys are looking for Stephanie, and one is an investigator and the other is a lawyer. This is more or less an unfriendly crowd. Bob jumps up and I realize what a boneheaded thing I had done."

The bartender made a fast walk from behind the bar to where the customers were. Templeton, always quick on his feet, assessed the situation in a nanosecond and suggested strongly they get out of there – like now.

At the time, Templeton, all 5-foot-8 of him, was in his early 60s. LaFavers was 20 years younger, and built like a high school football lineman. As a former cop, possible confrontation was not his first rodeo.

"I was chapped, and I was really mad at myself," LaFavers said. "I started to slowly walk to the front door when the bartender comes around. I point to him and say, 'No, you don't want to do that.' And he must have known I was serious and went behind the bar."

There was still the matter of the bouncer at the door which Templeton had skirted around with no problem.

"I was running to get out of the place," he said, "and here's Jimmy just taking his time."

"You don't ever want to run out of place like that," LaFavers said. "The bouncer started coming to me and I more or less told him the same thing in that you don't want to do that. He was kind of in this little booth. He looked at me and kind of backed away."

When he finally made his way out of the club, Templeton already had his Mercedes in the middle of the lot with the passenger door open and one foot on the brake.

"My God, Jimmy, what are you doing?" Templeton yelled. "Let's get out of here."

"Bob," LaFavers said, "running out of that place is the worst thing you can do."

"You do if you really need to get away."

Templeton's car squalled out of the parking lot. Bottom line: They never located Stephanie Lozipone.

Shortly after the two returned to Amarillo, a trial with more than 20 defendants began in Amarillo. It went like Templeton thought it would with all but two convicted. So that made getting Oliver's case transferred to her hometown of Wichita Falls even more important.

The case sat dormant for a period. The prosecutor there didn't have much enthusiasm for a trial. So Templeton worked out an agreement that Oliver would plead guilty to Misprision of a Felony. That occurs when a person knows a felony has been committed, but does not inform authorities. It's a seldom used charge since it could overwhelm a legal docket by merely failing to report a crime.

But in this instance, Misprision of a Felony could greatly reduce time in prison. The maximum sentence is a fine and three years in prison, though Templeton, in offering that for his client, knew Oliver would not get that harsh a sentence.

The hearing was held in February 1994 in the U.S. District Court for the Northern District of Texas in Fort Worth. The judge was David Belew, Jr. He was an Army captain during World War II. He was physically a huge judge, and as Templeton and Oliver would soon discover, a compassionate judge.

Templeton brought Oliver's 14-year-old son with them at the hearing where he asked for probation. Templeton told Belew that Oliver was the sole provider for her four children and was the daughter of a Baptist pastor.

Belew gave Oliver a probated sentence – but with unusual terms. They were terms that made national news when a reporter for the Fort Worth Star-Telegram happened to be in the courtroom.

Belew ordered Oliver and her family to attend Sunday church

services for a year. They could only miss if illness or a major problem prevented them from attending. A probation officer in Wichita Falls would make sure that Oliver lived up to her part of the bargain, Belew told Oliver.

"She's a good woman," Belew told the Star-Telegram. "I thought if the children got in Sunday School, and she into church, it would be beneficial for all of them."

Belew told the newspaper that he expected to receive some criticism, but he did not believe that he violated provisions of the First Amendment or the constitutional guarantees separating church and state.

"I think we've gone too far on this separation of church and state," he said. "This country was founded on religious freedom, and it's getting to where we have less and less of it."

As for Oliver, she was relieved to get the probation and had no issue with the returning to church during her probation.

"It was a blessing. And as for the judge, I think he's a wonderful, loving, kind man," she told the Star-Telegram.

At the end of the hearing, Templeton urged Oliver, a rather attractive woman, to go to the bench and thank Belew.

"He said, 'Oh, that's not good enough,'" Templeton said. "And he reached over and grabbed her and hugged her."

Belew then gave the single mom some unsolicited advice: "Don't go having any more kids without a husband."

Belew later said he told Oliver that because he was tired of unwed mothers having children and being on welfare.

"I'm very opposed to these children being born out of wedlock and nobody except the government being able to support them," he said. "That's what's wrong with this country right now. There's too much of this going on."

That didn't solve Oliver's difficult life, but the probation allowed her to keep her life and remain a mother present for her children. Compared to those in a similar bind at the Amarillo trial, Emma Jean Oliver certainly came out ahead.

"Jimmy and I, we did something that was outside the box. We did the best we could to help our client," Templeton said. "I'm not sure how many lawyers would have gone to those lengths in a court-appointed case."

A few months later, Templeton was in conversation with Robinson, who told him that Kimball, the prosecutor, didn't want to face him in court. That was likely why she didn't object to moving the trial to Wichita Falls.

Five years later came Felicity Lopez. She was younger than Emma Jean Oliver by at least 12 years. She had been wronged and needed help. Templeton, John Smithee and Brian Heinrich combined to help her with stakes much higher than that of Oliver.

Lopez was just 14 when she was a patient at the Quest long-term nursing facility at 9th Avenue and Coulter Street in 1997. Lopez had a difficult life. She never knew her father. Her mother was a drug addict. She was basically left to the streets and was taken in by several foster homes.

"She had no ability to maintain a relationship with anybody," Smithee said. "She was a smart lady, but had some problems which were understandable considering her background."

Lonnie Thrower, Jr., was a worker at Quest. He had a criminal background. He was also about 15 years older than Lopez.

"Quest should have never hired him and put him in that capacity," Heinrich said. "Texas has a statute that I wasn't aware of at the time, but it concerned sexual exploitation by health care workers. You typically see this more in the counseling area, but it applied here."

Thrower was charged with sexual assault of a child when Lopez became pregnant in 1997. He was alleged with sexually assaulting her on multiple occasions.

"He disputed the baby was his. We did a paternity test," Heinrich said. "Those don't ever come back 100 percent, but this was 99.99 percent that he was the father. So really there wasn't any question about that."

The Templeton firm represented Lopez in the lawsuit against Quest, citing negligence. That Lopez was a minor, Thrower had a criminal background and the paternity test came back positive didn't bode well for Quest's insurance company. But they didn't back down. A mediation to settle the case was scheduled – and it was a bit unusual.

Smithee said it's comical now, but not then when Lopez, about six months before the trial, became pregnant by another man. She was showing. She needed to be present too. What to do? Templeton gave Lopez a blanket and told her to keep it around her. Never mind it was the summer. If anyone asked, she had a cold.

"The jury would later find out she was pregnant, but it didn't bother them," Smithee said. "We didn't lie to them."

In the mediation, Kevin Oncken from Austin, an attorney for Quest, came off as abrasive and arrogant to Smithee. He offered Lopez a paltry sum of $5,000.

"He had the money in $100 bills and put it on the table and said if you will take these 50 $100 bills right now, we'll dismiss your case. It will be all over and you can buy your daughter new clothes and take her to Disneyland," Smithee said.

"She said she would take it before I had a chance to say anything. I grabbed her and took her outside and said, 'Felicity, you can't do that.' She said that I couldn't guarantee her I'd get her get $5,000. I told her I would pay her $5,000 out of my own pocket. This case is too good, too valuable, so she backed off."

The settlement failed. The trial was set in Judge Robinson's court. This was a different era, long before Harvey Weinstein, Bill Cosby and the Me Too generation. Typically, defense lawyers went after the victims in these cases.

"The big thing is, as bad as the evidence was, as bad as the facts were, the insurance company persisted in denying everything and attacking her," Heinrich said. "Their attitude was, 'You chose this activity, you voluntarily engaged in these activities.' That was their defense. They attacked her at trial. That was their whole strategy. It really inflamed the jury."

Thrower was already incarcerated at the Middleton Unit in Abilene. Smithee drove to Abilene to take Thrower's deposition. Thrower had an attorney who told him not to answer any questions.

"He read a statement after every question that he was advised by legal counsel not to answer. He answered every question that way. I was disappointed thinking we didn't get anything out of it," Smithee said.

Robinson let the jury see the video tape, but the video was not of good quality. So Robinson allowed Heinrich to ask the video questions and Templeton, playing the role of Thrower, answered them.

"I turned to the jury and said, 'Oh, no, I wouldn't do anything like that,'" Templeton said. "The defense objected to the way I was answering the question. But Mary Lou overruled. She was very much on our side in this case."

Robinson had been a federal judge since 1979. She was just coming off presiding over the highly publicized Oprah Winfrey trial in Amarillo in 1998. Templeton and Robinson went back to the 1950s when she was a judge for the Potter County Court and Templeton was an assistant Potter County attorney.

"One thing Bob knew about Judge Robinson is that she could determine the outcome of a case without saying a word, just her mannerisms," Smithee said. "The jury really respected her. You learned pretty fast if she were sympathetic to your case just by her demeanor, the way she treated the lawyers.

"That made a big difference how the jury looked at that. She was very fair, but she saw what was going on and she didn't like the idea of attacking Felicity. It didn't play to their benefit."

The trial took a dramatic turn when Lopez took the stand. Templeton carefully guided her through some difficult questions during cross examination. The courtroom was still when she described one of the occasions when Thrower forced himself on her.

"One of those occasions, there was a little gym at Quest," Templeton said. "There was a little bathroom next to the gym, and that's where he took her. I asked Felicity about that. She started to cry. I asked her, 'Did he push you down? Did he push you on your knees?' She really started to cry then. The jury, gosh, everyone was crying. It was pure pathos. Highly emotional.

Then I passed the witness."

"Bob did a masterful job," Smithee said. "The jury empathized with her. They saw her as a tragic figure in this case. He painted that picture as well as anybody could have."

Off that emotional testimony came cross examination. No one expected a tender repeat of what Templeton did, but no one expected what John Wilson did either. Wilson, from Austin, represented Thrower. Wilson asked her if she had an orgasm during the assault. Templeton rose to object, but didn't have to.

"Mr. Wilson," Robinson said, "that is an inappropriate question. Move on."

Wilson did for a few questions, but then, to the shock of everyone except Wilson, came back to the first one. Again, he wanted to know if Lopez had an orgasm, an indication that she was a willing participant, that she enjoyed it.

"Judge Robinson lost it," Heinrich said. "She said there will be no more questions. Ms. Lopez you can sit down, and Mr. Wilson will not be allowed to ask any more questions. It was very offensive to everybody."

Just about every moment in the trial underscored the question of why the defense did not offer a better settlement. The case just seemed overwhelmingly in favor of the plaintiff. The defense hoped to score points with the paternity suit by raising the question her pregnancy could have been from someone other than Thrower.

A DNA expert from North Carolina testified on the results of the positive paternity test and the statistical analysis from it.

"He made the statement that based on the DNA there were only five males in the world who could be the fathers," Smithee said. "So their lawyer said, 'So you're telling me the father of this child could be five other people?' This is not Amarillo, but in the world.

"The odds of those other five having access to Felicity Lopez at that precise time, you'd have to say were ridiculously small. I looked at the jury and they were laughing. It was ludicrous to suggest that."

In closing argument, Heinrich compared Quest and its insurance company to the behavior of his young son.

"I ask my 4-year-old son something and he puts his finger in his ear and says, 'I can't hear you. I can't hear you,'" Heinrich told the jury. "That's what these companies did in this case. That had ample warning this guy shouldn't be there, and yet we see no evil, hear no evil.

"Even now, after all this time, after all these facts have come to light, what have they done in this trial? They continue to ignore what really happened, and continue to act like they haven't heard anything or seen anything."

The jury, it seemed, was out to send a message, a message not only on the negligence of Quest, but to the tactics of the defense.

"I remember walking down the steps of the courthouse," Heinrich said, "and one of the jurors, a woman probably in her late 50s, was in an old van in the front. I made eye contact with her. She just had this resolute look on her face and nodded her head up and down. That's how motivated this jury was."

Templeton left on a scheduled cruise with Martha before closing arguments. But he was confident in Smithee and Heinrich. On the cruise, he got word the jury ruled in favor of Lopez. The amount awarded in damages was $3 million.

The settlement was for $1.8 million. Templeton acted as a trustee for Lopez, setting aside a portion of the money that could not be accessed until she was older.

"She was kind of helpless with money, so we saved some for her to get to later," Templeton said. "Years later, she wrote me a note thanking me for helping her save that money. She moved to the Pittsburgh area, settled down with a guy and had three or four kids."

The case would have been won likely with any judge, but with Robinson, as Templeton said, "it was a case where the judge fit the case."

"I remember Mary Lou's voice where she shut John Wilson up," he said. "Judges don't do that often, shut up someone like that and say that's it. I never saw Mary Lou do that before or since. She was someone though who advanced the cause of women."

CHAPTER

14

The Best Case He Never Tried

It had drugs, bribes, and prostitutes. It was as one oilfield worker described, "24 hours of paradise." It was legal wrangling and maneuvering that was more than a decade from start to finish.

It may have been Robert Templeton at the top of his game. He was at his creative legal best, pulling one legal rabbit out of his hat after another. In some ways, it was desperate times that called for desperate measures to help avoid as much as $1 billion in liability.

"The things that Bob was able to do," said Jack O'Neill, a Houston attorney, "were really brilliant."

And it all started with a natural gas oil well in the eastern Texas Panhandle. The early 1980s were the final few years of the oil and gas boom. Drilling was at a fast and furious pace in the eastern Panhandle and western Oklahoma.

The Apache Key 1-11 natural gas well in Wheeler County was completed in July 1981 at 16,000 feet. The well was a 50-50 lease with non-operating partner El Paso Natural Gas. The operating partner was Apache Corporation. Following the drilling, it was then shut in for 90 days to make the pipeline connection.

All believed this was a good deep discovery well that would produce millions and millions of cubic feet of natural gas. But on Oct. 4, 1981, before the pipeline reached the well, all hell broke loose.

While waiting the pipeline connection, the well blew out. Did it ever. It shot the surface pipes and valves 80 to 100 feet into the Wheeler County air. Gas spewed unabated for several months after the blowout. Templeton later estimated 30 million cubic feet of gas were lost every day, amounting to a daily loss of a staggering $240,000 initially. The well was finally killed in 1983.

Over the next 11 years, numerous legal cases would involve up to 130 parties – royalty owners, leaseholders, and vendors of supplies to the Key 1-11 gas well. Indeed, the litigation was about as explosive as the well. It generated millions in legal and expert fees, made some discovery law, and touched on widespread corruption in the oil fields in the early 1980s. Hollywood even toyed with some of this as a movie.

"It was the biggest lawsuit to ever hit the Panhandle," Templeton said.

The first of the lawsuits arrived in less than two months after the blowout. Adjacent royalty owners and lessees next to the Key 1-11 well believed the blowout was depleting their gas reserves. They brought suit against Apache, the Houston-based operating partner, for millions.

Apache in turn brought suit against the tubing and casing head manufacturers. Discovery began that lasted almost two years. Meanwhile, Apache dug down about 2,000 feet to determine where the tubing and casing had broken off. A long line of bulldozers were side by side to dig out a massive hole around the wellbore in an attempt to reach the end of the crack in the casing.

Around that same time, Apache got permission from the Texas Railroad Commission to place special funnel-like equipment over where the well explosion had occurred, recapturing the gas, and, Templeton said, receiving enormous sums of money in the recapture.

From the fall of 1981 until the spring of 1983, Apache settled with adjacent land owners and royalty owners for about $18 million. In turn, Apache received settlements from tubing and casing manufacturers for an undisclosed sum.

While that may have seemed like the end of lawsuits, it was really just beginning. In Apache's inspection of the gas well, investigators looked at the casing relief valve and believed it was defective and a reason for the explosion.

Investigators said there was no insulation between the aluminum tubing and brass fitting. With no insulation, electrolysis will set in to the joint of the aluminum and brass, forming a powder and sealing the tubing and causing the pressure relief valve to fail. That was the conclusion of the Apache investigators, that the relief valve failed and that caused the blowout.

Axelson, Inc., was the manufacturer of the pressure relief valve. Just prior to the end of the statute of limitations in 1983, Apache sued Axelson as a third-party defendant. It wasn't for a little bit either, but the eye-opening sum of $500 million.

Enter Bob Templeton.

"Almost all the local lawyers in town were either representing the royalty owners, like Tom Morris, or they were local counsel for the casing and tubing manufacturers," Templeton said.

How Templeton came to represent Axelson took some connecting of the dots. Axelson, a small manufacturer, was acquired by U.S. Industries. U.S. Industries was then acquired by a British conglomerate, Hanson, whose American headquarters were in New Jersey.

Bill Attebury, Templeton's friend since childhood, was co-owner of a flat storage company, Houtex. Attebury sold Houtex to U.S. Industries.

"So when Axelson got sued, Bill recommended that U.S. Industries hire Robert Templeton," he said. "Bill got me the job. He believed in me."

Apache certainly had a head start. They had all their experts and evidence lined up. Templeton would be playing catch up, but at least they would have the resources. When Hanson acquired U.S. Industries, it agreed to indemnify and defend U.S. Industries of any lawsuits or claims against them. Hanson had insurance with AIG and Kemper.

Templeton somehow got the two insurance companies to pay for the entire defense costs without so much as a peep. Maybe it was because the case was so complicated, but over the next eight years, Templeton and his firm billed at $150 an hour in legal and expert fees and rang up $6 million in legal fees.

"Nobody questioned any expenses or fees because they couldn't understand the case," Templeton said. "Kemper would not do anything but pay the bills. I'd go to New York periodically to talk with AIG. They had a young woman up there who knew as much about the oil and gas industry as a hog does heaven.

"I then started reporting also to the counsel for Hanson. They were good lawyers, Ivy League graduates. But as far as the actual insurance companies were concerned, they never gave me any trouble because they couldn't understand the litigation."

Good news: Unlike many cases in the past, there was no contingency fee. The firm was getting paid, and paid well. Bad news: They still faced a severe uphill climb.

"It was the kind of potential liability that an attorney who regularly defends companies would have been sweating blood over," Templeton said. "I was probably too ignorant to sweat blood. We had no business with this size of lawsuit. But when we got into it, we weren't going to let them whip us."

It didn't start that way, however. Lead counsel for Apache was Harlow Sprouse with the Underwood firm. Mark Packard was assisting him. The case was pending in Judge Granger McIlhenny's 31st District Court in Wheeler County where the gas well had blown out. One of the first orders of business for Templeton was to request discovery information from Apache.

"Harlow, being Harlow, wasn't about to give Robert Templeton any information until compelled to do so," Templeton said.

Templeton would file a motion for discovery. The sides would have a hearing, and McIlhenny would invariably rule in favor of Apache. It didn't hurt Sprouse that he hired a Pampa attorney that McIlhenny trusted and respected.

"We'd have these hearings and Harlow would object to this and that," Templeton said, "and Granger would rule for him – 'Yeah, you didn't do this right or that right.' And this Pampa fella would get up and talk like a sage — 'Well, you've heard this and that, Your Honor, but here's what I recommend you do.' And, of course, Granger did exactly that."

In a way, this case of Apache v. Axelson seemed to Templeton like a basketball team going on the road and facing not only a talented team, but one with referees that wouldn't give the visitors a fair shake.

"If Mayberry had a judge, he would have been Granger McIlhenny," Packard said. "He was just a country judge, as nice as he could be, all warm and sunshine. When he finally did rule on these discovery motions, Bob would file a motion to rehear them all, and Granger would say, 'OK, we'll hear them all. Let's come back in two weeks or next June.'

"It got to be a boring discovery fight that should have been resolved pretty quickly. But that was Bob's strategy to just delay, delay and delay until something good would happen."

Something had to happen to turn the case. Something finally did. Templeton had nothing to do with one of them. With the help of a young associate, everything to do with the other.

Templeton had the financial backing of AIG and Kemper. They didn't question any expenditure. The other side wasn't as fortunate. Sprouse had used up all of Apache's insurance carrier's money that has been set aside for the defense. Any money now for Apache's attorneys would have to come from Apache's own pocket.

Apache hired new counsel, who quickly clashed with Sprouse. Apache didn't like spending money and wanted this resolved as soon as possible. Sprouse knew it wasn't going to happen quickly. He sent a letter to Apache with a contingency fee contract. Apache responded by firing him.

"He was very Napoleonic. That's just the way Harlow was," Templeton said. "But firing him was one of the best things that happened to me because Harlow understood the case and knew how to win.

"Harlow Sprouse, as I've said many times, in my opinion, had a wonderful mind. As far as grasping complicated matters in oil and gas, he understood the engineering, he understood all of that. He was a great planner and organizer of a lawsuit. They fired a guy who may very well have won that lawsuit."

Packard, who was assisting Sprouse, thought the case was in good hands – until Apache ended its legal relationship with Sprouse.

"Harlow was one of the smartest men I ever met. Just brilliant," Packard said. "He had this deep voice that sounded like God talking. Harlow had been on that case for such a long time, and knew so much about it. I guess I never thought he'd get fired."

There remained in the lawsuit a few adjacent royalty owners and working interest owners. One was Tom Scott. Previously, Apache attempted to settle with Scott and family for $100,000. Templeton talked him out of it by meeting Apache's $100,000 and promising to pay Scotts' attorney fees if he would stay in the case. He would repay the $100,000 from any funds recovered from Apache.

"I got permission from Kemper and AIG to pay Scott's and Leo Moore's (a royalty owner) attorney fees," Templeton said. "The effect of this was to leave Apache as a defendant.

"Otherwise, Apache would have settled with those small owners and it would have Apache as plaintiff and Axelson targeted as the only defendant. The psychology of having Apache as a defendant changed the whole case for trial."

Apache's settlement offer to the Scotts was crucial because of a proviso that the Scotts would assign their experts to Apache, who could then designate them as "consulting only" experts whose knowledge would not be discoverable by Templeton or anyone else.

"Harlow had a master plan, part of which was to maintain control of all experts," Templeton said. "His experts had been 'consulting experts,' and I could not get discovery from them unless designated as a witness.

"But Harlow didn't stop there. When Apache settled with the others, he put a requirement in the settlement agreement that all these experts were assigned to Harlow."

The settlement requirement would be a grave threat to Axelson and Templeton. He believed that a number of experts had targeted the tubing and casing as the cause of the blowout. So to show that, Templeton needed to get the reports.

"Harlow's master plan was to change course. Instead of claiming the tubing and casing caused the blowout, he blamed Axelson and the casing relief valve," Templeton said. "But if I could get the experts' opinions, I could stuff it down Apache's throats."

While the undesignated experts' opinions are privileged and need not be disclosed, Templeton believed these experts had factual knowledge, which would not be privileged. He called them "two-hat experts." If he could obtain their factual knowledge, it would expose their opinion. At least that's what Templeton believed and pursued.

"But Granger refused to let me get their factual knowledge. You try to stay on the good side of a judge as much as you can, but I was at a tremendous disadvantage," Templeton said. "This thing went on for years in discovery.

"I'd go over there in the winter to Wheeler in the snow and walk back with my tail between my legs, trying to figure out what I could do. What I was trying to do was delay the case. Delay it as much as I could and try to figure out a way to win the case."

After Sprouse was fired, Apache was represented by Jess Hall and Scott Hogarty of Liddell and Sapp in Houston. They came on for a $1 million fee. They were no Harlow Sprouse. They never asked for any of Axelson's discovery, and as Templeton knew at the time, it was a good thing they didn't.

But it didn't really matter who represented Apache as McIlhenny ruled in their favor at every turn, especially when it came to Axelson seeking discovery. It would be comical if not so serious.

"They had sort of set up this routine where there was an Apache Day every month in the Wheeler County Courthouse," said Joe Lovell, a first-year associate in the Templeton and Garner firm in 1988. "They would hear our many discovery motions. It was just an endless battle on each side of not giving the other side discovery."

Lovell was a banker in Wichita Falls in 1981 when the well blew out before moving to First National Bank in 1982. He had a career change, attending Texas Tech Law School in 1984, graduating in 1987. He was clerking for the Underwood firm in 1986 as a summer intern when Sprouse took him to a deposition of a witness in the Key Well blowout. Opposing attorney was Templeton.

Now, a little more than a year later, Templeton hired Lovell, and put him on the Axelson case. It was Axelson all day every day. There was enough work on both sides, Lovell said, for 100 lawyers.

Packard was two years ahead of Lovell in law school at Tech. They had become friends, and Lovell knew how consumed Packard had been on the case before Sprouse was fired, much like Lovell was now.

"It had grown so burdensome and weary to him," Lovell said. "After Harlow was fired, at the first monthly hearing in Wheeler, during the lunch break, we were wandering around the courthouse square and there was a drugstore. It had souvenirs and postcards, including one from Wheeler and the Wheeler County courthouse.

"So I bought the postcard, wrote on it, 'Having a wonderful time. Wish you were here,' and mailed it to Mark. He kept that for years. He said he really enjoyed that because he was glad he was not there having a wonderful time."

Before the roadblock with the "two-hat experts," Templeton had gleaned some startling and useful information in discovery with Apache drillers. Jim LaFavers, investigator for the Templeton firm, had earlier been asking questions about employees and the working conditions at the Key Well. The more questions he asked, the more uneasy he felt.

"Such a lot of corruption," LaFavers said. "Prostitutes at the well from Oklahoma City, dope at the well, kickbacks. There was such a shortage of drillers at that time that they would get absolutely anything to drill on a well. One of the drillers testified if you want a house, you got a house. If you wanted a boat, you got a boat. Whatever these drillers wanted, they got."

Templeton sent LaFavers to Oklahoma City to see if he could locate any women who were prostitutes at the well. Templeton could only imagine how that testimony would play to a jury and how it might affect Apache's negligence.

More than 50 federal indictments were about to be issued in Oklahoma on corruption in connections with the Key Well blowout. Nothing was official yet as LaFavers, while in Oklahoma City, made a side trip to the Murrah federal building to talk with a federal prosecutor. Timothy McVeigh's fertilizer bomb would kill 168 people and destroy the Murrah building in 1995.

LaFavers spent an interesting late afternoon and evening with the young prosecutor in trying to get some information about impending indictments. He arrived at 3 p.m., but didn't see him until closer to 5 p.m.

"I got to befriending him, and before I knew it, he asked me if I liked basketball. I said, 'Yeah,'" LaFavers said. "Then he asked if I drank beer? So we went to watch his kids play basketball and then went to Pizza Hut for pizza and beer. Then he asked if I wanted to see his new house under construction – he was getting a divorce – and I just wanted to continue to be his buddy."

The prosecutor told LaFavers they weren't at the indictment stage yet, but they were close. Why not go by his office again, he suggested, and LaFavers could look at what he had and bring it back in the morning. Why not indeed.

"So I call Bob in the middle of the night and tell him I got this box full of documents that the U.S. attorney gave me. What should I do with them?" he said. "Bob said, 'Oh my God, copy them, copy them.'"

LaFavers went downstairs at the Best Western he was staying and asked the clerk if he could borrow his copy machine for a few minutes. It was much more than a few minutes, but LaFavers was able to copy almost the entire federal investigation.

"I took them back the next morning, and you could kind of tell he was already in trouble for just talking to me," LaFavers said. "He told me that he wasn't supposed to have done that, and see you later. You could tell he was brand new."

It proved to be treasure trove of information that LaFavers brought back to Amarillo. It showed Templeton and other attorneys the astonishing level of bribery that occurred at Key Well.

It fortified Axelson's contention that the kickbacks at the Key Well contributed to the blowout by allowing shoddy drilling practices and lackadaisical monitoring of the well by preoccupied and intoxicated workers. It's how they found out about Wayne Eller, a driller on the well. Apache had fired him prior to starting their own investigation.

"Here you are, after the blowout, and you fire the absolute key witness to all that stuff. That's one of the dumbest mistakes you can possibly make," LaFavers said. "There goes your loyalty."

In his deposition, Templeton asked Eller how good a driller he was. Would he ever dog leg a hole or would it be straight?

"You wouldn't drill anything but a straight hole?" Templeton asked.

"No, a straight hole is the only thing I'd drill intentionally," Eller said.

"You drilled a straight hole on the Key 1 well, didn't you?"

"I'd like to think I did, but the only problem was I had about $5,000 worth of cocaine in my head."

After that, Eller went through a long list of what was provided to oilfield workers – most of it drugs and sex.

"I said, 'Wayne, how was it?'" Templeton said. "He said, 'It was paradise. After it was all over, it was hell.' I asked him how he was now. 'I'm struggling and it's still hell,' he said. I sat there and felt sorry for the man."

Jack O'Neill, a Houston attorney, was brought in by Templeton to represent the royalty owners. They teamed together on a few depositions, including another oilfield worker, Donnie Snapp.

Apache hired Amarillo attorney Don Reavis as separate counsel for Snapp. During the video interview, Snapp can be clearly seen while Reavis' arm next to him is seen.

"I still think how dumb this was, but Bob asked a question about something he thinks is going on at the well, and you see this arm come out and give a piece of paper to the witness, and he said, 'I, Donnie Snapp, hereby invoke my rights under the fifth amendment against incrimination,'" O'Neill said.

"It didn't take Bob and I very long to figure out that no matter

Joe Lovell

Jack O'Neill

what we asked this guy, he was going to take the fifth and it was going to be admissible. Bob and I had a field day putting words into his mouth. You could have said anything to him – 'Isn't it true that there were 15 hookers on the job site and you had a big party going on while installing a 10 5/8-inch intermediate casing in the well?' 'I, Donnie Snapp, hereby invoke my rights under...'"

The net effect of that at trial in a civil case was telling. While taking the fifth amendment can not be used against a criminal defendant, it is admissible in a civil case. And Eller and Snapp weren't the only ones under the glare of Templeton and O'Neill.

"One guy was even in a work trailer with a hooker one night," O'Neill said, "when he found out his wife was on the way out there and was coming down the road. He ran out the trailer with his pants down. It was one witness after another like that."

But as juicy as all that would be to Templeton, he still needed discovery of Apache's experts. He assigned Lovell and John Smithee, a lawyer in the firm and a newly elected Texas state representative from District 86, to play a pivotal role in the case.

Templeton believed he had no choice. He finally decided to

petition for a Writ of Mandamus against McIlhenny. Mandamus is when an appellate court can order a trial court, in this case, McIlhenny, to allow discovery of facts if it is a clear abuse of discretion.

"We had just banged our head against a wall for so long that we wanted to see if the appellate courts would force Granger McIlhenny to give us discovery," Lovell said.

That crucial responsibility fell on Smithee and Lovell, who was barely a year out of law school. They did a bulk of the briefing. Since they were the petitioners for the Mandamus, they also had the burden of proof.

In May 1988, Smithee and Lovell argued the Mandamus before the Seventh Court of Appeals in Amarillo [755 SW2d, 170]. A month later, the court ruled photos were discoverable, but kickback investigation information was not nor were any expert witness testimony.

From there, the Mandamus went to the Texas Supreme Court in Austin. Smithee started the argument and Lovell handled the rebuttal.

"Bob was kind enough and confident enough in me to allow me to argue the rebuttal," Lovell said. "Yes, I was tense and scared, but no more than we always were. The thought of it was more intimidating than actually doing it. Once you get into court, once you're able to stand up, all of that goes away. It was exhilarating is what it was. It was an incredible and rare opportunity for a young lawyer."

The argument and rebuttal couldn't have gone better for the two with the Texas Supreme Court upholding the Mandamus against McIlhenny. It had key ramifications affecting discovery and how discovery was conducted in Texas.

"It stated what you can hide and what you couldn't hide," Lovell said. "The biggest effect was how you could use experts."

In Axelson vs. McIlhenny [798 SW2d 550] in October 1990, not only did the Texas Supreme Court say McIlhenny should have done an in-camera examination of the kickback documents before denying Axelson's attempt to discover them, but it ruled Apache's employees who were designated as "consulting only" experts weren't exempt from discovery.

The Texas Supreme Court's conclusion: "We hold the trial judge abused his discretion by refusing discovery of the kickback investigation without conducting an in-camera inspection; denying the request to depose the six experts redesignated as consulting-only experts; denying discovery of a witness who does not qualify as a consulting-only expert, and denying discovery of facts known by consulting experts.

"We are confident Judge McIlhenny will vacate his orders denying this discovery and will enter orders consistent with this opinion. Should he fail to do so, the clerk of the supreme court is directed to issue the writ of mandamus."

It ended the two-hat witness where not only expert opinion, but factual information, was privileged and unavailable to the defense or the plaintiffs.

Until then, what Sprouse had initially done for Apache had been effective. When Apache settled with all but Axelson, the settlement gave Apache the right to all the experts hired by the settling plaintiffs. Part of that settlement, Lovell said, was, in effect, buying the plaintiff's experts and designate them as "consulting only" experts.

"By re-designating them as 'consulting only,' they then hid what the experts had done and the conclusion the experts had reached to determine the cause of the well blowout," Lovell said. "The Texas Supreme Court said you just can't go out and buy experts and make them go away.

"They were hiding that so the remaining unsettled plaintiffs could not use it. More importantly, Apache was trying to recover back everything. So Apache was trying to get $500 million against Axelson, but hiding the work of the original experts in the case."

"And the original experts of Apache in the case," Templeton said, "believed the casing and tubing had failed, not the casing relief valve. They settled and got money out of them. But they didn't want us to find out that information."

So now the dam of discovery had been blown apart. Apache would have to release photos and documentary information helpful to Axelson. The ruling upset McIlhenny.

"The (Texas) Supreme Court had slapped Granger, and he took things personally," Templeton said. "He disqualified himself after that. But I don't think Granger would have ever tried it. He would have gone out of office before trying it."

William Sheehan, who had retired in 1989 as 31st District Court Judge in Dumas, was named visiting judge in the case. Sheehan, with his rulings, seemed to even out his decisions.

Three times in 1992 he would sanction Apache – for failing to comply with a court order in a timely manner of producing its own kickback investigation, for failing to provide all kickback documents, and for dismissal of Apache's deceptive trade practice claim against Axelson.

The trial, scheduled finally in the summer of 1992, was coming into view. The trial was originally set for Wheeler County. By then, McIlhenny had not only recused himself from the case, but had retired.

The big question in the case was what caused the blowout?" Templeton said. "Did the tubing fail at about 9,000 psi, or did the casing fail at about 7,000 psi? Or did the casing relief valve fail to work and allow the pressure to exceed the ability of the casing and tubing?"

Templeton hired an expert and had Paul McGuffey work with him, but they never came up with a proper answer. Templeton then traveled to Rice University in Houston.

"I hired a physics professor, and in one afternoon, he worked the physics problem on the energy to blow 81 feet of casing into the air and the pressure required. His opinion was that either the tubing or the casing failed to meet the stated pressure capacity. This in part allowed Jack O'Neill to blame the tubing and casing as well as sloppy drilling.

As the trial loomed, there was some nastiness in the air, particularly from the Apache end. Roxanne Armstrong was Apache's in-house attorney and general counsel in the case. The two sides met for the first time at a mediation in Dallas.

"I told Roxanne, 'I understand you used to practice with my friend, Jim Leahy, in Houston,'" O'Neill said. "She said, 'I didn't practice with him. He worked for me.' I thought to myself, 'The day Leahy works for you, Roxanne, is the day I eat gravel for breakfast.' So she was just incensed. I've never seen meanness like that in a case."

"She hated me," Templeton said. "Apache lawyers hated me."

That O'Neill came up from Houston to represent almost all of the remaining royalty owners who had seen this to the end was, he said, a tribute to Templeton's cunning and creativity.

"I'll flatter Bob a little bit," O'Neill said, "because the tactic that Bob thought of was quite brilliant."

That was to put Apache on the defensive. Apache was laying all the blame on Axelson in its suit. Templeton persuaded the remaining royalty owners not to settle, but to intervene in the case and sue Apache.

"The optics originally are bad for Axelson. Apache is beating them up and is the defendant. There is a great advantage in some cases to being the plaintiff," O'Neill said. "Apache would get to open and close. They get to voir dire the jury first. They get to make the opening statement first.

"Now, with the royalty owners, Apache is the defendant. Some of the advantages they would have had against Axelson they don't have any more. It just looks like they're laying all the blame on little old Axelson."

The trial, *Tom L. Scott inc. el v. Apache Corp. and Meridian Oil Production Co.*, was moved to Randall County in Canyon, Texas. There were hundreds in a packed courthouse.

"We were walking into the courthouse the first day to pick the jury and I could see this one-story white brick building next to the courthouse," O'Neill said. "Someone had painted on the side a mural, and it was very well done, of the arm of God holding the Ten Commandments.

"I was with two lawyers with my firm helping me try the case and I looked at them and said, 'I think we've come to the right place.' They are very conservative people with a strong sense of right and wrong. Apache miscalculated their sense of right and wrong and the abhorrence they would feel for Apache when they saw the evidence come in."

Templeton had offered Apache $6 million to settle the $500 million lawsuit. He had been turned down on more than one occasion. Now he had explicit instructions to settle from Hanson's general counsel, George Hempstead. He had stayed on top of the case.

Hanson, Axelson's parent company, had $25 million worth of insurance between AIG and Kemper. Those companies had never balked, but they were down to about the last $10 million.

On the day of the jury selection, O'Neill, representing the adjacent royalty owners, went first. He laid out a strong case against Apache. Then, Jess Hall, had Apache's counsel followed. He blamed Axelson. Between the two, they took up most of the day. At 4:45 p.m., Templeton got up for 15 minutes. "I don't know exactly what I said, but I was full of emotion," Templeton said. John Smithee, who was with me, said I made no sense at all, but I connected with the jury. I was later told that Jess Hall and Scott Hogarty, along with counsel for Apache, were literally seething at what I said, Anyway, I guess it worked."

Apache's attorneys saw Templeton's unusual tactics in the voir dire of the jury that unnerved them. They also knew their case against Axelson was not what it once was.

Charlie Tighe, an attorney from Midland, helped Templeton in representing a small companion company to Axelson. He could sense concern among the Apache representation.

"We ought to offer them $10 million and give them until 10 a.m. Friday," Tighe said.

"I said, 'Charlie, you convey it because they hate me,'" Templeton said. "They don't like me at all."

Tighe did just that, and Apache accepted. The case against Axelson was dismissed. Templeton was out of it.

"It was the best case I never tried," he said. "I did the best job on a defense of a case I ever did. Hanson never had to pay a dime. Not one dime, not in legal fees or on a settlement. It was all paid by insurance.

"I thought I could have won it, but we could have lost too. The risks were far too great, and I had the orders to settle anyway. The $10 million was nuisance settlement on $500 million."

But Scott v. Apache marched on – with a bit of a twist. Daisy Moore, one of the plaintiffs and a deeply religious woman, represented herself. She ran the business of the family farm and ranch near Dalhart.

"My Lord didn't have an attorney," Moore told Texas Lawyer in 1992.

But her family did, however. They asked O'Neill, who was already representing the Scott plaintiffs, to represent Leo Moore, her husband, and her sister-in-law, Bess Cole.

O'Neill laid out the case to the jury in his opening statement, detailing the blowout, the impact of the blowout, and what went wrong. He said in all his years of trying lawsuits, he'd never seen the evidence that he would present, particularly on the kickbacks.

"The basic question the jury was going to have to answer was who was responsible?" O'Neill said. "I told them Apache was laying the blame off on a small company that made a pressure relief valve, but the evidence would contradict that."

Jess Hall, lead attorney for Apache and also from Houston, was a former Church of Christ pastor. He was flamboyant – "a lot of Texan in him," O'Neill said. One incident in the long trial surprised O'Neill.

Sheehan ran the trial like clockwork. Trial started at 9 a.m., there was a 15-minute break at 10:30 a.m., and lunch break at 12:30 p.m. On one morning, Hall was in a direct examination of a witness as it approached 10:30 a.m.

"Hall asked a question, and Sheehan mentioned it was about time for a break," O'Neill said. "And Hall asked if the witness could answer the question, and Judge Sheehan said something like, 'Of course.' The judge let the witness finish the answer. Then he said it was time for our break."

The trial was set to resume after the break, but Hall asked if the jury could be excused, and Sheehan agreed. He then made a motion for a mistrial on the grounds that Sheehan interrupted his examination of a witness at a critical point to allow for a break.

"Judge Sheehan looked at him and said your motion is denied," O'Neill said. "The judge asked if I had a response, and I said, 'Your Honor, I don't.' My read on Judge Sheehan was he was a wonderful judge and a patient man. That objection was so unfounded and unreasonable and really a criticism of his judging."

As for Daisy Moore, who took two legal courses at Frank Phillips College in Borger, she continued to represent herself. She said that Jesus Christ was her lawyer. Her style, which included examining witnesses by using Biblical verses, wore thin.

"She was a character," O'Neill said, "but the jury didn't like her. We had jury consultants in the case, and in post-jury interviews, they didn't care for her."

The trial lasted two months. Its claims by the plaintiffs weren't nearly as large as what Apache sought from Axelson. Templeton, after the settlement with Apache, was advised to stay away from the trial, but he ducked in to listen to O'Neill's closing argument, much of which was based on the net worth of Apache.

The jury found for the plaintiffs in August 1992. It was the largest punitive damage awarded in Randall County history – $4.5 million. In addition, there was $81,292 awarded in actual damages for a negligence claim, and $191,713 in damage for a conversion claim.

Apache appealed and Scott settled with Apache. Moore did not settle, and punitive damages against Apache were removed.

"I walked into stuff I had not grown up with," Templeton said. "I wasn't a petroleum engineer. I wasn't a geologist. You had to make a quick study of the whole thing to understand it."

— Reflection —

"All good things must come to an end," Templeton said. "Goodbye to AIG and Kemper."

CHAPTER
15

A Lot Of Greed And A Little Revenge

Toni Banks and her husband, Max, were in the throes of a messy divorce in 1985. Why Templeton and Garner got involved, that's a good question. Divorces were legal matters the firm had a policy against. Let someone else chase those.

Max Banks, who drilled gas wells for major companies and independents, was supposedly worth around $50 million. He was 20 years older than Toni, who had made a local name for herself with a commercial for the Western Company in the 1970s with the memorable line: "If you don't have an oil well, get one!" They had two children.

"But after about 10 years of marriage," Robert Templeton said, "she had enough of Max."

Toni knew of Bob Garner and wanted to see if he would represent her in a divorce case. Garner knew of the firm's policy, but took the case anyway. He promised much, but couldn't deliver. After some months, Garner called a meeting with Banks and asked Templeton to join.

"This was another one of Garner's messes," Templeton said. "Bob proposed a settlement and Toni didn't like it. She said, 'If you can't get $20 million out of this, you're no kind of lawyer.' At the time, I was on a roll and I didn't think I'd lose a case. Like a fool, I said, 'OK, I'll take it.'"

The case could not be settled. Toni Banks wanted full custody of the couple's two children. Max believed she would move to Dallas.

Pat Boone of Littlefield was the judge, and he liked Max Banks. The trial was a disaster. It was tried in the summer of 1985 for an exhausting two months. Templeton found out how emotional a divorce with a fight over children can be. Toni was truly a victim, he believed, but it didn't come off that way.

Max's lawyers went after Toni Banks viciously. Templeton recalled Max Banks sobbing while on the stand. A video was played of him playing with his children that some were convinced was staged. Max was awarded custody of the children with Toni to have possession of them half the time. Toni received a substantial monetary award, but not $20 million.

Garner had a written fee agreement with Toni for $250,000, but she refused to pay. Templeton and Garner filed suit. Toni hired Dallas attorney Jack Cowley who then filed a cross-action against Garner for malpractice. Toni believed Templeton had earned his money and did not sue him. Raleigh Brown of Abilene heard the non-jury trial.

The morning of trial Garner capitulated, agreeing to pay the $1 million in malpractice coverage. Templeton and others were flabbergasted. Templeton, represented by Wayne Sturdivant, proceeded to trial with his claim.

Cowley didn't contest that Templeton had earned his fee, but the case was that Garner had released all claim to fees on behalf of the firm by telling Sam Kiser that Toni didn't have to pay, and Sam Kiser, by then a judge, testified as such. Judge Brown held that Garner had released the claim. Templeton appealed, but Judge Brown's ruling was affirmed.

"Sometime later," Templeton said, "Jack Cowley got Toni full custody and she never moved. I was always on her side, but I had it in for Jack Cowley. I told him that one day I was going to get him for this."

Templeton had no idea if that would ever occur. It would take an incredible amount of coincidence, fate, good fortune, and some skillful legal maneuvering — all of it twisted together in the next six years — but the two would meet again.

In between were Jim Lovell and his son John Lovell, Garner, Irving Melroe, and, a man from Kansas named Ed Baldwin and his wife. It was a web of intrigue and deceit.

"This is the only case I know of where somebody sued a lawyer for malpractice and conflicts of interest and after the jury heard the case, they said the lawyer didn't do anything wrong, and the plaintiff wasn't damaged, but the plaintiff defrauded his lawyer," John Lovell said.

It was 1984 and Lovell was not long out of Baylor Law School. He hung his first shingle in Clarendon, a town of 2,000 about 60 miles southeast of Amarillo in Donley County. He practiced by himself, taking whatever came along in a small town. It was not an easy way to make a living, especially with a wife and three young children.

Jim Lovell, his father and an attorney in Dumas, offered his son a steady client – Jim Lovell. He had got into some financial trouble and needed legal help.

"I mean, he's being sued by everybody on earth," John Lovell said.

In the late 1970s, Jim Lovell got into the land trading business. In the days of high inflation, Lovell believed he could borrow money cheaper than inflation and buy land, leverage it, wait about five years and make some money.

Lovell got more into land trading than practicing law. He had land all over the Texas Panhandle, New Mexico and Colorado. He had a quarter section near Del City close to Guadalupe Peak. At one time, he bought and sold around 100,000 acres.

About the time John Lovell graduated from law school, President Ronald Reagan and Paul Volcker, the chairman of the Federal Reserve, moved the prime interest rate to 21 percent. That about ruined Jim Lovell.

"Dad went broke in a few months," John said. "The most valuable asset in those years was cash. Nobody wanted land. Economically, land was stupid. The value of his acres went to nothing. You couldn't finance it. You couldn't sell it. He was overleveraged to begin with.

He was upside down instantly."

One of the purchases Lovell made was 800 acres that Bob Garner and Templeton held. Garner had talked Templeton into initially buying the farm land near Stratford. The two had a note on the land, and Lovell purchased it on a wrap-around note. When Lovell went broke, he owed about $220,000 that he couldn't pay.

"We had to pay it off to keep the land, and I paid it off," Templeton said. "I guess I was stubborn. I could never get mad at Jim Lovell. Jim was a friend of mine."

But Templeton was about the only one. Everyone else had creditors lining up to get their money. Lawsuits were flowing in. Lovell refused bankruptcy, or more accurately, his wife wouldn't stand for bankruptcy when that seemed like the prudent thing to do.

"I'm sure his creditors thought there must be some secret out there," John said. "The secret was my mother was a knucklehead."

In the flood of lawsuits, Jim Lovell called upon his son to defend him. Why not? After all, it was his dad who was in trouble. He would also pick up some income, some welcome income, for his help.

"My job literally was to raise hell with the creditors who sued him to make sure it was a non-profitable venture," John said. "A lot of it too was he wanted me to defend him so he could work. He had good work with good clients. But if he spent all his time dealing with discovery by these creditors, he couldn't work very well. I was cheap defense. I kept creditors at bay. They began to realize it wasn't a paying proposition to go after him."

One of those who did not realize that was Ed Baldwin. He and wife Irene were from Kansas. Baldwin was a creditor, but also in the land business. Baldwin, through a series of trades, now held the note on some farm land east of Dumas near Etter that Jim Lovell had purchased.

Lovell, in turn, eventually sold that land to Irving Melroe, a man from Colorado, who was helping Ed, his son, in the farming business. In the arrangement, Melroe assumed paying the notes from Lovell. But when the economy turned and interest rates skied to more than 20 percent, Ed Melroe went broke. Irving Melroe said he's broke too.

The Baldwins traveled to Amarillo, met with Garner, and it's there, they decided to file suit in federal court in 1984. Garner was hired to represent the Baldwins. According to a fee agreement, Garner received a $20,000 initial payment, and the firm of Templeton and Garner received 20 percent of any amount recovered against Jim Lovell or Irving Melroe.

Jim Lovell told his son in December 1984 that he was being sued by the Baldwins and the trial was on the horizon. Some Christmas present. Lovell had only two months to prepare for his first trial which was set for February 1985.

"I'm thinking, 'What is the defense against a promissory note?'" John Lovell said. "At the top, it says, 'I promise to pay...' So how do you deal with that?"

Garner had taken a shine to the young Lovell, and pulled him aside to say that he couldn't defend it. It was basically hopeless. But Garner had an idea.

"What you need to remember," Garner told him, "is Melroe breached their contract with your dad. Melroe promised to pay that note and they assumed it from your dad. Here's what you need to do. Don't fight the Baldwins. Work with me and we'll both prove the Melroes are the one that owe both of us."

Lovell's reaction? "Well, you know," he said. "That makes sense."

A bench trial with U.S. District Court Judge Mary Lou Robinson was scheduled for March 1985. Garner had his plaintiff client, Ed Baldwin. John Lovell represented his father. Irving Melroe was represented by local counsel Steve Hoard and an attorney from the Denver firm of Cogswell and Wehrle.

The trial took only half a day. Jim Lovell testified that he did originally sign the notes, and the Melroes assumed them. Under the contract, they had the obligation to pay the Baldwins, and if they can't pay, Lovell told the court, they breached their contract with him.

Robinson gave a judgment to Baldwin for a little less than $700,000 against Jim Lovell and Melroe. Lovell, though, had a judgment of indemnity against Melroe, meaning every dollar collected against Lovell, he could collect that same amount against Melroe.

"It was the best possible result," John Lovell said. "And if Melroe is good for it, my dad is released."

It was thought Irving Melroe might be able to pay it. Roger Melroe, his brother, had been the inventor and had the patent for a front-end loader used by Bobcat. He was well off financially. Though it was not known at the time of the trial, Roger had helped his brother through the years, and was a source of much of his money.

While Baldwin looked to collect, so too did Garner with a contract that called for 20 percent of any money from Melroe or Lovell. At the conclusion of the trial, Garner also caught John Lovell off guard – by offering him a job with Templeton and Garner.

"I thought, 'Wow, that would be something,'" Lovell said. "I'm a solo practitioner, and Templeton and Garner are heavy hitters in Amarillo. In the legal community, those two guys were the top plaintiff lawyers in the area, no question about it. I just thought I'd never have another opportunity like this."

Only one problem. Lovell's wife Trudy didn't share the same enthusiasm. She didn't want to move. She liked Clarendon, and didn't want any part of the city.

Lovell told Templeton that he'd like to join the firm, but his wife was adamant about not moving. Templeton asked Lovell to see if Trudy would see him at some point soon in his office. He was going to recruit her. Trudy did, meeting Templeton by herself.

"She said, 'You need to work with them. I'm OK with it,'" Lovell said. "I said, 'Great.' And I was ready for an interview."

He heard nothing for three months. He thought they must have changed their minds until Templeton called in late July, asking Lovell if he and his wife could meet him and Garner and their wives at the Amarillo Club.

Over dinner, Lovell was regaled with previous cases from Templeton and Garner. After, they made him a job offer and asked for a start date. But there was also a sticky wicket – a seeming conflict of interest with Lovell and Garner. Lovell was still representing his father in the judgment against him, and Garner was representing the judgment creditor of Baldwin against Lovell.

Garner told him not to worry. He had it worked out. He would assign all collection duties to attorney Sam Kiser because his firm did collection work. As far as they were concerned, Garner told Lovell, the case didn't exist beyond that.

"He said, 'John, you and I are never going to talk about it,'" Lovell said. "He said that he wasn't going to tell me what they're doing, and I'm not going to tell him what I was doing. Garner said he talked to the Baldwins and they were OK with that. I said, 'Sounds fine to me.' I thought the conflict was worked out."

Lovell began work at Templeton and Garner and for a short while, work was fine for the young attorney. True to their agreement, neither he nor Garner talked about the judgment against Melroe and Jim Lovell and the collection. And then...

Irving Melroe filed for bankruptcy in Denver. The hope the Baldwins would be paid by Melroe disappeared in a bankruptcy court in Colorado. Now what? Garner said he was not a bankruptcy lawyer, and was not from Colorado, and suggested the Baldwins hire a bankruptcy attorney in Denver. They did.

Meanwhile, the bankruptcy trustee in Denver later sent out a Notice of Surplus Funds. There was also a note attached that stated when the bankruptcy was filed, it was a "no asset" case, that Melroe did not have any non-exempt assets. Since then, however, some non-exempt assets were discovered. That's why Garner received a Notice of Surplus Funds.

He called the Baldwins and asked what this notice meant. They sent back a letter that included Melroe's surplus of funds. In the letter, Baldwin informed Garner there's nothing to this surplus. There's not enough there to pay attorney fees. With that, Garner believed that despite the new surplus of funds, Melroe was broke. He ignored the letter and the Melroe bankruptcy.

In the meantime, the Baldwins were active and aggressive in the bankruptcy. They received word that Roger Melroe died, and obtained a copy of the will. They took it another step by calling Roger Melroe's widow who hated her brother-in-law, Irving. She thought he mooched off Roger way too much and took advantage of him.

She showed the Baldwins a codicil in her late husband's will. In so many words, the codicil read that Irving had transferred an investment interest called the Michigan Chestnut Partnership to Roger to hide from creditors.

"In essence, Roger said it was a fraudulent transfer and he would give it back to Irving," Lovell said. "The partnership was named for a real estate development in downtown Chicago at the intersection of Michigan and Chestnut Avenue. Downtown real estate in Chicago. You can just imagine."

When Irving Melroe had money in the 1970s, he began investing in that limited partnership. When he realized he was getting into financial trouble and creditors would be nipping at his heels, he hid the Michigan Chestnut within the portfolio of his brother with the agreement he would receive it back at some point.

"That's about as bad a fraud in a transfer as you can get," Lovell said. "The Baldwins get wind of that and say, 'Hot damn, we're going to get hold of that Michigan Chestnut asset. We're going to recover it and then we're going to sue his lawyers, Cogswell and Wehrle, for fraudulent transfer.'"

The law firm and Irving Melroe were sued in bankruptcy court in Denver. Cogswell and Wehrle were sued for assisting with their client on "fraudulent transfers." Fraudulent transfers are the transfers of assets by a debtor made with the "intent to hinder, delay or defraud creditors" or "transfers for inadequate consideration." The transfer was both.

The firm settled with the Baldwins for $250,000. Its insurance company insisted because it was that blatant. But there was more. A secret settlement was worked out in bankruptcy court between the Melroe trustee and the Baldwins.

The Baldwins received the Michigan Chestnut Partnership interest for $25,000 credit on a sham note. Cogswell and Wehrle are released and the Baldwins received all the assets. The value of that interest was a cool $1.2 million.

"Here's the real problem," Lovell said. "The Baldwins had a really good time in doing all that. They really enjoyed it. They enjoyed suing the lawyers and they enjoyed the conflicts of interest. They enjoyed the lawyers doing nasty things and they enjoyed the lawyers' insurance money. They enjoyed getting this hidden asset. They thought it was like shooting fish in a barrel. It was like, 'Shoot, let's do this again.'"

They apparently enjoyed it so much they couldn't bear to stop. So now they turned their sights to Amarillo, to Bob Garner and the firm of Templeton and Garner. They were just getting started.

"The Baldwins basically say," John Lovell recalled, "'Garner, you hired Jim Lovell's son and I bet he knows where all the bodies are buried and I bet he could have collected all these things that Jim Lovell had. And you didn't check all the mineral interests and you didn't check this corporation or that. And right down the hall is his son and lawyer and we think there's shenanigans there and we're suing your ass."

Game on.

One fact that would eventually become important, and crucial to the Lovells and the Templeton and Garner firm was how Jim Lovell handled some of the mineral rights on land he bought. He took the royalty interest from the mineral rights and conveyed them to a corporation he set up for the benefit of his children.

"John was handling that end of it," Templeton said. "They had conveyed mineral interest all over the country to a corporation. I didn't know about this until later on, right before the second trial."

"And Garner's deal was we're just not going to talk about your dad's case," John Lovell said, "and I didn't. As a matter of course, my dad had it figured out. The first thing you do when you buy land is convey all the mineral to a corporation he set up so that when he resold the land he could truthfully tell the next buyer I don't have any of the minerals – and he didn't."

"The point is, people would say, 'My God, there's mineral interest all over the country. They have to have some value,'" Templeton said. "Now, not all of them did, but some did. Garner should have gone ahead and collected those mineral interests. That was an issue in the litigation."

The Baldwins sued Garner personally and Templeton and Garner as a firm in 1990. John Lovell felt a responsibility. If not for them, he thought, they may not be in this situation to begin with.

"I told them they are getting sued because you hired me," Lovell said. "I appreciated them giving me a chance as I never would have left Clarendon and come to Amarillo otherwise. They did me a big favor. Now let me defend you."

So John Lovell did, defending both Templeton and Garner and Garner. It was not long into the case where a major development turned the case. Shakespeare once wrote, "There is something rotten in Denmark." Well, there was something rotten in Colorado.

More than 30 years later, in 2019, from his office in downtown Amarillo, Lovell produced the letter that Garner received from the bankruptcy court in Denver along with an attachment from Baldwin that this surplus of funds would not even cover attorney fees.

"The problem is that is a damn lie when they say there is nothing there," Lovell said. "This is not a 'kind of' lie. This is black-hearted malice because this is what they collected."

Lovell produced a sheet of paper that showed more than $1 million in assets and deposits that Baldwin made from the funds. In 1990, that's Baldwin's little secret. Not only did he avoid paying Garner 20 percent of what was collected from Melroe because of the contingency fee agreement, he showed off some big brass ones by filing suit against Garner for failing to collect against Jim Lovell, who was liable to pay if Melroe could not.

"He wanted to collect the same debt twice," Lovell said.

When Lovell first took over the case 30 years ago in defense of his bosses, he didn't know that. No one knew that. All he had seen was some paper work in Denver that Melroe had filed bankruptcy and a letter from the Baldwins stating they weren't netting anything beyond attorney fees.

In the meantime, coincidentally, Baldwin hired Jack Cowley, the same Dallas attorney who had represented Toni Banks when Templeton had sued her for failing to pay attorney fees in a divorce case, the same Cowley who Templeton had said he would one day get some payback.

"I don't know how he came to represent Ed Baldwin," Templeton said, "other than he smelled blood. I think he smelled $1 million without even trying the case."

To make the stakes higher, because of $1 million paid into the Toni Banks case, the firm's malpractice insurance did not get renewed. The stakes were high as they currently held no malpractice insurance.

The case plodded along for a couple of years in discovery. Then, one afternoon, Garner got a call at this desk, like it was straight out of a B movie. The caller did not identify himself.

"Bob Garner?"

"Yes."

"You need to get up to Denver and see what the Baldwins are doing to you."

Click.

Garner got up and went into Lovell's office and told him about the brief and mysterious phone call. Lovell began making travel arrangements to Denver.

"An ordinary fellow, not John Lovell, might have passed it off and said that I'm not going to worry about that," Templeton said. "But he immediately went up there."

Lovell didn't know what to look for when he got to Denver. For all he knew, that anonymous call could have been a practical joke or an exaggeration, but there was nothing to lose. When Lovell arrived at bankruptcy court, he first took a look at the pleadings to see who the lawyers were.

He called the bankruptcy trustee, and got nothing. He went to see the lawyers who defended Cogswell and Wehrle in the fraudulent transfer. They had a box of files that he sifted through but saw nothing out of the ordinary.

Then he went to see Irving Melroe's lawyer – and the case took a dramatic turn then and there. He had the complete file, including what was sealed by the bankruptcy court. Lovell was basically told here's all the files, knock yourself out.

"I probably should not have been allowed to see it," he said, "but they let me see everything."

He could feel his heart beat faster when he started reading the settlement sealed by the bankruptcy judge. There was a protective order that said no one could see it, but here was Lovell reading every bit of it. At this point, he could have hugged Melroe's lawyer.

It was all there – Cogswell and Wehrle's insurance company settled for $250,000, that Cogswell and Wehrle paid $25,000 for a release, that the Baldwins were assigned the Michigan Chestnut partnership interest of over $1 million. This wasn't a smoking gun. This was a smoking arsenal.

"I thought, 'you lying SOBs!'" Lovell said.

He made copies of critical evidence. He then hired a lawyer in Denver to unseal the settlement so he could use the evidence. Then he filed a counter-claim against Baldwin, claiming they were the ones being defrauded.

"One of my mottos is 'paper kills, and more paper kills more,'" Lovell said. "I like to dig down into the details and see what happens. I like to get down into the weeds."

So now, armed with the truth, Lovell took Baldwin's deposition. He questioned him about Michigan Chestnut, the settlement amount, and especially the crux of the counter claim that he hid 20 percent Garner was entitled to in the collection of money per the contract agreement between the two.

"I said, 'Wait a minute, you had an agreement with Bob Garner for 20 percent and he's entitled to that. So you were telling him that you couldn't collect anything and look at all the money you've collected,'" Lovell said.

Baldwin's defense was when he contacted Garner to lie that there was very little in Irving Melroe's surplus of funds was that Garner had told him previously he didn't want to be legal representation in the bankruptcy.

"Baldwin's attitude was that Garner didn't want to mess with the bankruptcy in Denver so he didn't have the duty to tell him anything else," Lovell said. "He believed he was entitled to all the money and he didn't have to disclose anything. The fact the letter was a lie when it was written didn't matter.

"So my question to him was in regard to the letter, you just didn't tell him, him being Bob Garner, you didn't tell him the whole truth, did you? And his answer was, 'There was no need to.'"

Lovell would eventually blow up that question and answer into one of several posters to be used at the second of two trials in 2001. The first one ended in a hung jury. "Two women jurors took a dislike to Garner," Templeton said.

The second trial in 2003 involved the same parties – the firm of Templeton and Garner and Garner individually. But there was also the counter claim against Baldwin. The second trial required some legal maneuvering by Templeton. Cowley was a formidable foe. He may have at one time wanted to settle, but the Baldwins insisted the case go forward, and because of the agreement, he had no choice.

The Baldwins had been upset with Garner's withdrawal of representation, so when they hired Cowley, they doubled his fee to $40,000 and 40 percent of recoverable assets, but with one major catch – he could never withdraw from the case.

"Cowley was a very good trial lawyer," Templeton said. "He could sell soap. He could be very persuasive. He had a way with juries."

At the second trial, at the 108th District Court at the Potter County Courthouse, Vann Culp, a visiting judge from Midland, presided. It became dueling posters for several days between competing lawyers. Lovell had several posters made of direct questions and damning answers from Baldwin in his deposition that he placed in the jury room. Cowley had his own posters.

When there was a break, Cowley would replace one of Lovell's posters with one of his own. After lunch, Lovell would change that for one of his. So it went back and forth.

"I think that had an awful lot to do with the jury's ultimate

John Lovell

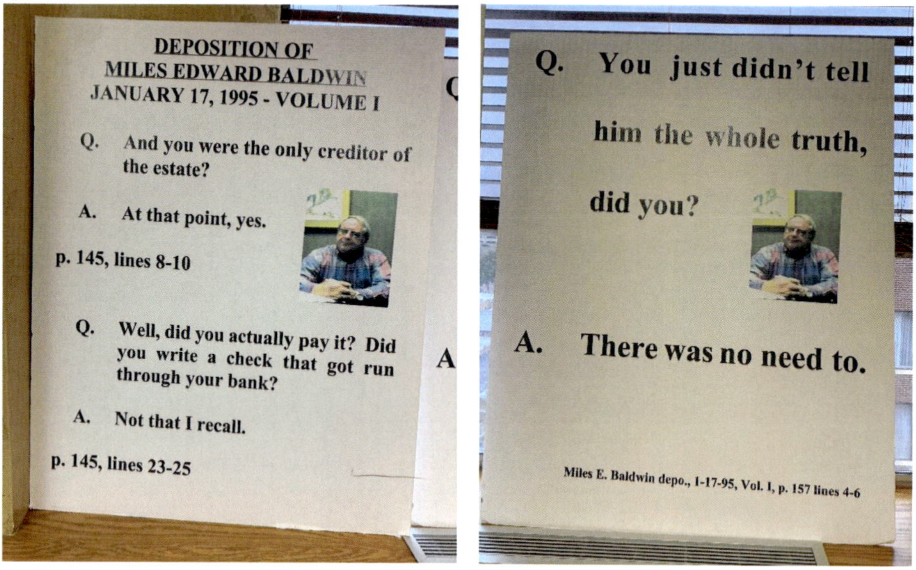

Posters of Baldwin's deposition that Lovell showed at trial.

decision that Baldwin was a crook," Lovell said. "For him to admit that he didn't think he had the duty to tell the whole truth obviously killed him in the case."

There was still the major issue of Jim Lovell's conveyance of minerals into a corporation for his children. Cowley suspected the minerals had been conveyed, but could he prove it?

Most of the transfers occurred in Sherman and Moore counties in the northern Panhandle from an old Hugoton field production. The wells didn't produce much, and there was small scattered royalty interest. Cowley went to the tax office of the two counties seeking the tax records, believing that would prove mineral rights ownership.

"He thought the tax records proved ownership," Lovell said. "What I knew and Bob Templeton knew is where title is a direct issue, you can't prove a direct issue with secondary evidence. What happens with tax districts is they don't do a title search. What the tax districts do is call the oil operators and ask what do your division orders show?"

Templeton had the idea of preventing evidence of transfer at trial. He spoke to Judge Culp, telling him that Cowley had not gathered any evidence of title, and making a motion therefore it should be excluded. Culp ruled in favor of Templeton.

"After the judge excluded that evidence, Cowley knew he was deader than a hammer," Templeton said. "He had no leverage. He wanted to mutually dismiss."

No, Templeton had been waiting for this moment ever since the Toni Banks case. There would be no walkaway.

"No, Jack, we're going to trial," he said.

"We're going to take our kill shot," Lovell said. "Bob enjoyed that."

In addition, some mineral rights were subject to judgment liens, which comes with an abstract of judgment. That's a brief synopsis of what creditors are owed. Templeton put on evidence that Baldwin was the 23rd judgment.

"Basically, Cowley failed to prove ownership of those minerals," Templeton said.

"Failed to prove ownership, failed to prove they hadn't been lost to judgment, and here's another thing – even if he had proved title, how would he collect it?" Lovell said. "How could you recover anything if you're the 23rd priority collector?

"We did do the title research. We knew what happened with all those mineral titles. We had charts of all the judgment liens ahead of the Baldwins in each county. Judge Culp knew that we knew what we were talking about – because we did."

Unlike the first trial, Lovell could not serve as counsel because he was a material witness. Templeton, as he did in the first trial, defended the firm in the second. They were helped considerably by David Langston from Lubbock, their expert witness on bankruptcy procedure. "A crackerjack witness," Lovell said.

"Oh, I had a ball in that case," Templeton said, "but John did all the work. He had it all prepared. All I had to do was be the mouthpiece. They put Ed up there (on the stand). My cross examination of Ed was basically the case. John had all these posters and all I had to do was make it clear. And I can make things simple and clear to the jury."

At the same time, Garner was an individual defendant and defended himself. He nearly sabotaged the entire trial, much of which hinged on keeping evidence of mineral transfer suppressed. Judge Culp had previously granted that motion.

"Garner gets up and is asking a witness some questions," Lovell said, "and he says, 'Well, you are aware of Pritchard and Abbott, they're the engineering firm that works for all the tax districts and they gather all this information and it's pretty accurate information they gather up..."

Templeton and Lovell, seating at the counsel table, were incredulous. They had worked to keep the evidence out and here Garner was talking about how accurate it was. Lovell wrote a note to Templeton which read: "Are you going to shoot him or can I?"

Templeton didn't shoot him, but he did object, primarily to keep Garner quiet. Judge Culp considered undoing his ruling, but let it stand. After the proceedings ended for the day, Templeton got

Garner alone and told him in no uncertain terms that he was not going to lose this case for them, and keep his mouth shut.

Garner did, but in closing arguments, he did not. That would score him points with the jury. Lovell called Garner the most emotional man he'd ever met, which helped make him an effective trial lawyer.

"He could project any kind of emotion very easily," Lovell said. "The reason he could project, it was it was always just a little below the surface. Garner didn't have to act. He just had to release.

"He was having an emotional event. He was totally upset that he would be accused of bad motives and cheat his client, and he never did. Garner maybe wasn't always smart, but he didn't do anything wrong. A lot of it goes back to he was so emotional, and had a hard time engaging logic at times."

In closing arguments, Garner essentially threw his fate to the decision of the jury. It was effective.

"It was pure raw emotion," Templeton said. "He said that if you think I did wrong, just give it to me. Give me what I deserve. Basically, he said if you award judgment against me, you're ruining me. If you want to destroy me, go ahead. You have that power.

"How do I know it was effective? A neighbor across the street was on the jury. She was a strong juror. After the trial, she told me she felt sorry for that poor man and what they were trying to do to him. They could see by the evidence that Baldwin had a bad lawsuit."

The trial turned on several points – that Baldwin had already collected through the hidden surplus of funds from Irving Melroe, the transfer of minerals could not be used as evidence, and Garner was a sympathetic figure to the jury.

The jury returned with a verdict that couldn't have been better if Templeton and Lovell had drawn it up themselves. The jury took it well beyond finding the Templeton and Garner firm and Garner not guilty.

"Where else can you have a case where a lawyer is being sued for malpractice end up holding up for the lawyer, and then allow him to collect attorney fees and find punitive damage against the plaintiff?" Templeton said.

The jury awarded approximately $900,000 in actual and punitive damages to Templeton and Garner. The verdict was upheld by the Amarillo Court of Appeals and the Texas Supreme Court declined to hear the case. It was over. Baldwin, who died in 2017, attempted more legal wrangling in the ensuing years, but it went nowhere.

As Cowley would later say, "The counter claim was the case."

The verdict and trial by themselves were rewarding enough. Add to that a little payback from the Toni Banks lawsuit and it was about as satisfying as a case can get.

"Oh, gosh, of course, I enjoyed it," Templeton said. "I don't know if I said, 'OK, I got you now,' after the trial. I know I said it later on. Jack said, 'Yeah, Bob, you got me.'"

– Reflections –

"In trying cases before a jury, there were times I never felt more alive," Templeton said. "When you're connecting with a jury, there's no greater satisfaction. That's the greatest satisfaction a trial lawyer can have."

CHAPTER
16

When The Brilliance Lost Its Luster

Steve Sterquell was brilliant.

That was the word that seemed to follow him. Oh, he could sell too in the way he convinced investors to join his latest project, made them believe they were missing out on a lucrative deal if they didn't put their money with him. But more than that, Sterquell spoke in a financial language that had many certain that he was gifted beyond their ability to understand.

"Just about everybody you talked to agreed, 'Wow, that Steve Sterquell, man, he's a smart guy,'" said attorney Joe Lovell. "'Brilliant' was the word repeated time and time again. The man was brilliant. That was across the board.

"I never sat in on one of his presentations, but I interviewed a number who did. Some people thought they understood it. Some people didn't understand it but they believed in Steve and knew he was smart. But some would say, 'Steve is brilliant and clearly he understands it, but I didn't and I don't feel comfortable making an investment in something I don't understand.'"

Sterquell's roots were deep in Amarillo. His father, U.C. Sterquell, graduated from Texas A&M at the end of World War II. Betty Wright, his mother, entered the University of Texas at age 16 and graduated with a double major and double minor. They married in July 1949, and shortly after, they moved to Amarillo where U.C.

was a certified public accountant.

The Sterquells fingerprints were all over causes and organizations in Amarillo, from helping start Camp Alphie for children with cancer to the High Plains Food Bank, from the Amarillo Symphony to the Circle of Friends for the Harrington Cancer Center. Betty, in particular, was a driving force in Republican party politics in Randall County.

Steve, one of three children, was cut from that same cloth. He was an Eagle Scout, and kept that lifetime association with the Boy Scouts of America. He graduated from Tascosa High School and from Texas Tech in 1974. The next year, he was in Amarillo, beginning an accounting practice. In 1978, like his father, he became a certified public accountant, forming the accounting firm of Sterquell Hill & Goelzer.

His life was a balance of career, hobbies and community involvement. He was an avid hunter and fisherman. On three safaris to Africa, Sterquell shot what is known in safari circles as "The Big Five" – elephant, lion, cape buffalo, rhino and leopard.

Like his parents, he was heavily involved in community groups and causes. Kiwanis Club president, High Plains Food Bank, chairman of the Children's Miracle Network telethon, president of the Maverick Boys and Girls Club, Jan Werner Adult Day Care Center,

Steve Sterquell

Amarillo Little Theatre. The list was a long one.

With wife Marshallette, they had two children. His life was full. But there were some professional cracks that should have given some pause. In the 1980s, he was on the board of directors of First Federal Savings and Loan where he chaired the loan committee.

The mid-1980s was a time of the savings and loan crash in Texas. First Federal, later Shamrock, was one of two in Amarillo to fail as a result of bad loans made to a number of developers.

"They would have these people go out and value these apartment complexes at extraordinary amounts of value and then First Federal loaned to people based upon these appraisals that were 'inflated,' which is a kind way to put it," Amarillo tax attorney Bill Hoy said.

Those highly inflated appraisals were predicated on non-recourse loans and no personal guarantees. On a default, the only asset a savings and loan like First Federal had to fall back on were the properties themselves.

"And if the properties are overinflated, they're never going to retire the loans," Hoy said.

Hoy said he advised a number of clients to stay away from these investments because many were "arbitrage partnerships," meaning there would be a shortfall in operating capital, but investors were told they would make that up in tax savings. Investors were then asked to remit a portion of that tax savings back to the partnership to meet its debt service.

"But we had a little problem," Hoy said. "In 1986, the tax statute was amended. The marginal tax rate went from 70 to 33, meaning instead of paying 70 percent of your investment, Uncle Sam is only going to pay 33 percent. The difference in the two was a shortfall in capital. Sterquell was heads and tails in the midst of that."

Hoy had a client that was entangled in one of those partnerships. He was a doctor.

"I'd known him for years and years. Good guy," Hoy said. "I said, 'John, how the hell did you get into this? Did you think of asking me if this thing was any good or not?" And he said, 'Well, I did ask Sterquell if I could show this to Bill Hoy? He said, 'Oh, don't show this to Hoy. He's too hard to get along with.' I had pulled the plug on a number of his investors before."

In the late 1980s, Sterquell began to use his financial acumen and philanthropic bent in a similar way that First Federal once did. It would be a way to make money for him and his investors and help others who needed it. It was the combination of an adrenaline rush in making a deal and the reward of satisfying the need of others.

The vehicle was affordable housing.

It was a complicated web of tax credits, limited partnerships, non-recourse loans, guaranteed rates of return – all these sleights of hand maneuverings that only Sterquell could master. The plan was vintage Sterquell – baffling, but seemingly brilliant.

American Housing Foundation was a Sterquell creation, a 501c3 nonprofit corporation that he founded in 1989 after he persuaded state officials to issue tax credits he could sell to help finance his plan to refurbish two Amarillo apartments formerly owned by the Catholic Church. He sold the tax credits to oil giant Chevron for seed money, a sign of things to come.

A tax credit is a tax incentive that reduces the amount of money a taxpayer owes to government. Unlike a tax deduction, which reduces taxable income, a taxpayer can subtract a tax credit from the amount of tax owed. Tax credits of up to 40 percent of the value of the property allowed AHF to grow rapidly with multiple apartment purchases.

By 1995, he sold his accounting practice to focus on his burgeoning nonprofit. His son and daughter worked for him. His mother was on the board of directors. For the next 20 years since its inception in 1989, AHF would define him. Sterquell operated AHF with almost fanatical zeal and earned money hand over fist, it seemed, for him and investors. He also operated AHF almost in secrecy, at least the details, which most of the nearly 20 employees and board of directors didn't find troubling until it was.

"Pretty much it was Steve who made all the decisions and the board was just there to validate and approve," said Glenda David, who prepared administrative work in financing and development for

AHF as well as recording secretary of the board. "I don't know how much they understood but only what Steve told them.

"Steve ran the company very close to the vest. Unless he wanted you to know something, you didn't know it. He was a smart man – very smart – but he only wanted to tell you what you needed to know. That was pretty much it. We didn't know the broad picture."

Rick Crawford had been with AHF for six years in various capacities, including executive vice-president. When he was promoted to president of AHF in 2009, he had to admit to the board of directors that he could not answer many of the questions they were asking him.

"He carried the foundation's business in his head," Crawford told the Amarillo Globe-News of Sterquell. "Sometimes he delegated to me or somebody else, but he was a perfectionist. He did a lot on his own."

Initial success with the two Amarillo apartments stoked his ambition for more. He expanded low-income housing purchases to Austin and Oklahoma City. Through the years, AHF grew to 33 cities in 10 states, some as far away as Kentucky, Georgia and Florida. More than 14,000 apartment units were under the AHF umbrella.

Sterquell sold bonds and used tax credits as equity to borrow for other projects in an effort to serve what he called "our communities." By 2007, AHF's financial statement showed a net worth of $81 million. What was not listed was a $2.3 million loss that year.

"I did something nobody thought I could," Sterquell said in a video in 2007 on the AHF website.

Alvin Johnson got about as close a view on how Sterquell worked his apartment deals as anyone when he came on board AHF in early 2008. Johnson was from the Dallas area and wanted to get into a similar business as Sterquell. An appraiser knew them both, and helped set up a one-hour meeting in the AHF branch office in Dallas in early 2007.

"He looked at what I wanted to do and told me that he'd assist me and loved guys that wanted to make the world a better place for other people," Johnson said. "After that meeting, I thought I was going to set the world on fire."

For a couple of weeks, Johnson called Sterquell to update him on some apartment deals he was working on. Sterquell told him each time it was not going to work. Then Sterquell quit returning his calls even though Johnson persisted.

Finally in January 2008, Sterquell told him no more calls. There had to be a better way. If he wanted to learn the business, be in Amarillo on March 1. He'd put Johnson in a hotel for 30 days and he'd show Johnson how AHF made it work.

So Johnson arrived, got a room at the Extended Stay Hotel and went to work. Sterquell sent him to look at properties in Waco and Houston. The properties were in really bad shape or had management issues. Johnson loved the work, and at the end of 30 days, Sterquell asked Johnson what he thought of his time in Amarillo.

He said he loved it, and wanted to stay. Sterquell hired him full time and Johnson found himself on the road again, back to those same cities in discussion with police departments, mayors and city planners.

"Really what I was there for was to try assist in building up some confidence with the mayor and city government agencies that AHF could with enough time turn those properties around," Johnson said. "Of course, it took money and I didn't know at that time there was none."

There was the traditional way of buying properties, and as Johnson discovered, there was the creative Sterquell way he guaranteed would make money for his investors.

The traditional way, Johnson explained, would be to purchase an apartment for $20,000 per unit to use round figures. If there were 100 units in a complex, that's $2 million. Remodeling may add close to another $20,000 per unit for a total of $40,000.

"If you stabilize it, it's probably worth $45,000 to $50,000 or more," he said. "In that case, it will do well for everybody. That's a real straight business model."

Sterquell would reverse that. As an example, AHF would pay $40,000 per unit for a 100-unit complex, but would reverse its way down to the basics of $20,000 per unit with the use of tax credits.

"Essentially, that could work but there were so many things that had to go your way – state approval, tax credit allocations being awarded, state reps having to approve any tax credits that go on in these markets," Johnson said.

"'NB' laws – not in my backyard laws – is another where you may have these properties in Austin that are in a really nice area, and the residents there don't want any more of 'those people' in their backyard. There are so many competitive things that go into a tax credit application that you would be ludicrous to do that. Absolutely ludicrous."

Sterquell records later showed he gave a healthy sum to elected state officials. The Amarillo Globe-News reported in 2009 that campaign donations filed with the Texas Ethics Commission over eight years showed that Sterquell gave nearly $375,00. Nearly half of that went to former state comptroller and gubernatorial candidate Carole Keeton Strayhorn. Another large amount went to her successor, Susan Combs.

Others who received smaller amounts included state Rep. David Swinford (R-Dumas), state Sen. Kel Seliger (R-Amarillo), and Attorney General Greg Abbott. Governor Rick Perry and Lt. Gov. David Dewhurst also received contributions.

Sterquell ranked No. 65 among the state's campaign contributors in 2006, which was curious to Andrew Wheat, research director at Texans for Public Justice, an Austin-based group that monitors campaign donations.

"Although he didn't give out millions of dollars like some did, the reason he came to our attention is because he led a nonprofit," Wheat said. "It's a mystery to us why he gave to those folks. It looked like he didn't have to."

The Texas comptroller's office oversees the status of Texas corporations. The attorney general's office is the state's chief civil law enforcement entity. The attorney general could pursue a statewide nonprofit corporation for any violation of state law.

In recent years, the Texas Legislature dealt repeatedly with property tax exemptions for nonprofit Texas housing corporations. The Legislature also makes the final decision on the amount of tax-exempt bond financing available to corporations like American Housing Foundation.

State officials had an obligation to examine the condition of AHF each time the foundation sought low income housing tax credits or tax-exempt bond financing for another apartment project. AHF purchased properties at a rate far greater than any other Texas non-profit.

"It is the lobbyists or special interests who give so much money because they want something in return, but a nonprofit?" Wheat said.

No question, approval of tax credits were the pistons in the financing engine for AHF. They could be as much as 40 percent of the purchase price of a property. They were a must.

According to a former AHF employee, who asked her name not be used, Sterquell would establish the purchase price of an apartment, and the appraised value would then come in right at the purchase price. Then he would build the basics for a tax credit application. That would be the costs associated with the purchase and financing and any construction costs.

Sterquell would bring in Larry Bunn, his son-in-law who had a construction company within a nonprofit he ran. He would be the developer as well in the transaction.

"The way he made money is when we went to do the financing, you got so much money for being a developer, so much money for construction, so all those costs added in would give you a higher property value which increased your credits," she said.

Sterquell would then submit a competitive tax credit application at more than the likely tax credit value or he would secure a bond purchase, a 4 percent bond purchase.

At that point, he would seek out investors to be limited partners or sell them in the open market. That money, the AHF employee said, would go for what was considered pre-development costs – the upfront costs for appraisals, any third-party reports, possible architect costs and any others associated with the pre-development.

"For the investor, the return was around 12 percent," she said, "and it was basically a short-term note. Once the financing came in, he could pay off the higher interest notes on the pre-development costs. The limited partners also have a long-term investment in the property based on the financing with the tax credits."

But for individual investors, all of that might be too much in how the sausage was made. Sterquell could talk over their heads – even one of his CPAs he had worked with said he didn't completely understand it all. But to entice them to give him their money, some of it into seven figures, he had to give them a language they could see and understand.

Sterquell would show them his personal financial statement of approximately $8 million. He'd show them AHF's audited financial statement of about $81 million, though at the time no one knew those books were cooked. There was also a financial statement from funeral director Maurice and Mary Schooler of $25 million and their guarantee to the individual investors.

So investors in the limited partnership would have received guarantees from Sterquell personally, American Housing Foundation and Maurice and Mary Schooler.

"He'd say I'm not going to pay you at least 12 percent, but I'm going to guarantee you 12 percent," said Lovell, later Templeton's lawyer in the bankruptcy case against AHF. "AHF will guarantee that you get your 12 percent in addition to the principal. He would say that I, personally, Steve Sterquell, will guarantee that. Look how rich I am. Here's the AHF financial statement. Look at how huge we are in the low-income housing market.

"And on top of that, we can get you a big tax deduction. That's different than the tax credits although in my humble view most people didn't understand that."

That was hard to say no to. And it got even harder.

In a complicated weave, investors would be limited partners in a partnership. The limited partnership would provide financing on approval of a project that included tax credits. That would be rolled into another entity to buy and develop the apartments.

"So when it was rolled into the next entity, the developing entity would pay the soft costing financing entity and that entity would pay these investors their principal, their guaranteed rate of around 12 percent and Steve would prepare what was necessary for these investors to claim a charitable donation deduction," Lovell said.

The deduction was the difference in what the project was worth when AHF found the deal – the contract entered into for an often run-down apartment – and the worth later when the property was developed to qualify for lucrative tax credits.

"He would have that difference in the appraisals and say that is a capital gain donation, and so the investors would take deductions based upon their respective interests in that capital gain that was donated to the development entity," Lovell said. "Some of those were really really big based on the appraisals they got."

Sterquell prepared forms for investors to attach to their tax returns at the outset to show such a deduction. Then one of his clients got audited.

"And, lo and behold, they survived the audit that Steve did with the capital gains property. It passed," Lovell said. "So, man, oh man, Steve had what he really needed. Steve got permission from the guy who was audited and made copies of all of that available to them.

"That was his main marketing tool. In addition to his financial statement and AHF financial statement, when he sat down for a presentation with an investor, he would show them the audit that was passed. People would scratch their head and ask how it is possible that all I do is loan money and get interest in return and also get a charitable deduction on top of the interest.

"That's a very good question, but he would have the answer for them with this audit. He could say it works because we've done it before and this guy has made a trainload of money and the Schoolers are rolling in dough. He would give them a guarantee and say all these people are making money hand over fist plus they're getting tax deductions. They are getting rich."

Robert Templeton later learned that Sterquell would often get a friendly appraiser – one in Houston – to put high value on a piece of property. He would also get a non-recourse loan, meaning if AHF could not make payments on the property, then all the lender could do was take the property back. There would be no judgment against AHF.

Private investors had a 15-year deal on tax credits. While AHF had contingent liability to these private investors, meaning they could back out on an agreement and sue the nonprofit if losses mounted, none were going to do that.

"When it came to pass, after several years of being invested, no one would exercise that contingent liability," Robert Templeton said, "because if they did, they would lose all of those deductions for the first four to five years they were in it, and they would have huge tax consequences."

Templeton knew none of that of course when he first met Sterquell in 1997. Sterquell was a Tascosa classmate of John Smithee, Templeton's law partner. They were in Smithee's office. At the time, AHF was rocking and rolling, at least it seemed that way.

Sterquell had acquired some low-income apartments in Oklahoma City. He began to make a sales pitch to Templeton, who had heard his share of sales pitches in his life. Sterquell was persuasive.

"He said that if you'll put up $25,000, I'll get you a return in less than two years of $75,000 and I'll get you a tax deduction of a like amount," Templeton said. "It sounded too good to be true. But Steve would get up there and start writing.

"He'd say, 'Well, I'm not having to pay 18 percent because of this deduction here and that deduction there and my true interest cost is about 4 ½ percent. To me it made sense at the time."

Templeton made about five investments periodically into a limited partnership within AHF, none that exceeded $100,000 at a time. He would eventually double his money, while receiving IRS-approved tax deductions and tax credits.

David Miller, a friend of Templeton's, was an oil and gas producer. They had made a number of lucrative investments together. Miller joined his friend in investing with Sterquell but something didn't sit right with Miller after a period of time. He pulled out.

Templeton continue to invest over a nine-year period, nearly $5 million in the limited partnerships. Why not? Through the end of 2008, everything that Sterquell had promised had been delivered.

"I had great faith in him because he had performed all this time. Through the end of 2008, any payment obligation he had on those earlier partnerships he had met in a timely manner,"Templeton said. "It was a great boon to me from a tax and income standpoint. I thought Steve Sterquell was a genius."

In addition, Sterquell would furnish investors an audited tax return on AHF done by Brown, Graham and Company, P.C., certified public accountants. The last one that Templeton said he saw was in 2007. It showed a net value of $74 million. It all looked solid. Few knew then what they would later learn.

"Steve exercised substantial influence over those auditors," Templeton said. "The truth of the matter, we later found out, it wasn't an $74 million evaluation. They were about $74 million in the hole."

It's hard to know exactly when the ball of financial string started to unravel, when all the balls that Sterquell had to keep in the air began to fall one by one. But 2003 seemed to be when AHF began to get into trouble.

Expansion had been in high gear for a decade or more when the financial fuel began to run low as financing deals fell through. The Travis County Housing Finance Corp. in Austin rejected an AHF bond proposal to finance five apartment complexes. It was for just under $100 million.

That was just the beginning. With the national economy starting to sour before the housing bubble burst in 2008, and with apartment occupancy rates declining, AHF struggled to pay everyone from bondholders to individual investors to banks who funded its buying spree that peaked in 2003. From 2004 to 2007, AHF reported losses of $11 million.

"If you recall, in late 2002 and early 2003 the housing boom began which ultimately produced the debt bubble that exploded in 2008," Hoy said. "So Sterquell had at that point in time four or five low income housing apartment units that were reasonably successful and he was managing with some degree of care. But he became enamored with the notion that he could acquire more of these because of the extremely low interest rate."

The prime interest rate was 3.25 percent. Low income housing on non-recourse or recourse loans was about 1 to 1.5 percent above that. Sterquell could use the equity in the other apartments as collateral, and with a personal guarantee began an aggressive buying effort.

The AHF debt exploded from $32 million in 2002 to a whopping $340 million by the end of 2004. The interest rate was variable and so his debt was floating.

"Sterquell had thought some of this through and he went to Bank of America and got a guarantee that if the interest rate or the amount of payments exceeded a certain sum, then Bank of America would step in and pay the difference," Hoy said. "Now it wasn't 100 percent, but it would still be tremendous savings. It was like a credit default swap."

That did not come into play until 2008 when the housing debt bubble exploded and everything hit the fan. Bank of America told Sterquell there was not going to be a guarantee. It got worse because from the time he began a massive buying spree in 2003 to 2006 to when he called Bank of America about the guarantee, the prime rate almost doubled to 6.5 percent.

"Now when you're dealing with low income housing," Hoy said, "rental payments are fixed by the government, but your expenses of operation, your debt service, is not. So all of a sudden, you have this tremendous squeeze between the two. And he's running out of cash."

Sterquell sued Bank of America, but even if successful, this was going to take time. He needed a Plan B.

"Sterquell's concept was not completely out of line," Hoy said, "but he had to tell people. The problem is he didn't tell people what he was doing. Had he told people and been above board, and actually faced the consequences of this horrible situation involving the squeeze between the debt service and the income stream, he would have come out of this without any problem."

In 1999, Sterquell established a limited partnership for Maurice and Mary Schooler. AHF was the managing partner, guaranteeing Maurice had been a client of U.C. Sterquell, Steve's father. The Schoolers both had been involved in a litany of civic organizations throughout the decades.

Mary was named the 1996 Amarillo Globe-News Woman of the Year, that honor highlighted by her recovery from breast cancer and her work helping others who had faced the same health crisis.

"You would have a hard time finding a family more respected in Amarillo than those two," Templeton said.

Because of Maurice's previous business relationship with Steve's father, he trusted his son with a proposed business arrangement. He agreed without hesitation. It was a limted partnership, AHF Development, of which the Schoolers and Mary's sister, Louise Conley, owned 99 percent with AHF as the managing partner.

Sterquell talked Maurice Schooler into personally guaranteeing repayment of AHF's loans and guaranteed investments. The guarantees were absolute. If the foundation didn't repay the lenders and investors as agreed upon, the Schoolers would be totally responsible. But there seemed little risk of that. AHF's sound financial health and Sterquell's record of sound management made that extremely unlikely.

Or so they thought.

That would eventually take them into financial ruin, but for many years, it operated smoothly. Sterquell would show investors that AHF Development Ltd. (the Schooler partnership) was worth about $25 million and investors would get 12 to 18 percent return flowing out of that partnership.

The AHF Development/Schooler Partnership raised enough money from new investors to bring outstanding loans on properties current and provide rehabilitation and remodeling of many properties in disrepair, getting them to federal government standards. Eventually, Sterqeuell sought to sell them or syndicate them to corporations desiring low income tax credits. But then it played out.

"At the end of 2005 AHF Development, Ltd. sold its one remaining property and therefore was nothing more than a shell," Hoy said "Sterquell used that shell as the vehicle to initiate the scheme that he was perpetrating on the investors. He understood how everything worked, but the only problem was he was as crooked as dog's hind leg."

And in 2006 is when it began to go dark. Whatever line that wouldn't be crossed in previous years got crossed many times for the next three years.

"This is where he said, 'OK, I'm going to use this shell partnership as the vehicle to transport the money I'm getting from my investors, banks and operations from other properties and basically sanitize them for whatever purpose I want and not necessarily dedicate it to this particular project or property that it was initially given," Hoy said.

"He induced these investors, individuals like Bob and banks into thinking it was going for targeted projects. So he had this tremendous inflow of capital and if he hadn't had such an aggrandized ego and not been so arrogant, and actually used it for the right purposes, Plan B might have actually worked.

"But he spent it on hunting trips to Africa, private jets, spent it on other trips and all sorts of things that had nothing to do with AHF."

Later, during the bankruptcy proceeding, a forensics accountant testified later during the bankruptcy proceeding that his calculation showed that Sterquell flowed approximately $145 million through Schooler's AHF Development partnership between early 2007 and March 31 2009.

Things reached critical mass for Sterquell and AHF in 2008. He needed to make a big move – and it had to succeed. Most of AHF properties were financed in two major portfolios. They were cross-collateralized, which made it even tougher.

"That was very important," said Johnson, who worked for AHF fulltime beginning in that tumultuous 2008. "They were two portfolios with one lender, and all the properties were cross-collateralized. So you could not take one of the portfolios, take the best property and sell it and add more money to the bottom line. The bank will say you're diminishing the value of the whole portfolio, and essentially you were. That prevented us from doing any of these 'one-off' deals."

Debt was mounting. For the first time, he had to lay off a few employees. But Sterquell had been juggling financial balls all his career. This was another neat trick, or as Johnson called it, "his last shot in the dark."

His plan, Johnson said, was to refinance these 15 properties with more tax credits. That would allow him to go to Bank of America and show the bank that all of these apartments were ready to be financed with tax credits.

AHF had last been able to qualify for low-income housing tax credits in 2006. The office at 1800 S. Washington Avenue worked at a feverish pace in 2008 on more than a dozen tax credit applications in several states. The stress was high.

But problems arose. The foundation had compliance issues on several properties with the Texas Department of Housing and Community Affairs. In fact, AHF was on a probationary period for some of them, meaning their application was flagged. Beyond the application, those issues had to be resolved.

Another key issue was whether the original purchase of the properties had been an arm's length transaction. Larry Bunn, Sterquell's son-in-law, owned a development entity within another 501c3. It appeared this was going to be seen as a conflict of interest.

"That just lowers your (tax) basis because TDHCA looks at your costs with a fine tooth comb," said a former employee. "They want to make sure you're not padding anything so you can get more tax credits and it's like a swap in-house. They want it to be a true arm's length transaction."

There was another issue as well in how Sterquell structured the partnerships for tax exemptions. Legislation changed often with regard to tax exemption for real property. AHF needed those tax exemptions to be profitable.

"The structuring of the partnerships was just so confusing to the state," the employee said. "They would get their attorney and get into a long process with Steve on this. So if you have something that's really complicated like this, they don't want to work that hard. They would rather find a way to turn it down if it's so complicated if they can't present it to their (TDHCA) board and make them understand and approve it."

As the calendar turned to January 2009, the tension at AHF as palpable. Sterquell waited on word on the tax credit approval. Then came Jan. 31.

And he did not get it.

"Steve came into the office where the development team was, and when he found out we didn't get the credits, he just put his head in his hands," Johnson said. "You could tell that's when the ship came all the way out of the water. There was no hope."

It was quiet and businesslike in the AHF office from February into March 2009. Sterquell took some vacation time along with his son, "Sterq," but in and around that, he was working. In fact, he asked Templeton for a loan in mid-March and he provided AHF a $500,000 loan from the estate of Frances Maddox, one of his clients, at 8 percent interest.

One of the deals Sterquell quietly worked on was changing the beneficiaries of $27 million worth of Key Man life insurance, and in March of 2009 he blatantly and openly changed the beneficiaries on the $27 million in Key Man life insurance to his family. Jim Fletcher, who was then president of AHF, signed off on the change, as did a couple of other employees. Sterquell exercised complete control. That change would loom large in 2009.

"I would imagine for the next 60 days, he probably worked really hard to plan his death and get his affairs in order," Alvin Johnson said. "It was just really somber because no one was used to seeing him like this. He was a larger than life guy most of the time. For the next 60 days or so, it was really really bad."

March 31, 2009 was a Tuesday. Sterquell asked Johnson and about five others to go to lunch at a favorite Mexican restaurant in east Amarillo. The conversation was awkward, especially when Sterquell mentioned he was probably worth more dead than alive.

"He was real somber," Johnson said. "He looked at me and said, 'Alvin, are you going to be here?' And I said, 'Yeah, I'm going to be here.' He said, 'No, are you going to be here? I said again, 'Yes, I'm going to be here.'

"He said it's going to be really rough for the next few months, but he thought everybody could get through it. He didn't say 'we.' He said, 'I think everybody can get through it.' None of us really knew what that meant."

They left the restaurant. Some went back to the office. Johnson left for Waco on a business trip. The next day, April 1, was clear, calm, warm and dry.

– Reflections –

"People talk about how brilliant Steve Sterquell was. I don't know how much was brilliance. He was salesman," Templeton said. "He could sell you on about anything. Looking back on all this, there are several who say Sterquell didn't start out the way he ended. I don't know. I think if you have larceny in your heart, you have always had it. He just seized the opportunity.

"The change of beneficiaries took place in March, 2009, before Sterquell took his own life. But the theft by fraud started much earlier. From nothing in his 401k, he stole money out of AHF and built up his 401k. In a financial report to his bank, he claimed it was worth over $8 million. The money that was stolen to build up the 401k started several years before."

CHAPTER

17

A Bird's Nest On The Ground

The morning of April 1, 2009 looked like one of those rare spring days in Amarillo when the wind was light and the sun was bright. Even though it was a Wednesday work day, it was a day to find reason to be outside.

Steve Sterquell had found a reason. One day after having lunch with a number of employees, he headed south on I-27 to the second family home at the Palo Duro Club between Amarillo and Canyon. The grass needed cutting.

He never got that far. His 2007 Lexus SUV slammed into a concrete overpass pillar at an estimated 80 to 85 mph. The car was on fire. Sterquell, 56, was pronounced dead at the scene.

It didn't take long for the awful news to spread among family, friends, and to the employees and investors at his 501c3 nonprofit, American Housing Foundation. The creator and leader of one of the country's largest companies of low-income housing was tragically killed.

Glenda David was one of a handful of employees who was at work around 7:30 a.m. Word filtered in not long after that Sterquell had been in a serious accident.

"I did remember his comment the previous day about being worth more dead than alive, and it was shocking," she said. "It was like, 'What's going on?'"

Alvin Johnson, who had joined AHF 15 months previously, was in Waco on business. His phone rang about 9 a.m.

"At first, they called and said he was missing and they could not find him," Johnson said. "About 30 minutes later, I got another call to say that his car was on fire and Steve had died."

Coincidentally, Robert and Martha Templeton had also been in Waco at their second home. It was the city where they met as students at Baylor. It was about 9 a.m., and they were already on I-35 on a return trip to Amarillo. About the time Johnson's phone was ringing, Templeton's phone was too. It was from Don Storseth, a longtime friend and fellow AHF investor.

Sterquell had been killed in a car accident. That gave Templeton a lot to think over as he made his way seven hours back to Amarillo.

Sterquell's memorial service was three days later at a full First Presbyterian Church. Templeton was seated next to an aisle where the family walked down to begin the service. Betty Sterquell, Steve's mother, surprised Templeton when she stopped and quickly whispered, "Bob, we need to talk."

"She was concerned about some things as was I," Templeton said. "Betty was the strongest influence Steve had in his whole life."

They never did talk, at least not in the way Templeton thought. Very quickly, it was about to get messy – and stay messy.

The cause of the accident was suspicious from the outset. That morning was clear and dry. Traffic was moderate. No other vehicles were involved. People were talking. Templeton sent his ace investigator Jim LaFavers to investigate the crash scene. While that upset a few AHF employees who fervently believed in Sterquell, LaFavers had company. Local authorities were doing the same.

Forty-eight days later, on May 19, Randall County Justice of the Peace Clay Houdashell ruled the death a suicide. This was after investigations from the Randall County Sheriff's Department and the Texas Department of Public Safety. A witness told investigators the vehicle appeared on fire before the impact. Forensic reports indicated a measurable amount of accelerant was found in the interior of the vehicle. There did not appear to be any evidence of braking.

But questions arose well before the official ruling of Sterquell's death. It started with insurance. Sterquell had approximately $30 million in Key Man life insurance. A Key Man policy is one a company purchases on a key executive's life. The company is the beneficiary of the plan and pays the premiums.

The insurance is needed if the executive's death or incapacitation would be devastating to the future of the company. That was certainly true with Sterquell. The $30 million question was where was the life insurance money going. It was supposed to go to the company, but was it? There was a growing belief the beneficiaries of the Key Man life insurance were the Sterquell family.

Templeton led a group of creditors to hire David Mullin of the Mullin, Hoard and Brown law firm to lead a pursuit of the insurance. No one who knew was talking.

"We were very concerned," Mullin said. "There was a connection between Sterquell and a guy that lived in the Caribbean. We didn't know for a fact there was anything going on there, but we thought there might be something that would happen to that money if it were paid to the Sterquells. We were very concerned."

In a hearing with Potter County Judge Arthur Ware, he ordered depositions into the insurance mystery. In a deposition with local insurance agent Miles Harris, he revealed that Sterquell had changed the beneficiaries in the $30 million Key Man life insurance to his family. Previously, Harris had steadfastly refused to state if the beneficiaries had been changed, and, if so, to whom.

Templeton urged Mullin to get a restraining order on the release of the insurance money. The day before the suicide ruling on May 19, U.S. District Judge Robert Jones granted the motion to stop payment. It was very likely had that not happened, that $30 million was headed to an untouchable off-shore account in the Virgin Islands.

"People would say, 'My gosh, Steve, you're so brilliant, what happens if something happens to you?'" said attorney Joe Lovell, who would later represent Templeton in the bankruptcy trial. "He said, 'Oh, you don't have to worry about that. I've got $27 million in life insurance. He touted that, and everybody relied on that."

"Lo and behold, during the window of time in February and March, Sterquell started these fraudulent transfers with the life insurance to essentially his kids, and he transfers all the assets he can to his family," Lovell said. "These people he made all these promises to would be left out.

"It wasn't, 'Gee whiz aren't I a great guy? I'm going to take my life so there's plenty of money to pay off these investors.' Oh, no, it was, 'I'm going to take my life and I'm going to steal – I've already stolen this money from the investors – now I'm going to steal the life insurance from them for my family."

Something else that seemed curious to Templeton were the premium payments, or apparently the lack thereof. Attorneys began to look closer at the Key Man Life Insurance. Premiums for the bulk of the insurance, as many as $12 to $15 million on the policy, had lapsed the previous year before they had resumed in the last months of Sterquell's life.

In a hearing before Potter County Judge Arthur Ware, the judge ordered depositions into the insurance mystery. In a May 2009 deposition of local insurance agent Miles Harris, Harris revealed that Sterquell had changed the beneficiaries in the $27 million Key Man life insurance to his family. Previously Harris had steadfastly refused to state of the beneficiaries had been changed, and if so, to whom.

It was discovered that not long after AHF was denied tax credits on a refinancing deal on January 31, 2009, Sterquell began making plans. He planned his suicide, but he also planned to take care of his family through the beneficiary change that left employees and creditors in the lurch.

After the Harris deposition, Templeton urged Mullin to get a restraining order to prevent release of the insurance money. On May 19, the day before the suicide ruling, U.S. Judge Robert Jones granted the restraining order. Had that not happened, it was very possible that $27 million was headed to an untouchable off-shore

U.S. District Judge Robert Jones

account in the Virgin Islands.

The Mullin firm filed a lawsuit in early May 2009 against the AHF directors for gross mismanagement because of the beneficiary change. In depositions, Jim Fletcher, chairman of the board, admitted that the and others agreed to the change in beneficiaries.

"The bankruptcy counsel from Austin asked Mr. Fletcher if he realized he was admitting to what could be a criminal case," Templeton said. "And Jim said, "Well, that's what we did."

Something else that seemed curious to Templeton were the premium payments, or apparently the lack thereof. Attorneys began to look closer at the Key Man life insurance. Premiums for as much as $12 to $15 million of the life coverage were not timely paid the year before so those policies had lapsed, but they were reinstated in the last months of Sterquell's life with funds derived from investor. The insurance company allowed Sterquell to reinstate the lapsed policies without a renewal.

"Under Texas law, when a policy is lapsed like that, they're supposed to go through the whole process of renewal like it's a new policy," Templeton said. "Also, it starts the time running anew on a two-year period so that if he kills himself within that two-year period, suicide is a complete defense. After that, there's no defense. The major insurance company, for some reason, just let them pick up the payments without a renewal."

Lovell said had Templeton chosen to do so, he could have made a serious legal claim for $12 to $15 million of the insurance money for himself. This was because the last money that Templeton sent to AHF as an investment was traced, and that money was used to make premium payments on the life insurance policy that had lapsed.

"If I pay you for something and you defrauded me through that, and I can trace the money that I gave you to wherever you put it, then you have something," Lovell said. "It's like if I give you some money, and you go buy a house with it, even though you don't have the money any more, if I can trace that money down to the purchase of the house, I can say, 'That's my house. My money bought it.'

"Same thing with life insurance. There's a law that says if they take your money and use it to pay a premium on life insurance, the life insurance money is yours – all of it." When Templeton tried to recall why he didn't take that route, Lovell said the goal was to help all the creditors.

"Bob said the right thing to do was get the money and put that in the bankruptcy estate so it's protected and everybody can make their claims. Bob would have been in a better position to take care of Bob had he gone for the money himself as he likely had a legal claim to do at the exclusion of everyone else, but he didn't do that. I want people to know Bob did that."

Once the insurance money was prevented from transferring to the Sterquell family – and that took about a year -- Templeton, Mullin and other creditors believed they were in good position to mitigate financial losses. "We were feeling comfortable and confident," Lovell said. "We had the life insurance money. We had these guarantees. We had it all papered up. It should be pretty simple. We may lose a little bit of money but at least there's $27 million out there to go toward our claims that totaled $46 million or so."

In January of 2010 Templeton and Mike Powell, an Austin attorney representing Marshallette, Sterquell's widow, reached an agreement for Marshallette to receive a $3 million policy and the Palo Duro Club property over and above the exempted property, and by agreement the balance of the $27 million in insurance proceeds went to American Housing. That filled the bird nest. "I believed she was innocent of her husband's shenanigans , Templeton said.

That was one of the few decisions that would seem fair in the ordeal. Going forward from recovering the Key Man insurance money, nothing seemed logical or simple.

"It was a comedy of errors," Templeton said, though he was not laughing. "Had no bankruptcy ever been filed, and we collected only the $27 million, that would have repaid a high percentage of the local investors."

Templeton said his first mistake was to request the Mullin firm file a bankruptcy petition against AHF even though the foundation could not be put into bankruptcy. Since a 501c3 has directors and no stockholders, it can not be put into involuntary bankruptcy. As the case unfolded, counsel for AHF decided to convert to a Chapter 11 as a debtor in possession, and they filed a Chapter 11 debtor in possession proceeding in May of 2009. In a Chapter 11 bankruptcy a company is a debtor in possession, meaning the board of directors still had control. Fletcher hired attorney Tom Boyd to represent the board.

"He was not the kind of lawyer to get things done quickly," Templeton said. "I'll say that about him. So this thing just rocked along without anything really happening."

A debtor in possession must come forward with a plan to pay the creditors. If the debtor, American Housing Foundation, fails to do so, they lose control.

"Failure to get a plan was the monumental failure of the bankruptcy," Templeton said. "That led ultimately to why bankruptcies benefit usually one group – bankruptcy lawyers. The Gardere Wynne firm and Steve McCartin came in and saw this huge bird's nest on the ground, and helped themselves to about $12 million in insurance money.

"The directors, employees and officers of were spending most of their time just talking to creditors and really not getting anything done. I was trying to get some things done, trying to get a plan through, but I was totally inexperienced in bankruptcy."

Alvin Johnson had been appointed to the board after Sterquell's death. Templeton appealed to Johnson to devise a plan, one in which the debtor in possession, which was AHF, and the creditors committee, headed by Templeton, would present to the bankruptcy judge for a method of distribution. That was how it was supposed to work.

"I said, 'Alvin, we got to agree on a plan,'" Templeton said. "We're going to face some downstate lawyers and we're going to be in a lot of trouble. He said, 'Bob, it's out of my hands.' I said, 'Alvin, it's precisely in your hands.'"

Bankruptcy attorney David Langston, from the Mullin firm in Lubbock, eventually provided an old plan to Templeton that had been utilized in a similar bankruptcy. Templeton and Glenda David sat down in October 2009 – six months after Sterquell's death – and using that old plan as a guide. They changed the language and tweaked other areas to write a plan.

"There were other people who should have been on top of it and should have seen to it the plan was written well and went forward to the court so the board of directors could retain control of the company," Templeton said. "But they didn't do it. I'm not excluding anybody, including my lawyers, from the failure to develop a better and more timely plan."

Meanwhile Mullin, after initially working to stop the insurance money from going to the Sterquell family, continued to represent the local investors in the bankruptcy. Judge Robert Jones of Lubbock was the bankruptcy judge and the Mullin firm had experience with him.

It became clear that AHF was not really a candidate for full bankruptcy because, other than Texas Capital Bank's $5 million claim, most of the lenders on the more than 13,000 rental units of property had no recourse against AHF. When AHF borrowed the money from the lenders, the debts were non-recourse.

"If there is any lesson to be learned, it's never put the company in the hands of bankruptcy lawyers." Templeton said. "Creditors have to do everything they can to work it out. Otherwise, when the smoke clears, the entire process benefits the bankruptcy attorneys. In this case it benefitted the Gardere Wynne firm."

Mullin said AHF was Sterquell's creation, and the organization and management of it was weak.

"Steve had really run this like a dictatorship for years," Mullin said. "He had a board obedient to his will. If you look at the board minutes, the only one who ever challenged him was his own mother. She did not seem to be completely confident in her son's integrity. Everyone else just went along with what he said.

Texas Capital Bank of Dallas, one of the creditors, wanted a trustee almost from the beginning. The bank filed a motion to appoint a trustee, which was pivotal in the bankruptcy case. It would prove to be a turning point to Templeton and the rest of the local individual creditors.

"The appointment of a trustee in a Chapter 11 case where the control of the company was still with the board of directors was almost unheard of," Templeton said. "David Mullin made an impassioned plea to Judge Jones against the appointed trustee on April 27, 2010. David made a brilliant argument for two or three hours, but by then it didn't make any difference."

Judge Jones sided with Texas Capital Bank and appointed a friend, Walter O'Cheskey of Lubbock, as trustee on April 30, 2010. Templeton believed O'Cheskey to be unqualified for that level and complication of a bankruptcy case. But it didn't appear to stop O'Cheskey from wanting to be paid handsomely.

The insurance money is sitting in the bank and so O'Cheskey wanted 5 percent (commission) for doing absolutely nothing," Templeton said. "So that would have been \$1.35 to \$1.5 million. Even the way the judge was inclined, that didn't set too well. So finally Walter dropped that claim and wanted \$10,000 a month and other compensation. O'Cheskey had been a trustee for wage earner bankruptcies. He was totally in over his head."

But O'Cheskey impacted the case in a way that would reverberate to the end. He hired the Dallas firm of Gardere Wynne, and with that, its lead counsel, Steve McCartin. The bankruptcy would never look the same again. McCartin immediately took full control. It became apparent that O'Cheskey was nothing more than a figurehead.

"That changed everything," Lovell said. "And by changing everything, I mean literally everything. We entered a whole new universe at that point."

To represent the trustee in the Sterquell bankruptcy case would be any lawyer's dream. There were about 30 million reasons to dive into this case – the dollar signs were everywhere.

"McCartin submitted bills of $600 to $700 an hour with all kind of attendants and co-counsel," Templeton said. "McCartin will never again have a case like this. It was a bird's nest on the ground, no doubt about it – a bird's nest on the ground."

One of McCartin's first acts was to fire the Mullin firm, which was representing the creditors' committee. One of his next acts was to attack all the local creditors and break up the committee.

"One of the first things they did was to actually file a bunch of lies claiming I was a co-conspirator with Sterquell in the whole thing, and that got me kicked off the creditors' committee without me knowing about it," Templeton said.

It was just the beginning on a contentious battle between McCartin and the local creditors, especially Templeton, that continued into late 2010 with competing plans. Finally competing plans went to a vote in September of 2010.

Steve McCartin

The manager of a Dallas investment company that had invested $15 million with Sterquell and had voted for the creditors' plan called Templeton telling him that he was going to change his vote which would have allowed Jones to approve the trustee's plan. Templeton then realized he had to make the best deal he could before the December 10 hearing on the approval of the plan.

So Templeton and John Lovell, Joe's attorney brother, along with Langston, went to Dallas to negotiate the best deal they could. They were able to get some concessions, including a special committee that was supposed to have strong influence over O'Cheskey and McCartin. A compromise was reached and the creditors agreed to Gardere's plan with some changes.

"We felt reasonably good about our ability to be properly represented from that point on," Templeton said. "I had David Mullin question McCartin, and in December of 2010 McCartin said in open court that he would abide by the compromise."

If Templeton felt "reasonably good" about representation going forward, it was a temporary victory that evaporated quickly. Judge Jones said that he was not bound by any of those recommendations.

"That was my third real warning of how the judge would treat us," he said. "And after that, McCartin ignored the committee, and, in fact, tried to organize another committee to do the same job. Essentially he ignored the committee and failed to abide by the agreed changes."

Jones was a graduate of Texas Tech and the Tech School of Law. He was one of six federal judges on the bankruptcy court for the Northern District of Texas. He was appointed to the bankruptcy court in 2000 for a 14-year term. Each of the 94 federal judicial districts in the U.S. have a bankruptcy court. Bankruptcy cases can not be filed in state court.

"(U.S. District) Judge Mary Lou Robinson recused herself because of me and our friendship," Templeton said. "If Mary Lou had retained the case, she would have had control of the damn case, and it would have gone entirely different. No question about it.

"We were dealing with a stacked deck. It was the worst stacked deck you could find. We knew if there was any discretion or opportunity, the judge would rule for Gardere, and he did it time and again and again and again."

After McCartin fired Mullin, Joe Lovell – "one helluva lawyer, a natural," Templeton said – was tabbed to represent his former boss on claims by Templeton and other local investors. It was going to be a challenge since Lovell had little to no bankruptcy experience.

"Poof, you're gone," Lovell said. "They were fired. The Mullin firm is just flat out. O-U-T. Out."

Since Mullin represented the entire creditors' committee, the firm could no longer represent an individual. It was seen as a conflict of interest. So it was up to each creditor to secure an attorney. Mullin encouraged John Lovell, Joe's brother, and the firm of Lovell, Lovell and Isern to represent the creditors.

"It was like we don't know what to do," Joe said. "We're not bankruptcy lawyers. Mullin said we will help you."

With a plan that got rammed down the throat of the creditors, representing Templeton's claim would have been the challenge of a career for even the most experienced bankruptcy lawyer.

"It fell to Joe to try and help me," Templeton said. "Though he wasn't a bankruptcy lawyer, he did as good a job as a man could do. Very loyal. Every time we had an issue Jones always ruled in favor of the trustee and against us."

On the opposing end, the way Templeton saw it, McCartin's tactic was pretty simple. That was to deny any limited partnership claim by local creditors. Stretch it out, make it expensive for creditors to continue to pursue their legal claim to get their money back. McCartin even told Templeton and Lovell, straight out, that he and his client did not have incentive to reach an agreement to pay any of the investors. "We get to fight you with your own money," McCartin said, referring to the insurance money that Templeton and the investors had collected and placed with the bankruptcy court.

One of the creditors was Terry Horton. His case was the first one tried. Sterquell had taken advantage of Horton's Christian faith. Sterquell had talked Terry into making a $1.4 million guaranteed investment in HURIKE, Ltd. Terry Horton's claim was denied.

Templeton said "When the judge did that, even I, Robert the optimist, realized what we were up against."

The investors' claim was to get paid back by AHF for the guaranteed portion of their investment. Some of them had their life savings in the investments, but they believed they had documents with guarantees they would be paid back by AHF.

"Here's an example. A Mr. Scott has $1 million in a limited partnership and had an agreement he would be paid back with a guarantee of 12 percent of the increased value of the interest," Lovell said.

"So the basic claim would be 'Well, I loan you $1 million. You agree to pay me back. If you go into bankruptcy, I get to go to the bankruptcy court and say that here's my note right here, and it says I loaned Sterquell $1 million and he has to pay me back $1 million plus interest. So I have a claim to whatever is there in the estate so I can get repaid.'"

Creditors heard Gardere Wynne attorneys claim the creditors did not give AHF equivalent value for the guarantees, even though it was undisputed that Sterquell took the investors' money and ran it through AHF Development to pay AHF's and Sterquell's debts and expenses. The local creditors put up their savings. The money went to support AHF, pay mortgage payments, pay employees, etc. This was just another specious attack. They were also accused of being part of a tax scheme, of being part of a Ponzi scheme, of "clawbacks" by the trustee, of subordination. Templeton, more than any creditor, had his character attacked.

"They accused me of every wrongdoing they could find," he said. "They lied about me and continued to lie about me. They said I was a co-conspirator with Sterquell in all of this. I was their enemy. I was the force of their opposition, at least in the way they perceived it. Looking back, I don't know how I endured it, but I did."

There was the incident of the tax returns. In July 2010, McCartin began to urge the court to require Templeton to produce his personal income tax returns for a number of years. As the 5th

Circuit stated in oral argument, since the loss was real any claim on a tax return was immaterial. Put simply, if a thief steals your money it's the theft that counts and nothing else.

At the same time, Jones had a female briefing clerk who for a while seemed to be seeking the attention of McCartin, to say the least, according to several in the courtroom. Some might have called it borderline flirting. Templeton said she was making "goo-goo eyes" at the Gardere attorney.

"It was pretty obvious she wanted a job with McCartin," he said. "After a while, she quit making 'goo-goo eyes' and I could see a real change in her attitude. I asked her at one point if she were going to work for Gardere and she said an emphatic 'no.'"

On July 6, 2010, a Tuesday, an order came from Jones office, which Templeton is convinced was authored by this briefing clerk, ordering him to produce tax returns from a number of years back by Friday. On July 7th, the next day, she joined the Gardere firm.

"Then she makes her little announcement that she is going to work for Gardere," Templeton said. "What do you know? These kind of things speak volumes of what we were up against. The order was overreaching, and Joe filed a motion to set it aside.

Templeton's claim was tried over eleven months, two to three days a month, a total of 25 trial days during that time. "Pure hell," he called it.

Gardere first took the position of questioning whether AHF received equivalent value of the investments and whether the investments were made by Templeton in good faith.

"That became the defense to the claims," Lovell said, "you didn't give value for that – you did not make the investment in good faith, and that really became a fight – whether or not these investments were good faith investments. That ended up turning on the fight over the tax deductions."

The trustee took the position that the deductions were part of a tax scheme claiming they were not made in good faith. Lovell got jammed with that time and again, the investment was not made in good faith and therefore the trustee did not have to pay that.

But Amarillo tax attorney Bill Hoy, who could not testify for Templeton because he represented another plaintiff in a partnership, disagreed. He said the court never analyzed what the creditors were faced with in regard to their liability against the tax code. Hoy said "Those like Bob, and many others with claims, said, 'Sterquell stole the money from us. We should be participants in the bankruptcy estate like anybody else because he owes us money.'

"The trustee countered, saying, 'No, no, no. You invested in fraudulent tax shelters.'

"It's only fraud if you knew Sterquell was stealing your money and you took the deductions anyway. And even if you did know the guy was stealing your money, you are probably still entitled to the deduction because he stole it from you. So if Bob Templeton puts $200,000 into an investment and gets zero out of it, it ain't no tax shelter."

A second argument McCartin made was for "clawbacks," the position that over the years the investors in previous deals got paid money – got their interest payments and got their principal paid back. The argument was that the investments were part of a Ponzi scheme, and so before the investors could be paid, they first had to pay back into the bankruptcy estate all of the money they had ever received on their earlier and existing AHF-related investments.

For the trustee to clawback any money from Templeton or the other investors, the judge would have to find that their investments were not made in good faith. In other words, that the investors knew the investment was a fraud or part of a Ponzi scheme.

The limited partnership contained a clear promise to pay back the investor. It was guaranteed by AHF, Sterquell personally, and by the Schoolers. The Schoolers could not escape the guarantees and took bankruptcy.

"Truth of the matter, it was both," Templeton said. "I even got up one time to talk, haltingly, when I knew Jones was going to rule against me, and said, "It's not 'either or,' it is both. The limited partnership was a hybrid document that was authored by Sterquell.

"It was in part a limited partnership and in part a promise to pay back the debt guaranteed by Sterquell. But the judge never ruled that way, never saw it like that. He came down on the ruling. Look, this judge was disposed for that trustee and Gardere Wynn from the word 'go'. Period. Paragraph."

The dye was cast in the first creditors case. Terry Horton invested $1.4 million in a limited partnership with AHF. Jones ruled that Horton's claim was "equitably subordinated because he did not give equivalent value" even though he gave AHF $1.4 million for the investment. The judge ruled it a tax scheme, not in good faith, and denied Horton's claim.

Subordination means a creditor doesn't get paid until all creditors get paid in full. "Which means for all intents and purposes you're not getting paid," Lovell said. "There wasn't enough money there to pay the approved creditors and everybody knew it.

"We won on most of the technical issues, but Judge Jones would still come around at the end of the day and subordinate the claims. In my viewpoint, he was trying to be consistent in the face of ever more troubling evidence that maybe he had not made the completely right decision in the beginning. But that didn't do any good for our people who were subordinated."

Another case which illustrates the depths that Sterquell went to was with a man from New Mexico who trusted him. Robert Duncan, former state senator and Texas Tech chancellor who later was a guiding force in the Texas Tech vet school, represented the creditor. "Bob Duncan called it 'steal and re-steal'," Lovell said. "That's because what Sterquell was doing was defrauding this guy early on, paying him back, then defrauding him out of money again and then killing himself.

"McCartin's argument was that, even though Sterquell had originally defrauded the investor of his trust funds, now the trustee was entitled to claw back from the investor the amounts Sterquell had earlier returned to the investor. 'Steal and re-steal' again, but this time by the bankruptcy trustee. That is hard to swallow. I mean, that is hard to swallow."

The Gardere Wynne firm claimed Ponzi scheme in all of the cases, alleging that other victims of the Ponzi scheme were harmed by the principal and interest payments AHF made to Templeton and the other guaranteed investors, even though they, too, were victimized by Sterquell's fraud.

"McCartin made these clawback claims based on a Ponzi scheme against Bob," Lovell said. "We won all of those because it was not a Ponzi scheme and because it was a legitimate business. Of course, Bob didn't get his claim either because it was subordinated."

Sterquell's fraud was never a Ponzi scheme. A Ponzi scheme is a form of fraud that lures investors and pays profits to earlier investors with funds from the most recent investors. Victims believe the profits are from legitimate means and are unaware of the source of the funds. The most famous Ponzi scheme in history broke in New York in 2008, the year before Sterquell's death. Bernie Madoff was later sentenced to 150 years for bilking 4,800 clients out of $19 billion. But here's a difference in the Madoff and Sterquell bankruptcy. In early 2019, Bloomberg reported about 70 percent of the $19 billion – roughly $13.3 billion – had been recovered for the victims by the New York attorney overseeing the liquidation of Madoff's firm in bankruptcy court.

"McCartin kept saying, 'It's a Ponzi scheme, it's a Ponzi scheme, it's a Ponzi scheme,' and we were always fighting that, saying, 'No, it's not a Ponzi scheme,'" Lovell said. "AHF was a legitimate business. It owned 13,000 to 14,000 rental units. A legitimate business can not be a Ponzi scheme."

If there is a consolation – and it's a small one if it is – Jones agreed with Lovell's argument.

"That's what I mean when we won on most of the hard issues, but ultimately, the judge would decide to be consistent with the Horton decision and that these claims were subject to equitable subordination, which means they don't get paid.

"That's what happened to Bob. McCartin believed they were going to tag Bob for$1 million in clawback liability. Bob was put up as the ultimate great case they had. They thought they could win that coming and going, that no matter what, they could clean Bob's clock. In fact, they did not.

"They looked at it as a loss because they didn't get anything against Bob. They got no clawback. Of course, we looked at it as a loss because Bob's claim was subordinated.

It was hard for Mullin – and many others – to understand how lending institutions could come out of the bankruptcy in much better shape than individuals, many of whom got taken in by Sterquell's salesmanship and credentials.

"He didn't trick everybody, but he was a compelling speaker and could be mesmerizing," Mullin said. "He could trick a lot more than he didn't. It wasn't fair to deny these everyday people their claims."

Templeton eventually appealed to the Fifth Circuit of Appeals in New Orleans. Lovell made the oral argument in front of the bench. Templeton felt reasonably well when the court said his tax returns were irrelevant and the focus appeared to be how much he had lost.

"We went out of the hearing thinking we had won," he said, "but there was this one little case that said if this limited partnership that I had invested in was somehow connected to AHF, then the claim was subordinated. If it was subordinated, there wasn't enough money to pay all the creditors.

"That meant I got nothing. That was the end of it. That was the end. I fought it all the way and on a claim that the partnership was somehow an affiliate of AHF, that was it."

In essence, Lovell won a number of battles in his oral argument in front of the Fifth Circuit Court of Appeals, but he ultimately lost the war.

"In oral arguments, we saw the three-judge panel shoot down the Ponzi scheme argument, the relevance of any tax returns, and give attention to the actual loss," Templeton said. "But as so often happens when an appellate court wants to approve and affirm a local court, they seized on the tern 'affiliate'. Walden II, under any definition, was not an affiliate; it was clearly a limited partnership by its own terms and was never an affiliate. But once the Fifth Circuit ruled, it was over."

Ten years after all of this went down, Templeton said if he knew then what he knows now, he would have walked away from it all the moment he got a call from Don Storseth that Steve Sterquell had died in a car wreck south of Amarillo. But his motivation, in addition to recovering his money, was to help his fellow creditors who had been taken.

Plumber Bill Scott of Scottco. Susie Miller. Maurice and Mary Schooler. Terry Horton. Don Storseth. It's a long list of people who fell by the legal wayside in the fight against Gardere Wynne.

"There was a terrible injustice done to some of the local creditors," Mullin said. "Susie Miller, David Miller's widow. She had $600,000, which was basically her entire life's savings, everything she had in the world, and she put it with Sterquell.

"Lost it. Judge Jones basically said she can't recover anything because she's in on it. She was an equity holder or whatever. Come on, it was a fraud. She was defrauded. She was an unsecured $600,000 creditor. Sterquell took that money from her under the guise of being in church with her."

The Schoolers were the biggest monetary victims. They had total trust in Sterquell. He got them to invest millions in a limited partnership, and then to guarantee other investors. In all they signed for about $46 million in guarantees. They thought there was nothing to be worried about. They had seen Sterquell's financial statement, the AHF financial statement. The 2008 audited financial statement for AHF showed net assets of $84 million, which was false. There were millions and millions in both, but those were paper lies.

The Schoolers took bankruptcy.

Perhaps the most cold and heartless transactions was conducted within family. Randy Sharp, Sterquell's brother-in-law and who was on the AHF board, sold some land in New Mexico with an approximate value of $6 million. Sterquell told him to avoid a capital gains tax, he should give him the $6 million and it would be sheltered. Not only would he avoid taxes, but he would realize a return on it.

"Such nice people," Templeton said of the Sharps. "Such victims."

"He takes the whole $6 million," Mullin said "He just stole the whole thing. All of it. All their money."

As for Templeton, he worked on two claims connected with Sterquell. One was a malpractice suit against Sterquell's accounting firm and the other against American Housing Foundation's accountant for providing misleading audits on the financial well-being of AHF.

Templeton settled with Sterquell's widow on January 10, 2010. He met with Mike Powell, Marshallette's lawyer, in Amarillo. Sterquell had a retirement plan that at one time he said was worth $8 million. Sterquell invested mostly in limited partnerships in Dallas. Powell told Templeton that Sterquell's retirement plan had some limited partnership interests. Powell said they had no value, and he offered them in settlement.

"We took those assets in the retirement plan, and we put them into a new corporation called 'PSF'," Templeton said. "Gradually, over the years and through a separate lawsuit, we found that at least three of those partnerships were valuable."

Hoy set up the corporation and listed all local creditors, giving them a percentage of the corporation based on the claims they had made to AHF.

"It gradually unfolded," Templeton said. "There was the Denton Crossing agreement. There was the Lubbock 82 Partners and one other through protracted litigation and collection from the limited partnerships." Those creditors have received approximately $4 million of which the final distribution was made in the fall of 2020, more than 11 years after Sterquell's death.

"My cost was seven years out of my life pursuing the malpractice cases, the Schooler bankruptcy, the limited partnerships and finally defending myself. I was trying everything in the world to help my fellow creditors," Templeton said. "The bottom line is it was seven years out of my life.

"I guess there are forms of medieval torture. I always heard it is the anticipation of that torture that drives a man mad, and not the actual torture. I lived like that for a long time."

That lasting impact of Steve Sterquell and AHF is wide and almost unending. The heartache was immense – to his family and employees, not all, but most of whom were in the dark. There were the victims – the private investors who placed their trust in a charming, seemingly brilliant accountant who could help them while helping others, but lost millions.

But not everyone lost, not everyone had heartache. Bankruptcies often benefit one group and just one – bankruptcy lawyers. The Gardere Wynne firm and trustee Walter O'Cheskey were the financial winners. That Key Man life insurance of nearly $27 million the creditors fought hard to keep from the Sterquell family? Gardere Wynne swooped in and helped itself to at least $12 million of it.

A bird's nest on the ground? Well, yes, but more than that, it was a pot of gold at the end of the rainbow, and this one was real.

Nearly all of his life Templeton's thoughts become organized and crystallized at different times. It's something he can not force of will. It just happens. It happened in almost all of his biggest trials and it happened in this one, the Sterquell bankruptcy trial.

A decade after its completion, hard feelings linger. They linger because when right is weighed against wrong, and wrong wins, those feelings are not easy to dismiss. In the final days of the book's completion, after hours of discussing American Housing Foundation, its victims, the trial, the lawyers, it was thought the whole thing was put to bed. Then Templeton's thoughts crystallized once again in an unfiltered and honest observation:

"Early on in the bankruptcy, before the December 10, 2010 hearing in which Steve McCartin and Walter O'Cheskey were approved, McCartin took control of the trustee, O'Cheskey. I visited with McCartin briefly and asked what he specialized in.

"I solve puzzles," he said.

"I didn't know at the time what that meant. At the appointment of O'Cheskey and McCartin, David Mullin, my counsel was there, and I was between David and McCartin and put a hand on the shoulder of each of them and said, "Welcome to my new friend."

"McCartin shot back, 'If you want a friend, get a dog.' I didn't know exactly what he meant at the time, but I got the message. I later learned what he meant by solving puzzles.

"There wasn't much of a puzzle about this bankruptcy. McCartin, as a bankruptcy lawyer, was supposed to represent the client. The trustee is supposed to represent the client. But, really, who was the client in this case? Sterquell was dead. American Housing Foundation was a 501(c)3 corporation that had no stockholders, only a board of directors who had been appointed.

"So, really, it was like a nonexistent client. To whom do you give your loyalty? What does a bankruptcy lawyer do? One thing he has to do is make a living. How did they make a living out of this particular case? It was as obvious to a good bankruptcy lawyer as the nose on his face.

"One, he has to spend time on the case and he has to get the court to approve his fees. McCartin billed at $700 an hour and $500 an hour for the second chair and on and on and on. But how could he justify those fees? What was involved.

"There were basically only a few creditors. The lenders who had financed the purchase of the 13,000 to 14,000 apartment complex units were on what is called a 'non-recourse debt'. That meant all they could look to would be the foreclosure of those properties, and most were not worth the purchase price when Sterquell bought them.

"The second category were those who had purchased all of those tax credits and had been on those tax credits for five or six years. It was a given by anyone who understood taxes that they could not renege on those tax credits. If they did, there would have been a tremendous tax burden, so that wasn't going to happen.

"Now who else was involved? Well, there was a bank or two, and there was an investing company in Dallas that had given AHF $15 million in a jicky way. Then there were local creditors who were the true victims in this case.

"Texas Bank, one of the banks involved, had pushed very hard for a trustee in April of 2010. The bank was on the good side of

McCartin as was later shown. The investing company was a $15 million creditor that should have been disallowed because it was a jicky deal from the start. McCartin chose not to fight them. So who did he have left that he could spend time trying to disallow their claims.

"Obviously, these victims – mostly local people, lifelong friends of Sterquell who had put their full trust in him, and what could you do there? Oh, yeah, well, you could contest those claims on many levels in any way you could, and that's what McCartin did.

"In fact, on one of the Schooler claims, which should have been allowed, the counsel from Austin representing the Schoolers when McCartin filed their objection to the claim tried to say, 'OK, we'll drop our claim and you drop your claim against us because there is really no basis for that.' Would the Gardere Wynne firm, of which McCartin was a partner, do that? Of course not. They went through a considerably long trial where they ran up fees after fees after fees.

"The same thing happened in my case. In my case they fought it for 13 months, two or three days each month, in every way they could. So they were able to run up some major fees. The total amount charged by just the Gardere Wynne firm, not including their experts and their hangers-on and their paid witnesses, was at least $12 million.

"Now in this bankruptcy as it was when McCartin and O'Cheskey came on, we had already recovered $27 million of Key Man life insurance. We creditors put that back into the bankruptcy, naively thinking we would be the beneficiaries of that as creditors. And then there was the $3 million against the directors for gross negligence.

"Believe me, if there is any way you can describe negligence as being gross, this was. It was totally run by Sterquell, totally dominated by Sterquell, and totally ruined by Sterquell. So there was $30 million sitting there where Gardere Wynne took over. McCartin, through various efforts against some of the victims, extracted money from them – some from David Miller, some from the Sharps – which added to the $30 million.

"A part was from a few properties that they were actually able to sell that had a market value over and above the amount owed. But those were simple things. Those were not difficult things. No. Had Gardere Wynne and McCartin come in and said, 'Well, we can make this simple and do this quickly,' they might have had about $2 million in fees, not $12 million. But that wouldn't have done McCartin much good. He needed to show come income for the bankruptcy section of his firm.

"This was truly a bird's nest on the ground – not just a bird's nest on the ground but a bird's nest full of golden eggs that needed to be gathered. What did he need? He needed to spend time contesting all of those people who finally gave up one by one, and he needed to have a judge say, 'OK, do it.'

"Early on, we should have realized how it was going to be. I remember the December 10 hearing when McCartin got up and said he agreed to these terms where there is an oversight committee and you do this and that and give us creditors some kind of protection. But Judge Jones said at the hearing on his own from the bench, 'Well, I don't have to abide by any of these terms,' and he didn't.

"Little things, I remember in the course of one of these two-or three-day hearings against me, a second chair for Gardere Wynn was the primary examiner of a witness putting forward some evidence. He wasn't doing the job to suit McCartin who stood up and took over examination of the witness.

"There is a fundamental rule in Texas and in most jurisdictions that a side gets one lawyer to a witness. It's a given in trial court and very few exceptions. I said to attorney Joe Lovell, 'Joe, get up and object. He doesn't have the right to get up and take over the examination.' Joe got up and made an objection. The judge said 'Oh, no. I wouldn't keep Mr. McCartin from going ahead and questioning the witness.' And it was the way he said it too. One can't describe in written words how sweetly the judge said that.

"There were other things that took place. Obviously in the Terry Horton case, which was clearly a $1.4 million theft and fraud upon Horton in December of 2008, the judge some way found reason to hold – and I don't know how – it got 'subordinated,' which meant Horton didn't get a dime. There was $30 million sitting there less the $2.4 million that Mullin had charged.

"Now McCartin could have stopped right there and said, 'OK, we are going to make distribution to those victims so that you don't suffer.' I mean, even the Bernie Metaph. victims did much better. And these victims were justified in what they did – totally justified. There was not a single person who put money with Sterquell who didn't have a good reason for doing so, and didn't have a good reason to trust him. So would stopping there have been the lawyer-like thing to do, the moral thing to do?

"Of course, I have my opinion, and the answer to that is an obvious 'yes.' But McCartin went way past that, especially as to me because at the start he claimed I was part of the conspiracy. He claimed that I was a conspirator with Sterquell in trying to defraud people, which was an out and out lie.

"Just like a lot of things said in court, there is this 'qualified immunity,' and lawyers can say things in pleadings and in court that are libelous and slanderous and get away with it because they are 'immune' from that in a lawsuit. They were smart enough to never open their mouths outside of court.

"So here we are. I'm writing this little book, and I have the right to tell it like it was. The readers can draw their own conclusions. My conclusion is to avoid bankruptcy, avoid bankruptcy court, and avoid greedy bankruptcy lawyers."

– Reflection –

"Joe Lovell fought hard. He worked like a Trojan even though he had no experience in bankruptcy. He never lost his temper. He totally respected the Courts."

CHAPTER

18

Family, Clubs, Cards And Slim

A blind date lasted 64 years of marriage. Actually, it was one day shy of 64 years. Martha Williams was the Baylor suitemate of Mary Tom Templeton, Robert Templeton's younger sister. He was in his second year of law school at Baylor.

At the encouragement, or maybe even the insistence of Mary Tom, Martha and Robert went out together. She had the only car. Templeton didn't have much money, so they sneaked into a Waco drive-in theater. They didn't watch much of the movie, but they didn't do what a lot that age did at a drive-in theater either.

Instead, they mostly talked. Martha proved to be a good listener. One date became two, and two became three, and three became... They loved the other for who each was, and accepted each other's flaws. They married on June 12, 1954 in her hometown of Austin.

Linda was born in November 1955 in a two-year stretch when the Templetons were in Ohio. Robert was fulfilling a commitment at Wright-Patterson Air Force Base.

The other two children were born after Templeton returned to his childhood hometown to begin practicing law. Martha, because of a low thyroid condition, miscarried when she was 5 ½ months pregnant in 1958. She miscarried again before Tom was born in 1960. Luanne, the youngest, was born in 1964.

In 1967, home was at 1510 S. Rusk, a home that banker Coney

Burgess once owned. It was where the Templeton children grew up, went to school. It was a time of growth in different ways for all five of them.

"There were good times there," Templeton said. "Loved that place. It was a great house."

Even though her husband had a difficult time leaving a lawsuit at the office, Martha tried to keep the two separate and distinct. She was a mother, a housewife, a good tennis player. She got her real estate license and dabbled in that bit.

"Martha was always sensible, conservative about money, a good solid thinker," Templeton said. She said I could be gullible and naïve, and she was probably right. Sometimes she would see the glass half empty. I always saw it half-full."

But like any busy home, there were real-life issues. When Martha was pregnant with Tom, she was given hormone injections. Since then, there have been numerous studies on the link with progesterone and the sexuality of a new-born baby.

A study in 2017 by the Department of Public Health of the University of Copenhagen in Denmark said there are "clear indications" that an adult is more likely to identify as bisexual or homosexual if the mother received progesterone while pregnant.

"For 32 weeks, Martha was given hormone injections by her doctor," Templeton said. "Tom's brain was not masculinized because of those shots. He was born gay."

They knew he was different. He wanted to wear girls' clothes as a young boy. It was hard for parents to understand other differences, but they still loved him.

"I loved that boy and he loved me," Templeton said, "but there was no one as close as he and Martha. Tom realized he was gay when he was about 15. He told me about it. That's a hard thing for a young man to do – a hard thing."

Tom fought depression from the age of 15. He received therapy and Robert and Martha talked to counselors in the mid-1970s to get a better grasp on what their son was facing and how better to help him.

"It was very stressful," Templeton said, "and that was during some years when I had some of the toughest lawsuits I had."

Tom was smart, nearly 6 feet tall. He studied art, graduated from SMU in Dallas. He was in Dallas when he died in July 1988 at age 28.

"We never got over Tom dying," Templeton said. "Just never got over it."

Linda Cunyus has been the bookkeeper for her father's firm, in his words, "forever." Luanne is a certified occupational therapist, graduating from Texas Tech. She had four children, and in 2019, moved from Amarillo to East Texas.

To escape and get some balance in his life, two of Templeton's pursuits have been golf and card games, namely poker and gin. Golf has taken him to such courses as Augusta National in Georgia, home of The Masters, and the renowned courses on the California coast like Cypress Point and Pebble Beach.

Templeton never had time or the inclination for golf until after Baylor Law School when he was at Wright-Patterson Air Force Base in Ohio. He never took a lesson. He began playing right-handed, and did so for about 10 years.

But he's also cross dominant, meaning his right eye is his master eye, and his left hand is dominant. After a decade or so, he switched to play left-handed which required all new clubs. He eventually played the best golf of his life left-handed, getting down to a 9-handicap.

"I might have had three lessons in my life," he said. "I was self-taught, which was terrible. But we had a lot of fun in those days."

He had a lot of fun on the golf course mainly with a character named Conley Bishop. He grew up in Clarendon, and worked as a printer at KFDA television. Templeton can't recall exactly how he met him, but Lon Moser, his old law partner in the 1960s, had KFDA as a client, so that likely was the reason,

When Bishop was 16 he lost his right arm due to an accidental discharge from a shotgun. It didn't slow him down much. He didn't have an enemy, and after his wife died, he went through a series of girlfriends. His name for his friend? "Templeton, you turkey."

"He was just a fun guy, that's all there was to it," Templeton said. "He really enjoyed life. He could do so much with that one arm. The only thing he couldn't do was tie his shoes."

He never could get a ball all that high in the air, but had a sixth sense on where to hit to get it to roll and roll. He was an extraordinary putter. If Bishop had a 30-footer on the final hole, he'd take bets on whether he'd make it, and usually get odds. More times than not, those long putts would roll in.

If the weather was nippy on a cold morning of golf, Bishop might have a little nip with him tucked in his golf bag. One morning at Ross Rogers Golf Course, he packed a bottle of whiskey for a foursome that included Templeton and his former partner R.C. Hamilton, a pretty fair golfer himself. Bishop and Hamilton were betting on each hole.

Bishop took a swig, and passed it to Hamilton, who, likewise, took a swig. Hamilton won every hole through the first eight holes. Bishop kept doubling after each lost hole and found himself down about $700.

"I remember it like it was yesterday," Templeton said. "They get up to the ninth tee. R.C. had been drinking and playing lights out. Conley knew how to hold his liquor pretty good, but on the ninth tee, I could see R.C. swaying back and forth pretty good.

"R.C. missed his tee shot and couldn't hit a thing. He was drunk as could be. He took a 9 or 10 on the last hole, and Conley bogeyed. Conley won all his money back, and then several hundred dollars from R.C. He was a lot of fun."

A former client in Los Angeles got him on famed Cypress Point and Pebble Beach in California. He played Augusta twice and saw The Masters three times. He and several from Amarillo were guests in the 1970s of Billy Morris, owner of Morris Communications, parent company of the Amarillo Globe-News. Morris Communications was headquartered in Augusta, Ga. Morris was a member of Augusta National Golf Club.

"I don't know why they picked me at the time, but they did,"

Templeton said. "Dick Harris (president of First National Bank) and I slept in the Eisenhower cabin. We were in two beds next to each other. Dick had a habit of talking in his sleep that I didn't know at the time. In the middle of the night, I heard Dick say, 'Get up, Shorty!' And he said that two or three more times. So I got up. I thought he was talking to me. Shorty was his wife."

Templeton broke 90, and won a bet with Bishop before he left that he couldn't break 90. The contingent played from the club tees, but the undulating fairways, the fast greens, the challenging second cut, that was all the same.

"You had a caddy, and he knew where to tell you to hit your approach shot on the green, which direction to putt, how hard to putt," Templeton said. "Otherwise, you wouldn't get close to the hole. He'd have you 10 feet to the right of the hole, and if you didn't do exactly what he said, the ball would end up 10 feet to the left of the hole."

Templeton had four holes-in-one – two at Amarillo Country Club, one at Tascosa Country Club, and one with his lawyer friend, Tom Morris, on what Templeton said was a "postage stamp" green on the famed Prestwick course in Scotland.

"If I ever say anything about that hole-in-one, Tom says, 'Yeah, that was the worst looking hole-in-one I ever saw. It hit the front edge of the green and rolled 50 yards into the cup. Terrible looking,'" Templeton said. "And I just say, 'It was a hole-in-one, Tom.'"

For most of his golf-playing life, Templeton was a 13-14 handicap – "I just willed it in," he said. By the time he began to really learn the game, his shoulder got so bad he couldn't play.

But his shoulder didn't affect his shuffling cards. More than even golf, it's been poker, and later, gin, that have been his playtime pursuits. Templeton began playing poker some at Baylor and at Wright-Patterson and accelerated the pace when he moved to Amarillo to start his law career.

He was in his 20s, and would sometimes stay up half the night playing with Bishop, and a man named Claude Killingsworth, among others. He had the energy to get up at the usual time the next morning and put in a full day's work. They didn't play for much money because no one had much money. But he got good at the game

He later played with Jay and Billy O'Brien, Leon Cizon, Kenny Wagner and Dr. Rick Clark. Jay O'Brien kept recruiting players to the game, players who usually weren't as good as the regulars. They had a table at the Amarillo Country Club. It was supposed to close at midnight, but they'd be betting and calling until as late as 3 a.m.

While Templeton didn't play for much money in the 1950s, that changed 20 years later. There were nights when Templeton would win as much as $5,000. He got the nickname, somewhat kiddingly, somewhat not, of "The Professor." Clothier Eric Corbyn called Templeton "the best poker player I ever saw."

They would often play draw poker, in which after drawing hands, one card, a "goofus," would be turned up for all players to have in common. It was in draw poker that Templeton and Billy O'Brien had a memorable showdown.

Both had good hands. Templeton's hand was full of hearts. He drew a card that gave him a high heart flush, one short of a straight flush. The two bet. O'Brien put all his money in, and Templeton put most of his in. O'Brien bet, and Templeton called.

"He turned over a full house, maybe aces high. Billy started dragging in the pot," Templeton said. "I said, 'Billy, that's a heckuva hand, but not quite good enough.' That goofus card gave me a straight heart flush. Billy took one look at that, bolted out of his chair and left the game."

Templeton discovered strategies in poker that were similar to those in trial – facts, opponents, intuition, boldness.

"In poker, you're doing everything," he said. "You're calculating percentages, and it's like a lawsuit in a way. In lawsuits, you're looking at facts. Then you're looking at what chips you got compared to them. Then you're studying your opponent and let your intuition help you on whether to call, raise or fold.

"If you're a really good poker player, you could make a really good lawyer as far as trying lawsuits. It's people and courage. I know why people do nothing but play poker. But I could never do it. It's just something I did."

Poker is its own unique game. Players good at one card game doesn't always mean an easy transition to poker. Morris "Snake" Bailey was an exceptional gin player, and started playing poker. On one memorable night, Templeton won $20,000 off Bailey.

"He sent me two or three checks for the amount," Templeton said. "I tore up two and cashed one for $8,000. I said, 'Morris, I don't think poker is your game.' He agreed with me and never played again. He tried to bull the game."

Templeton expanded his competitive card nature beyond Amarillo Country Club to Las Vegas and elsewhere. He and Martha were frequent visitors to Vegas. Most of the time it was random playing at various casinos. But he also got to know "Amarillo Slim" Preston, whose celebrity as a poker player exploded in 1972 when he won the World Series of Poker tournament. He appeared several times on "The Tonight Show" with Johnny Carson and never said no to a publicity stunt.

Slim made Amarillo his landing base. It's where his three children were raised and where he lighted when he wasn't traveling the country plying his trade. Slim, who would become one of Templeton's clients, first got him into some major poker tournaments.

He got him into one in Mississippi where he played Omaha poker and finished third out of 150 players. He went to Reno, and didn't do much. But twice he was in Las Vegas tournaments where he placed both times. Once he did well enough to get his entry fee back, and another time he did well enough to finish 11th out of 250 entrants.

Templeton's best day of poker in Las Vegas may have come out of desperation. He and Martha were having breakfast with Slim. Johnny Moss was a legendary player who was now getting up in years. The three-time World Series of Poker champion, including the first one in 1970, had mounting bills. His wife was also in a nursing facility. Moss was attempting to sell some of her jewelry, which included a

Templeton's family at Christmas in the 1970's: (from left), Luanne, Tom, Linda, Martha and their dogs.

A contengent of Amarillo golfers prior to teeing off at Augusta National Golf Club in 1975. Templeton is second from right between banker Gene Edwards and attorney Bob Sanders. Billy Morris (third from left), of Morris Communications, was an Augusta member.

Templeton, wife Martha, their children, sons-in-law and grandchildren on a family cruise.

Amarillo Slim, the renowned poker player, was a friend and later a client.

gold bracelet, an emerald, and a couple of diamond rings.

"Damned if Slim didn't talk me into buying $8,000 worth of jewelry," Templeton said. "I had no more use for it than a man in the moon. But Slim could talk you into anything. Martha said I was crazy."

Later that day, he got into an Omaha game against some of the best players in Vegas, which included Moss, a charter member in 1979 in the Poker Hall of Fame. He won $10,000 which paid off the bracelet. He gave the bracelet to Frances Maddox, wife of one of his most prominent clients, W.A. Maddox. She had recently had an emerald and gold bracelet stolen.

In one of the hands, it was just Templeton and Moss. That was mighty big company for a lawyer from Amarillo. The amateur vs. the legend.

"I felt sorry for him," Templeton said. "You could tell he never mastered that game (Omaha) and had got old. I knew I had the best of him. I said, 'Mr. Moss, don't call. I got you beat.' So he didn't, and I turned over my hand. You don't do that in Vegas. Moss never did that to a soul in his life."

Templeton and Slim were casual friends who became closer later in Slim's life. On occasion, he'd come to the law office.

"One time, I got him and (former partner) Bob Garner together," he said. "Slim was about 6-3 ½ and Garner was about 6-2. Long and skinny, both of them. Both full of the gift of gab. It was like two dogs circling each other. They could have been brothers."

In the early 2000s, Slim was riding a bit of a hot streak. His autobiography, "Amarillo Slim in a World of Fat People," was a best seller. There was serious talk of a movie based on the book with Nicholas Cage playing Slim. Slim was also trying to get an online poker operation off the ground. He talked his friend into investing $100,000.

"That was the only time I put any money into Slim," he said. "I never let him hook me for anything except that. Slim took that money and bought a $70,000 truck. My money had gone to buy him a truck. Later I found out that I was only one who put money into the thing."

Templeton was convinced the online poker would have got off the ground and made a lot of money until a shocking charge later in 2003. Slim was indicted on a charge of indecency with a child. It was big news that didn't play well.

"I never heard him do anything like what he was charged with," Templeton said. "He was always good with his family. He helped them out in every way."

The charge was reduced to a misdemeanor through a plea bargain. He pleaded "no contest" to the reduced charges which included a $4,000 fine, two-year probation and counseling. In an interview in 2009, Slim said he was innocent of the charge, but chose the plea bargain to spare his family the ordeal of a trial.

"I helped him through that and never charged him a dime," Templeton said. "I pulled the strings on the criminal case. All his friends dropped him. They had no use for him. The movie was gone. Everything was gone. If that had not taken place, Slim would have made millions off online poker and the movie. Made millions."

Slim was in failing health when he approached 80. The glitter of Las Vegas had faded. He died of colon cancer on April 29, 2012 at age 83.

"Slim died broke. No money," Templeton said. "I probated the will. He didn't have anything."

A busy law practice makes no concessions though. Time has to be carved out of the day and night for gambling and golf, for family. Work has to be juggled especially for one like Robert Templeton, who turned 88 in March 2020 and still practices law.

In 2009, Martha had a cold virus that settled into her heart. She lost half of her heart efficiency after that. A good Ejection Fraction to test the efficiency of the heart is 65. Martha's hovered around 35. As the years wore on, she got weaker and weaker. Because of that, she had falls that resulted in a broken back, broken ankle, broken wrist.

"She finally got to the point where she said, 'Bob, I want to die,'" Templeton said.

On June 10, 2018, a Sunday afternoon, Martha's condition

worsened. Her husband called Luanne, and they agreed to take her to the hospital. A blood test revealed sepsis and serious damage to her kidneys and liver. She died the following day, June 11, one day shy of their 64th anniversary at age 84.

For the first time in his life, Templeton is alone. Growing up in Amarillo and Frost, through Baylor, through his more than 60 years of law practice in Amarillo, friends and family were at arm's length.

Oh, they are still there – there was a roomful at his 88th birthday party at the Tascosa Country Club – but it is different. Gin has replaced poker as the card game of choice. Many afternoons find him playing with his friend Marty Fenberg at Tascosa Country Club. There are three dogs at home, his two little ones and Charlie, the Golden Retriever that's on loan from grandson Nicholas. Gloria, a maid, comes for half a day during the week. And there's still work, of course.

"I don't know if I've adjusted or not," he said. "You learn to live alone. I've got these dogs and that helps. I don't get out much, but I'm not a loner. I'm still working on some lawsuits. I feel like I'm behind all the time."

But loss in the immediate family has been profound. A son, a wife of 64 years, the loss leaves holes that can't be sewn.

"Martha, my wife, was..." he said.

And the pause was a long one. His mind, which served him well in trials into seven decades, was searching and searching.

"..She was not just an anchor. She was not just the ship captain. She steered our boat. She was a natural leader in whatever she did. Women loved her. Men loved her too. I know I loved her."

ABOUT THE AUTHOR

Jon Mark Beilue worked for 37 years with the Amarillo Globe-News. He spent his first 25 years in the sports department, the last 17 of those as sports editor. From 2006-2018, he was a general news columnist for the Globe-News. His work has been recognized both statewide and nationally. A native of Groom and 1981 graduate of Texas Tech, he has two books on his collections of columns. He and wife Sandy, parents of two grown sons, live in Amarillo. Thankfully, he has never needed Templeton's representation – not yet anyway.